FRONTIERS:
THE LIFE AND TIMES OF
BONNIE BIRD

Choreography and Dance Studies

A series of books edited by Muriel Topaz and Robert P. Cohan, CBE

Please see the back of this book for other titles in the Choreography and Dance Studies series

FRONTIERS:
THE LIFE AND TIMES OF
BONNIE BIRD

AMERICAN MODERN DANCER
AND DANCE EDUCATOR

Karen Bell-Kanner

harwood academic publishers
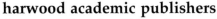
Australia • Canada • China • France • Germany • India
Japan • Luxembourg • Malaysia • The Netherlands • Russia
Singapore • Switzerland • Thailand

Amsteldijk 166
1st Floor
1079 LH Amsterdam
The Netherlands

British Library Cataloguing in Publication Data

Bell-Kanner, Karen
  Frontiers: the life and times of Bonnie Bird: American
  modern dancer and dance educator. – (Choreography and dance
  studies; v. 17)
  1. Bird, Bonnie 2. Women dancers – United States – Biography
  3. Dancers – United States – Biography 4. Modern dance –
  American influences
  I. Title
  792.8'092

  ISBN 90-5755-034-2 (softcover)

Cover illustration: Bonnie Bird in *Chronicle*, 1936. Photo: Paul Hansen (Bonnie Bird Collection)

The only way you can get into heaven
is to dance there

Brigham Young (1801–1877)
Mormon leader

CONTENTS

INTRODUCTION TO THE SERIES

Choreography and Dance Studies is a book series of special interest to dancers, dance teachers and choreographers. Focusing on dance composition, its techniques and training, the series will also cover the relationship of choreography to other components of dance performance such as music, lighting and the training of dancers.

In addition, *Choreography and Dance Studies* will seek to publish new works and provide translations of works not previously published in English, as well as to publish reprints of currently unavailable books of outstanding value to the dance community.

Muriel Topaz
Robert P. Cohan

ACKNOWLEDGEMENTS

I want to thank Dr Marion North, Executive Director of the Laban Centre for Movement and Dance, London, for her greatly appreciated encouragement during the writing of this book; Heidi Gundlach Smith, Bonnie's daughter, for gathering many of the personal photos from California that Bonnie had hoped to get ready for publication; Laurie Freedman, for Lionel Freedman's famous photos of the Merry-Go-Rounders; and Toni Nandi, for preparing the photos from the Bonnie Bird Collection at the Laban Centre.

There are many people with whom I have been in contact who have been generously forthcoming. But I especially want to thank: Peter Bassett, librarian and archivist of the Laban Centre Library; Madeleine H. Nichols, Curator of the Dance Collection of the New York Public Library for the Performing Arts; Professor Leta Miller, University of California, Santa Cruz, for generously sharing with me her research work relevant to chapter 7; Laban MA student Stacy Lee Prickett, whose paper *The Dance is a Weapon of the Class Struggle* helped open my eyes to political dance in the 1930s; Els Grellinger, dance notator; Professor John Mueller, University of Rochester Dance Film Archive; Harold G. Balridge, Director, Neighborhood Playhouse School of the Theatre; Dorothy Bird Villard; Manon Souriau; Professor Marion Ross, Mills College, California; and Bonnie's Laban Centre associates Dr Dorothy Madden, the late Dr Peter Brinson, Ilana Snyder, Antony Bowne and Sian Prime.

And most of all, with my deepest gratitude, regrettably posthumously, Bonnie Bird herself, who was so very wonderful and giving, not only during the year or so of the first taping venture, but ten years later when we picked up the threads of her life again and concentrated on weaving together the rest of her remarkable story. Her adventures and achievements are the stuff of dancers' dreams.

LIST OF ILLUSTRATIONS

PREFACE

This book started with a year-long series of taped conversations I had with Bonnie Bird in 1981 when she talked about her life and work. She was a wonderful story-teller with a prodigious memory, and I was fascinated by her first-hand accounts of her work with America's dance pioneers Martha Graham, Louis Horst, Doris Humphrey and Merce Cunningham, with whom I myself could relate from my own studies in the New York dance scene of the 1950s.

The transcribed tapes were intended to go into the archives of the Laban Centre for Movement and Dance in London, where she was then head of the Dance Theatre Courses. But in later conversations the concept of a book emerged, and in 1991 I began to write. There were many further interviews over the next three years and Bonnie also made available her innumerable letters to her family in Seattle from New York when she was working with Martha Graham between 1931 and 1937. The Laban Centre gave me access to her entire archive of American dance periodicals from the 1930s through to the 1960s which she had brought with her when she came to England in 1974. The archive included very early *Dance Observer* editions, many of which she had worked on with Louis Horst. I was also given access to her copious notes and plans while she was working with the Centre.

The book is, therefore, largely a compilation of Bonnie's own words from our many conversations, from her letters home to her family and her later letters from London to her friends all over the world, backed up by research to verify dates and places and to give a broader background to her story. I have tried to contain the length of the book by not mentioning more than a handful of the myriad students, colleagues and friends who were so much a part of her life. I hope that those of you whom I have inadequately treated will understand.

Finally, a short note on the spelling variations of *theater* and *theatre* in the text. Samuel Johnson's dictionary of 1755 adopted the French-derived spelling, *theatre*, and so popularized it in England. But Noah Webster's landmark dictionary of 1828 led Americans to settle on *theater*. For the most part, however, the *re* ending was retained in America for the names of purpose-built buildings. I have been as faithful as possible to the two different spellings.

Dr. Bonnie Bird Gundlach in her office at the Laban Centre for Movement and Dance, London, England. Photo: Toni Nandi.

1

EXTENDING THE FRONTIERS OF DANCE

BONNIE BIRD: 1914–1995

"Still busy as a bird dog!" was the response from 78-year-young Bonnie Bird in 1992 when I asked her about her latest activities. Although her work had been based in England for almost two decades, her speech still revealed a deep attachment to her American roots – a tie kept fresh by frequent visits to see her three children, old friends, attend conferences and look for fresh American dance talent. Over the years her warm smile, twinkling eyes and achievements in the field of dance persuaded generations of her American colleagues, former students and new dance acquaintances to work with her at London's Laban Centre of Movement and Dance. There, in tandem with Marion North, the Centre's executive director, the breadth of Bonnie's dream for a "dance university" inspired a new range of training courses for dancers that also led to the pioneering of Britain's first dance degree courses in higher education.

Bonnie's last years with the Centre were especially occupied with giving a creative impulse to choreographers. Following her establishment of a charitable trust fund for new choreographies, she presided over the commissioning of more than 30 new works by young choreographers from both sides of the Atlantic who composed their dances on fourth-year student members of Transitions Dance Company, of which Bonnie was the founder and tireless artistic adviser. Working closely with the Company she often traveled on tours through Great Britain, Europe, Asia and the U.S.A., where its success attracted new supporters, teachers, students and choreographers. It was her care and devotion, a hallmark of her work, that has made Transitions a unique undertaking in British dance education.

Dr. Bonnie Bird Gundlach's life in American modern dance covered more than 60 years of its rich history. As a young professional dancer in the 1930s she was a member of the Martha Graham Dance Group. Later, she became a teacher sensitive to the needs of changing times and attitudes, an imaginative and inspiring colleague and a visionary endowed with outstanding organizational skills. For more than 40 of those years she was a leader in extending the frontiers of dance as a major art form relevant to modern society and its problems.

This is the story of an American dancer, choreographer and dance educator, the times and places in which she lived, the artists who influenced her, and how she guided generations of young people from many lands through the rich and changing world of dance.

2

DANCE PRELUDE

Only by stretching far out over the porch railing of the home her parents had recently bought in Seattle, Washington, was ten-year old Bonnie able to see into the front room of the house next door. A tall, slender young man was standing by the window, touching the sill with one hand while tracing magical movements through the air with the other. Her eyes eagerly followed him as he moved around the empty room. She was fascinated. He seemed to have come from another world: she had never imagined anything so wonderful.

This was her first glimpse of Caird Leslie, a professional ballet dancer recovering from an injury. During his convalescence he decided to build a new career as a ballet teacher and his little neighbor became one of his first pupils.

Caird Leslie had performed in Chicago-based productions and in short touring programs with a small company called Ballet Intime, led by Russian-born Adolph Bolm. Bolm had been a leading dancer, choreographer and ballet master with Diaghilev's Ballets Russes and had partnered Anna Pavlova. Caird's experience with Bolm was to serve him well as a teacher.

When Pavlova and her company came to Seattle, Caird took Bonnie to a performance. Afterward they went backstage and Bonnie, in a moment never to be forgotten, was presented to the great ballerina herself. When this beautiful being asked her what she wanted to be when she grew up, all Bonnie's earlier dreams of becoming a doctor were forgotten and she answered, "I am going to be a dancer!" It was as if she had taken a vow; from that moment on there was no shaking her from her ultimate goal of a life in dance.

3

A CHILD OF THE PACIFIC NORTHWEST

The Bird family history was typical of the rich mixture of twentieth-century Americans. In 1860 Bonnie's paternal great-grandparents, Hannah and Joseph Lapish, left their village near Leeds, England, to make the long and difficult journey to Florence, Missouri, the gathering point for members of the Church of Jesus Christ of Latter-Day Saints on their way to Utah. Also known as the Mormon Church, it had been founded by Joseph Smith in New York in 1830. Its religious beliefs were based on revelation and an interdependence of spiritual and daily life, but because of its practice of polygamy, as well as its increasing political and economic power, the Mormons were continually hounded westward.

By 1844 the community had settled in Navoo, Illinois, but their leader was lynched after having been jailed on charges of provoking a riot. Shortly afterward, Brigham Young, Smith's successor, led 12,000 Mormons in covered wagons deep into the West. In 1847, they finally settled in the Salt Lake area of Utah, one of the most barren places in America, where they hoped they might be left to live and worship in peace.

From the new settlement Young sent word to those who still wanted to join the community that they would be welcome and there would be houses for all. In the mass immigration that followed there were many recent recruits from England, including Hannah and Joseph with their new baby and three young children. Many immigrants were too poor to buy a horse and wagon, so the church provided them with handcarts which they pushed and pulled on the two-and-a-half-month walk from Florence to Salt Lake City. "The long trek," in the words of Brigham Young, "was the gathering of Zion; the heartiest testing of both people and organization." The four thousand who made this journey, including the Lapish family, became known as the Handcart Brigade and immortalized in American art and literature.

The Mormons continued to practice polygamy until it was banned in 1890; whether Hannah Settle Lapish was Joseph's only wife is a matter of family speculation. She did not approve of polygamy, but was not allowed to say so. This tiny woman, weighing 96 pounds, raised a large family and lived to be 92. She had a farm in American Fork, just south of Salt Lake City. The Homestead Act of 1862 granted settlers 160 acres each of public land on condition they cultivate it for five years. Hannah, being a canny lady, obtained a tract of land she thought the railroad would eventually want to purchase. Within a few years she did indeed sell part of it to a railroad company to support her family. When Utah became a state in 1896, she was one of the suffragettes who fought for and won the vote for its women. She was a vigorous battler.

Bonnie's paternal grandfather was William Bird, a lawyer from a landowning and farming family that had settled near Wilmington, Delaware, at the time of the American Revolution. The U.S. government sent him to resolve a dispute with the Mormons and he and the community developed a strong respect for one another. A widower with two children, he stayed on in Salt Lake City as a lawyer for the railroads and later married Bonnie's grandmother, a daughter of the American Fork homesteader, who was considerably younger than he. Because she was marrying outside her religion she chose not to continue as a Mormon. Protestant churches had begun to proliferate in the city and it was as Protestants that she brought up their children.

Bonnie's maternal grandfather came to America from Ireland as a stowaway. Starting as a railroad laborer he became an engineer and married a Connecticut Irish girl. Bonnie's mother, Josephine Earle Powers, was one of their eight children. While most of her sisters and brothers worked in factories or on the railroad, she went to a teacher-training college. After graduating she was selected to join a team of demonstration teachers who were sent to the West Coast to raise teaching standards. It was there, in Seattle in 1912, that she met Bonnie's father, Scott Elliot Bird, who had left Salt Lake City for San Francisco to help out after the devastating earthquake of 1906. He had various jobs and slowly gravitated north to Seattle. He was planning to continue north to prospect for gold in Alaska, but when he met Josephine Powers his plans changed. They were married in 1913.

Scott Bird took his new wife two hundred miles south to Portland, Oregon, where he sold automobiles to the local farmers and lumbermen. Those were the days when a car salesman also had to teach his customers how to drive. From the moment she was married, however, his wife could no longer teach. Although it was not said outright, it was considered, especially in city schools, that women who had experienced sex were not fit to teach. It took a long time to change that way of thinking.

Bonnie was born in Portland on April 30, 1914. Her brother William was born two years later, followed by Scott Elliot, who was born in Seattle in 1924 after her father opened his own automobile agency there. Bonnie's family background was an interesting one: one parent from the East and one from the West. In her subsequent career, having family on both sides of the continent was to serve her well.

Seattle, on the West Coast of the United States, looks out onto the sparkling blue waters of Puget Sound, a natural gateway to both the Orient and Alaska. Its cool summers, mild, mist-laden, rainy winters, lush fir trees and surrounding mountain ranges – to the west the snow-capped Mount Olympus surrounded by the largest rain forest in a temperate zone, to the south and east Mount Rainier and the Cascade Mountains, to the north Mount Baker – create a dynamic environment for its hardy inhabitants.

By the time Bonnie was twelve she was driving an automobile around Robin Hill, the ranch her father had purchased just outside Seattle, and she easily switched from wearing pink slippers and pirouetting in ballet class to sporting long-haired chaps and riding her own horses. It was second nature for her to ride and train horses and she loved the wild west shows and rodeos her father, as president of the American Rodeo Association, ran with his two partners, auburn-haired Strawberry Red Wall and his wife Rose. Red and Rose, nationally famous as trick riders, were also Bonnie's tutors. Every spring she anxiously awaited the arrival of the cowboys who came to all the ranches and stayed through autumn, practicing their bucking, trick riding and roping. The young teenager dreamed of becoming a trick rider and roper, perhaps even a rodeo queen. Her mother thought it was crazy to try to combine being a rodeo star with her aim of a career in dance.

4

THE CORNISH SCHOOL

The Cornish School of Fine Arts was founded in 1914 by Miss Nellie Centennial Cornish. From its early days in rented quarters in the Boothe Building, the school offered an education in all the arts for students of any age, mostly from the Seattle area. In 1921 a new building with excellent facilities was erected on Roy Street at Harvard North. Nearly a thousand students were passing through its doors each week when Caird Leslie was invited to integrate his own school into Cornish and contracted to head its ballet department from January, 1927, for two years.

Miss Cornish, familiarly called Miss Aunt Nellie, or Aunt Nellie, was a respected and innovative arts educator who had started her career as a music teacher. She spent two or three months every year traveling through America and Europe to see for herself the most effective new developments in arts education. In the course of her travels she also recruited professional artists who brought a wide variety of experience to the school faculty. The Cornish School was highly regarded by the people of Seattle, as well as in such distant places as Dartington Hall in Totnes, Devon, England, where Miss Cornish was a friend and adviser to Dorothy Elmhirst, née Whitney, Dartington's founder and patron.

The heart of the school lay in its excellent, 250-seat theater. It was here that faculty members made their greatest impact on the student body through their participation in regular Friday evening concerts. Miss Cornish also kept a sharp lookout for artists who happened to be visiting Seattle and invited them to perform in these programs. Bonnie heard the folk singer John Jacob Niles, the pianist Berthe Poncy and many other first-rate artists. These performances were always followed the next morning by special school programs for the younger students given by the same artists using much of the material from the previous night's performance, sensitively adapted and informally presented.

Caird Leslie was stimulated by working among so many artists and the number of ballet students greatly increased as his reputation for excellence spread. Bonnie regularly appeared in his Russian-influenced productions, such as *Poupées Russes*, in which she danced *Petruska in Box*. His student dance group also performed in other venues in and around Seattle. Caird considered Bonnie a worthwhile student and supported her aim of becoming a professional dancer.

A course in the national dances of Spain taught by the wealthy, socially correct Cornelia Niles was Bonnie's only folk dance experience at Cornish. She lost interest in Spanish dancing, however, from the moment Miss Niles' swirling skirt revealed her plain, knee-length bloomers. Niles also fancied herself as an 'interpretive' choreographer in the style of Isadora Duncan, and she made a series of dances in which Bonnie, dressed in a short tunic and trailing diaphanous draperies, wafted through performances given in ladies' clubs and at garden tea parties. In retrospect, Bonnie mused that perhaps Miss Cornish, in her haste to sign up a well-known artist, had mistaken Cornelia for her sister, the internationally famous Spanish dancer, Doris Niles.

Because Miss Cornish saw all the arts as interrelated, she understood the need for a wide range of studies for young, potential artists. From 1915 eurhythmics was an obligatory subject for all music and dance students. Performing two different rhythms simultaneously on opposite sides of her body at first caused Bonnie some difficulty, but she came to appreciate the training it provided. Drama classes were also part of the curriculum.

From her first year of high school, Bonnie attended the Cornish School every afternoon from three to seven o'clock in preparation for the full-time, four-year course in dance. The course compared favorably with a college education, and was what Aunt Nellie, who took a close personal interest in Bonnie's education, had in mind for her.

There was one particular lesson having to do with good taste that made a lasting impression on the teenager. With her fellow students, Kenneth Bostock and Nelle Fisher, Bonnie created an apache dance for an informal school party. They knew nothing about this violent dance that had originated in Paris, but based their ideas on photos they had seen in popular magazines. During the dance Kenny Bostock flung Bonnie around by her hair and hands, but finally it was he who ended up face down on the floor. In a gesture of victory Bonnie planted her foot triumphantly on his bottom. The next day Miss Cornish called Bonnie into her office and asked if she had, as was reported, "kicked or put her foot on Kenny's bottom." Bonnie explained that she had placed her foot there to show she had won the battle. Accepting that Bonnie had not meant it as a vulgar gesture, Aunt Nellie said, "The margin between good taste and bad is very narrow." A lesson never forgotten.

Near the end of the 1928 autumn term, Miss Cornish called the dance students into her office one by one to tell each of them personally that she had decided to abolish classical ballet and replace it with 'modern dance'. She had witnessed tremendous changes in dance and dance education since the first pioneers of American modern dance, Ruth

St. Denis and Ted Shawn, had established their Denishawn Company and School in Los Angeles in 1915. Now some of the younger Denishawn Company dancers, Martha Graham among them, were beginning to make a name for themselves as dancer/choreographers in the concert field. Indeed, Graham had recently become head of the dance department at the newly established Neighborhood Playhouse School of the Theatre in New York City. During her travels in Europe, Cornish had also seen performances by a new wave of exciting Central European modern choreographers and had visited schools where modern dance featured as a major creative art. There was a fresh wind blowing through the world of dance and as a leading arts educator she could not ignore the new developments.

Bonnie was stunned by Miss Aunt Nellie's announcement. She loved her classes with Caird Leslie and had absolutely no idea how the magical transformation into a fine dancer could be achieved other than by studying ballet. She challenged Miss Cornish, and remembered her response: "What do you know about a career in dance? Just how do you think you get started?" Bonnie could not answer; she could only visualize a single moment: the solo dancer in a white spotlight on a darkened stage, fluttering like a moth, with the audience transfixed and marveling at her beauty. She had only seen Anna Pavlova once and the only other high quality dance presentations she saw were at the Cornish School. During these last years of the 1920s the American ballet scene was barren and there was not much good dancing of any other type to be seen. Bonnie had once seen the tapping, high-kicking, skirt-swirling girls of the Fanchon-Marko Review, a down-market version of the famous New York City Roxy Theatre line dancers known as the Roxyettes, but they did nothing on point. Finally answering Aunt Nellie's question, she said she might first join Fanchon-Marko and then move on to the Albertina Rasch Girls, a touring company of toe dancers doing their own style of popular show dancing. And after that she might be ready to join a ballet company somewhere. But she had never thought about what she needed to know in addition to ballet technique in order to become a member of a fine ballet company – or whether one even existed in America. Miss Cornish told her she was convinced that the best way to educate young dancers was to stimulate them to make their own artistic decisions, and ballet training did not prepare them for this. Bonnie left the interview on the verge of tears. She could not imagine that modern dance, whatever that was, could replace her beloved ballet.

The new teacher for creative dancing and eurhythmics was Louise Solberg, the daughter of Miss Cornish's close friends and financial supporters in whose home she had lived for eleven years. When the young Louise had first participated in the Boothe Building classes, she found she was expected to call her favorite aunt 'Miss Cornish' instead of 'Aunt Nellie'. She quickly solved the problem by calling her 'Miss Aunt Nellie', and the name stuck. Louise was gifted in both dance and music and Miss Aunt Nellie willingly took on much of the responsibility for her education. Along with her regular classes, Louise had studied ballet with Adolph Bolm during his three summer sessions at Cornish and in preparation for teaching at the school she spent two years studying in Switzerland with Emile Jaques-Dalcroze.

To start her dance reforms, Cornish brought Louise back to Seattle to teach at the beginning of the January, 1929, term. Her dance classes combined ballet fundamentals with a broader movement vocabulary and made a bridge from ballet to modern dance for the stubbornly ballet-oriented Bonnie. She was very excited by the new classes in improvisation and composition, with their emphasis on the students making their own artistic decisions, and by the stimulating discussions that took place following performances of their own works. Louise Solberg was an intelligent and warm person for whom Bonnie came to have enormous regard. When Mrs. Bird invited her for a weekend at the ranch, Louise's ability as a horsewoman astonished Bonnie almost as much as her teaching.

Early in 1929 Miss Cornish also invited the European-trained Japanese dancer, Michio Ito, to give a four-week course at her school. Ito had trained with Dalcroze at Hellerau-Dresden from 1912 to 1914, and after his London debut in 1915 had been based in New York. He and his group of mostly advanced students had recently started on a concert tour that would eventually take them to Los Angeles, where he planned to stay and work. Bonnie and Louise joined his stimulating classes which also included his group members Pauline Koner and Georgia (Geordie) Graham, Martha Graham's sister. Ito gave a solo recital at Cornish and two group recitals in downtown Seattle before leaving for San Francisco, where Louise joined him for a further two weeks of classes.

A year later, Dorothy and Leonard Elmhirst, founder–directors of Dartington Hall, invited Louise to be a guest teacher for a term at their school from the end of April, 1930. Martha Graham, who had caught Miss Cornish's eye when she was with Denishawn and again in recent years by her own concert work, had been invited to teach at the Cornish Summer School from mid-June. Suddenly a modern dance teacher was urgently needed to cover the six weeks between Louise's departure and Graham's arrival. Cornish telephoned Martha asking for advice and she suggested Ronnie Johansson, then on leave from her work as director of the Swedish State Theater Ballet in Stockholm and teaching and dancing in New York City. Graham had seen Johansson in a demonstration for the Denishawn Company and been favorably impressed. She had been especially struck by Johansson's use of the floor for her opening exercises. Over the next few years Graham herself developed the idea of starting dance classes sitting on the floor. She devised exercises to master the control of the back and pelvis that made her dancers stronger and better able to tackle difficult standing and spatial movement. 'Floor work' soon became basic to Graham's movement technique.

Ronnie Johansson arrived at the Cornish School in time to see Louise off for England. "Ronnie was one of the most blithe and lovely dancers I can ever remember seeing," said Bonnie. "She not only had a sunny personality, but also a wonderful lightness which I suppose was a mixture of Swedish gymnastics and the Central European dance training that was already established in Germany. She based most of her technique on bound and rebound, so her dancing had a buoyant quality that was very exciting and made a great impression on me. I was beginning to be aware that there were principles of movement underlying how one approaches dance."

While Johansson was journeying west, Martha Graham was dancing the role of The Chosen Maiden in Léonide Massine's staging of Igor Stravinsky's *Sacre du Printemps*. The performance was conducted by Leopold Stokowski, who championed Graham's dancing. It was a rare showcase for her. Beginning on April 11th, *Sacre* had three performances at the Philadelphia Opera House and two more ten days later at New York's Metropolitan Opera House. "Over the next few years Martha showed us movement phrases from this dance. It was a demanding solo which she had actually created herself, full of leaps and jumping splits and very difficult movement sequences," Bonnie remembered. "Considering the limited technical skills that most dancers had in those days, it was astonishing."

Martha Graham, with Louis (Lōō'ē) Horst, her mentor, lover, musical director and accompanist, performed at Seattle's Metropolitan Theatre on June 2, 1930. Graham's name had come before a wider public as a result of articles about *Sacre du Printemps* appearing in such periodicals as *Theatre Arts Monthly* and in newspapers throughout the country. She was variously referred to as a leader in the modern dance movement and as one of the principal members of the Dance Repertory Theatre, which had recently had its first, short New York season. John Martin, *The New York Times* dance critic, described her as an unique dancer – one for the connoisseur.

The young Martha Graham. Photo: Bonnie Bird Collection at the Laban Centre.

Sixteen-year old Bonnie Bird, Graham's student on the 1930 Cornish School Summer Course.
Photo: Bonnie Bird Collection.

Dorothy Bird by Puget Sound, 1930. Photo: Bonnie Bird Collection.

There was great excitement when, in mid-June, Graham gave a solo recital in the Cornish School Theatre. It was the climax to a birthday celebration she had planned to mark the fifteenth anniversary of the founding of the school. The performance itself was a gift to Aunt Nellie from Martha and Louis. Fine rugs and tapestries were borrowed from the city museum and private collections and under Martha's direction were used to decorate the lobby, hallways and theater. Cornish wrote in her autobiography that this recital before an invited audience that filled the house was "...a revelation to all those of the guests who had never seen her dance before."[1]

When Graham came to Cornish she was going through a period of rethinking everything she knew about dance, but she had not yet found a solid framework for her own development as an artist. She was gradually escaping from the pseudo-oriental and mystical style of Ruth St. Denis and its successful vaudeville staging by her husband, Ted Shawn. They had together founded the Denishawn School, where

Graham gained her first important foothold as a teacher, and the Denishawn Company, in which she danced from 1920 to 1923.

Both programs in Seattle included a piece from Graham's first concert in 1926, *Tanagra* (Erik Satie), an unusual and exquisite treatment of a Greek Tanagra figurine of the Hellenic period. "Her handling of a wrap worn by one of the Hellenic ladies depicted in these small pottery figurines was extraordinary," Bonnie recalled. "Martha had learned the art of using fabric as a means of expression from 'Miss Ruth', who excelled in it. Her shawl was made of a very soft, lightweight pure silk, 'glove silk' as it was called, which had a certain amount of stretch. She threw it into space so that it went out at a right angle to her body and then, with the speed of lightning, she pulled it back before it fell so that it lay across her hand. It was a breathtaking gesture requiring great skill."

Other dances could only have come out of Denishawn because of their character and organization, such as *Deux Valse Sentimentals* (Maurice Ravel), *Maid with the Flaxen Hair* (Claude Debussy) and *Fragilité* (Alexander Scriabin). These dances, as Miss Cornish observed, "were more understandable to the layman than her later works."[2]

The first concert at the Metropolitan Theatre in downtown Seattle included two works, both created in 1928, that were not on the Cornish program. Both were two-part dances: *Immigrant: Steerage* and *Strike* (Josip Slavenski); and *Poems of 1917: Songs Behind the Lines and Dance of Death* (Leo Ornstein). "Martha had begun to translate into dance what was happening in the emerging artistic culture of America that had, until then, been receiving its inspiration from abroad," said Bonnie. "'Who am I?' she was asking. 'I am an American living in a vital and spirited country and that is what I want to express through dance.' It was the beginning of a profound appreciation of her roots. I think you have to live in the United States to understand just how deep are the crosscurrents of our experience."

"When this fierce, dynamic, startling woman – very small, very fiery – started teaching, the impact of her classes was extraordinary," Bonnie remembered. "She actually asked us questions that challenged everything we did. And her technique, which never allowed us to turn our feet out, did not dampen my enthusiasm, because I had already experienced so much that was new and different in the classes and recitals of Louise Solberg and Ronnie Johansson."

The first work in which Bonnie performed under Graham's direction was an entr'acte in a staging of Aeschylus' play, *Seven Against Thebes*, produced by Jean Mercier, a Swiss director who was the school's head of drama. It had three performances in the Cornish Theatre at the end

Bonnie (left) and fellow Cornish students. Photo: Bonnie Bird Collection at the Laban Centre.

of July, 1930. Cornish had hoped that Mercier would invite Graham to work with him on this production, but he planned the staging himself and drilled the student actors into set routines, leaving no room for experimentation, nor for Martha Graham. Instead, she created a dance interlude using Dorothy Bird (no relation), Nelle Fisher, Bethene Miller, Grace Cornell and Bonnie. With these five girls she caught the quality of figures on a Greek vase, especially in the way the girls entered down the side aisles of the slightly raked theater, moving along the walls to give a flat, two-dimensional image.

Graham made their costumes and headdresses very cheaply from a bolt of cheesecloth. From Ruth St. Denis she had learned the technique of making the fashionable, knife-pleated *Fortuney* gowns that were copied from the ancient Greeks. First she cut the fabric into lengths and dyed it. While still wet she twisted each length until it curled back on itself and became a tight ball. She then put the balls in an oven and baked them very slowly until they were dry. When they were unwound and draped from the shoulders, the knife-pleated cloth conformed to the shape of the body. Although stunningly stage-effective, the pleats soon softened. Had there been more than the three performances it would have been necessary to repeat the process. Bonnie learned as she worked alongside Martha Graham and, later in her career, she designed many costumes of cheesecloth for her own productions.

While at Cornish, Graham continued her custom of gathering dancers of promise for her own Group. She won the young Bonnie Bird to her cause by asking her for the impossible and getting it, willingly given and with joy. At the end of the summer session, Bonnie's dreams of also becoming a rodeo queen paled to insignificance in the light of Graham's invitation to join her in New York City after finishing high school.

5

PREPARATION

By the time Herbert Hoover succeeded Calvin Coolidge as President of the United States in 1929 there were millions of small investors sitting on paper profits from the speculative stockmarket boom. On October 24th, seven months after Hoover took office, the stockmarket crashed and heralded the Great Depression. The whole of America was crippled; many investors lost everything. Industry laid off workers and unemployment soon soared to eight million, but Hoover opposed both direct government aid to the unemployed and public works programs. By 1933 the number of jobless would reach more than 13 million.

The shock waves took a little time to reach the West Coast, but when they hit, they hit hard. Bonnie's father, who had expanded his automobile agency to include insurance and related businesses, went bankrupt. The Birds were only able to keep their home because Scott Elliot Bird had the foresight to transfer it to his wife as a gift so that it could not be taken away in bankruptcy proceedings.

When a letter arrived offering Bonnie a two-year scholarship to the Neighborhood Playhouse School of the Theatre in New York City, a plan Martha Graham had set in motion to prepare her for the Graham Group, Mrs. Bird saw it as an unique opportunity for their daughter to have the college education they could not otherwise afford. She had always clung to the belief that culture was more developed on the East Coast and was not afraid to let Bonnie go to New York, but Mr. Bird had misgivings about sending a naïve and innocent young girl to a big city three thousand miles away. Neither wanted their daughter to lead a humdrum life, so he finally agreed to let her go, largely because Mrs. Bird's family lived in Connecticut and her brother, Jimmy Powers, a conductor on the New York-New Haven and Hartford Railroad, was constantly in and out of New York City and could keep an eye on her. Years later, Bonnie was amused to learn that her Uncle Jimmy, faithful to his role as family guardian, had attended Graham's New York concerts to check on whether she was really doing what she said she was doing. He must have been very surprised at what he saw, but he was an extremely tolerant Irishman.

In the 1930–31 school year, Bonnie worked hard to complete her high school education. At Cornish her modern dance teacher was now

Lore Deja, the first graduate of the Wigman School in Dresden, Germany to be appointed to a regular teaching position in America. This was an unexpected development following a cable earlier in the year from Louise Solberg saying that she wanted to marry Richard Elmhirst, the younger brother of Dartington's director, but would return to fulfill her year's contract with Cornish if necessary. There had been no previous hint of a romance and the surprised but undaunted Miss Cornish cabled back, "Find me someone to teach eurthythmics and modern dance and you may remain in England."[1] Louise quickly signed up a graduate of the London branch of the Dalcroze Institute to teach eurhythmics, but her search for a modern dance teacher took her to Munich, where the German Dance Congress was in session. There she selected Lore Deja from among the dancers rehearsing with Mary Wigman for Albert Talhoff's production of *Totenmal*.

Bonnie found Deja's classes confusing and sometimes even mesmerizing, much to her dismay. She could remember following Deja across the floor on the diagonal, imitating what she did for what seemed like hours. With the repeated sameness of the drum beat and the almost unvaried monotony of the movement, Bonnie experienced her first trance. She did not like it because she felt she had lost control in a situation that someone else had created. Afraid of losing what had been gained through Graham's classes, she kept up daily practice in the Graham exercises. It took Deja almost a year to master enough English to answer Bonnie's question concerning the basis of her technique. When she realized that the young student had not fathomed that it was breathing she was furious.

"Lore Deja moved with an elfin quality," Bonnie recalled. "She was tiny and magically beautiful, with red hair, translucent skin and deep green eyes. Deja's German friends had prepared her for her three-year stay at Cornish by giving her some small aboriginal dolls. I think she actually expected to be teaching American Indians." Her successor at the school, Welland Laythrop, was deeply influenced by her teaching.

In December, 1930, just a few months after Deja joined the Cornish staff, Mary Wigman, Germany's leading modern dancer, arrived in New York to begin the first of three successive winter tours that were to popularize Central European modern dance in the United States. A reception was given for her by the Concert Dancers League and hosted by its organizers, Doris Humphrey, Charles Weidman and Helen Tamiris. Ruth St. Denis and Ted Shawn were introduced to Wigman as the luminaries of the American modern dance world. Martha Graham and Louis Horst were among the guests, as was a former Wigman pupil, Harald Kreutzberg, who had been giving concerts in America since 1928. After meeting the

American artists, Mary Wigman wrote in her diary, "Martha Graham's eyes alone speak of the art of the dance."[2]

Wigman's spellbinding solos captivated her audiences in New York, Boston, Washington, Philadelphia, Chicago and Montreal. Her visit, however, was not welcomed by professional American modern dancers, not only because of the box office competition in which foreign dancers of any kind always seemed to be favored, but also because of a plan by Wigman's theatrical manager, the impresario Sol Hurok, to follow up on the success of her tour by establishing the first American Wigman School. Under the direction of Hanya Holm, Wigman's assistant and a major teacher at her Dresden school, the New York branch of the Wigman School was opened in the Carnegie Hall Rehearsal Studios on West 57th Street in October, 1931.

Bonnie studied through the summer to obtain the rest of her high school credits and graduated in August, 1931. Her family had no money for the Cornish summer session so she did her Graham exercises and a ballet barre at home every day. Although Aunt Nellie had hoped that Bonnie would finish her dance education at the school, she understood the pull of Martha Graham for the determined girl and gave Bonnie her full support.

Because Graham wanted her prospective dancers to have as broad a training as possible in dance and drama before joining her Group, she arranged scholarships for them to the Playhouse School. In this way she could control and direct their development, not only through her own dance technique classes, but also in conjunction with Louis Horst's classes in dance composition. A scholarship was often accompanied by a small grant for living expenses which saved the girls from having to wander the streets of New York looking for jobs to maintain themselves. Graham also gave her Playhouse students free classes in her own Studio and had them dance in her larger works. They became her assistants and her teachers while progressing from understudies to solo dancers, all the time renewing their creative energy through their dedication to Martha Graham and her work.

Dorothy Bird, Bonnie's friend from the 1930 Cornish summer session, had already finished her first year at the Playhouse School. She came from Victoria, capital of Vancouver Island, British Columbia, a ferryboat ride from Seattle, where she had trained in ballet. Because their names were the same and they resembled one another they were often teased about being sisters. They soon became just as close. Dorothy was a year and a half older than Bonnie and had already finished high school when Graham arranged a scholarship for her at the Playhouse. During her first

year in New York City she danced with the Group in the premiere of
Primitive Mysteries (Louis Horst) in February, 1931. The dance was a
breakthrough for Graham and was immediately acknowledged as a work
of a choreographic genius.

   Years later Dorothy Bird remembered Bonnie as "a lovely, sunny young
student with pretty legs and coppery reddish-brown hair. Her mother
was a powerhouse and her father always wanted her to wear polka-dot
dresses. When we lived together in New York I was supposed to take
care of her, but of course no one ever had to take care of Bonnie. It was
kind of the other way around."[3]

In late August, 1931, Bonnie left Seattle on the first leg of the journey to
New York that started with a ferryboat ride northwest over Puget Sound
to Victoria to pick up Dorothy, home from New York on a family visit.
The boat was filled with hundreds of noisy, fascinating, indigenous
Indians – the Coast Salish, Nootka and Kwakiutl – on their way home to
their islands. In their midst she was captivated by the sight of a quiet
Japanese woman servant attending an elderly man as if he were an object
of worship. A new world full of splendors and surprises was opening
up for her that she wanted to share with her family. As soon as she could,
she put pen to paper and in frequent letters home over the next six years
recorded her adventures, vividly describing her feelings, frustrations and
accomplishments, along with finely drawn word pictures of the people
and events around her.

6

THE MARTHA YEARS

FROM THE LETTERS HOME

1931–1932: Launch

The two teenagers set off from mainland Vancouver on their 2800-mile transcontinental journey to Montreal, traveling on reduced-priced tickets obtained through Dorothy's family connections. To impress her parents Bonnie recorded every precious penny spent on food, as well as the exotic names of towns where they stopped. On one day they ate breakfast in Medicine Hat, lunch in Swift Current and dinner in Moose Jaw. They experienced Indian summer days and clear, cold nights as the landscape changed from the snow-capped mountains and deep valleys of the Rockies to the prairies and endless skies of Saskatchewan, and then to the rolling hills, blue lakes and evergreen trees of Manitoba and Ontario.

Other than the constant problem of coal dust from the steam locomotive spotting her dress, Bonnie enjoyed the journey. She saw her first rabbi, a rather grumpy man with a flowing red beard and bushy eyebrows, who ate only the food he himself cooked on the little stove in their carriage's own kitchen. The girls made good friends with their porter, a third generation Canadian descended from slaves, who was putting himself through medical school at McGill University. He took a great interest in what the girls were studying and contributed to their exercise regime nightly by letting them assist him in making up all the bunks, many of which were unoccupied.

After a year anticipating the moment of her arrival in New York City, Bonnie was anxious to see Martha and be welcomed by her. But there was no one to meet them the evening they arrived at Grand Central Station. She telephoned Martha and after a very warm greeting learned that she was teaching and also in the throes of moving house for a fussy Louis. Martha quickly but gently let Bonnie know that she was not going to be a surrogate mother, a role Miss Aunt Nellie had unstintingly filled, and that Bonnie would have to stand on her own two feet.

The girls spent their first night together in Manhattan at the Martha Washington Hotel on East Thirtieth Street. It had a reputation as a 'proper' hotel for young ladies and, to Bonnie's delight, was cheaper than the YWCA. Then Dorothy played city guide and took Bonnie for a long walk uptown to show her the Neighborhood Playhouse School of the Theatre and Broadway's Great White Way. Bonnie found the city quieter and the crowds much smaller than she had expected.

The next day they had lunch with Martha and Louis, accompanied by Max, Louis' dachshund. Martha was warm and lovely to Bonnie and told her that she had grown more ladylike. She invited her over to the Studio to take classes. Louis apologized for not having met them at the station and paid Bonnie one of his obliquely humorous compliments when he said that she was now "at least past the sweet girl-graduate stage." He took the girls to see his new apartment, along the way dispensing good advice and acting like a father. Afterward, Dorothy took Bonnie to the Graham Studio where she said hello to Group dancers Anna Sokolow, Lillian Shapero, Geordie Graham, Gertrude Shurr and Gertrude Ruiz. Then they visited the Playhouse School and Bonnie admired the "large, airy and elegant studios." She arranged to meet Mrs. Morgenthau, the school's executive director, and fervently hoped she would be liked.[1]

The Playhouse School Bonnie attended in September, 1931, was at 441 Madison Avenue, between 49th and 50th Streets. Other bits and pieces of it scattered around the city were later brought together at its present address, 340 West 54th Street. The Madison Avenue school occupied the third and fourth floors, each of which had a large studio, but the building had no theater, so the former Neighborhood Playhouse on the Lower East Side, by then called the Henry Street Playhouse, was used for school presentations.

Most of the two dozen students were high school graduates; a few had finished college. The five senior girls had almost all been brought in by Graham and included Dorothy Bird, Lil Liandre and Mary Tarcai. Bonnie described Mary as "a great big girl who looks like the statue of the Pioneer Mother." She felt that working in drama classes with the energetic and highly motivated Mary helped her lose her own self-consciousness. Bonnie found the seniors "simple, unaffected and real" and much preferred them to the 18 juniors, whom she thought of as "a society class, probably the result of the new, comparatively luxurious, school quarters."

Although there were some fee-paying students, the school was largely supported by wealthy patrons. Mrs. Morgenthau, a social worker as well as a wealthy woman, understood the importance of theater, not only as an art form, but also as a social force. Bonnie thought she was perfect in her role as "consoling arbitrator who kept everything going in the midst of constant skirmishes."

During her first year at the school, Mr. Bird could still afford to send his daughter $50 monthly. Food was Bonnie's major expense, but Dorothy quickly introduced her to Childs, a popular low-priced chain of restaurants where a satisfying meal cost only sixty cents.

It was Martha who helped the girls find the first of their many apartments together. It had only one room and the toilet was across the hall, but it was close to the school. Having grown up in a house with many large rooms, including a library into which her brother's horse had wandered, Bonnie was amused to find apartments in New York so tiny.

In the Depression years it was easy to find vacant apartments in good areas with one month's rent given free. This was an incentive the girls could not pass up and they moved often during Bonnie's first year in New York. Between apartments they would move back to the Martha Washington for a short stay and a decent bath, or spend weekends in South Norwalk with Bonnie's Uncle Jimmy and his sister Kate, where cake with thick chocolate icing for breakfast awaited them. After each visit they were slipped dollar bills and sent back to Manhattan with boxes of chocolates.

Fortunately their apartment hunting never took them near the city's Hoovervilles, the shantytowns that sprang up everywhere during the Depression. There was one in nearby Central Park right behind the Metropolitan Museum of Art with at least two hundred temporary structures. Many of its residents hunted for their dinners in the Park's bird sanctuary. In 1931 there were over a hundred reported deaths from starvation in New York City, but many more went unrecorded.

Shortly after the school year began, Irene Lewisohn returned from Europe to meet the students. Bonnie saw a slim woman of middle age with slender feet and a curious, sad, oval face. Her long hair was in a soft chignon knotted at the nape of her neck and she wore a mink coat that almost touched the floor. Bonnie looked forward to meeting the person who, on Martha's recommendation, was supporting her with a full scholarship, and the following year would add a small but necessary grant for living expenses.

When her turn came to be introduced, Bonnie, a strong, healthy Western lass, stepped forward to shake hands with 'Miss Irene', but her hand got lost somewhere inside the sleeve of the voluminous fur coat and she found herself energetically shaking Miss Irene's elbow instead. She felt as huge and overwhelming as an elephant and was very embarrassed.

In a matter of weeks Bonnie was participating in the senior as well as the junior levels of modern dance, dance composition and drama. Although she was soon officially promoted to the second year program, she insisted on continuing both levels with Martha and Louis. Because Graham was rapidly changing and developing her technique, Bonnie did not want to miss a single class. Martha taught nine hours a week at the Playhouse School; Bonnie would have liked nine hours a day.

The two courses in dance composition that Louis taught, Pre-Classic Dance Forms and Modern Forms, were formidable challenges for all comers. Louis said that these courses, begun at the school in 1928, had been inspired by Irene Lewisohn's insistence that a dancer should cultivate a more creative approach to music.[2] In the dedication of his book, *Pre-Classic Dance Forms*,[3] Louis wrote, "To Irene Lewisohn, whose foresight first made possible new experiments in these old forms." In the foreword to the same book, the dance critic Henry Gilfond described Louis' classes as based on new aesthetics in the composition of modern dances: formal structure, restraint, and an intellectual approach.

Louis pressed frightened, sometimes aggressive, but always hopeful students into transforming the essence of the early court dances such as the Pavane, Galliard, Allemande, Courante, Sarabande and Gigue, each with its own particular mood and rhythm, into modern dance compositions. It was often a painful experience for Bonnie, but she was able to find relief in the exhilarating classes in authentic court dances taught by the delightful, tiny Mr. Pirnikoff. In Modern Forms, in which she fared with more ease, the dances were based on modern developments in art and music, such as impressionism, expressionism, new tonalities, irregular rhythms and jazz.[4]

Bonnie had to prepare an average of two dances a week for Louis, who had a fearful reputation for shredding students after their showings. He might spend half an hour tearing her limb from limb with sarcastic, but nevertheless constructive, criticism as he did with her Sarabande. Even though he said her dance was good and technically right, he railed against her "lovely movements, full of that in-the-garden-fair stuff." She had to admit it was hard for her to capture the Lucrecia Borgia-like quality that Louis wanted. Mrs. Morgenthau, who often sat in on classes, agreed with Louis. On another day, when Bonnie did her dance in syncopated rhythm, Louis let out a big whoop and said that it showed "a glimmering of hope." Other times he made funny faces and called her endearing names like Blue Bird and Bonnet. "I like you so very much I can't always call you by the same name," he told her, making her laugh. She could not help liking Louis; he was so much fun.

Bonnie took part in many showings of compositions created by Louis' students when they were presented at the Henry Street Playhouse and other educational venues. Later, when she was a full-time member of the Graham Group, participation in Louis' programs was an integral part of the work.

From the beginning of her Playhouse studies, Bonnie was keen to accept Martha's invitation to take evening classes at the Graham Studio. Much to her dismay, Rita Morgenthau forbade her, as well as Dorothy, to go there. Mrs. Morgenthau thought that Martha might be tempted to use them regularly in the Group and she felt they were still too young for that. She said it was a "closed matter." The girls were very upset, but Martha quickly stepped in and worked her magic. She and Mrs. Morgenthau came to 'an arrangement' that allowed them to study twice a week at the Studio.

Bonnie was thrilled with the challenge of Studio classes, but there were so few students in them that she wondered how they could possibly be making enough money to cover the rent. She felt certain Martha was practically broke. Both she and Dorothy wanted to save some money from their own small allowances to contribute towards the cost of their classes. However, they were soon making their contributions by performing small chores around the Studio, such as taking Martha's dachshund, Mäd'l, whom Bonnie likened to a little black seal, for walks. When Louis was away, his Max and Martha's Mäd'l formed a duo. By the following summer, Alla, sired by Max, made it a trio.

The Graham Studio, having had several previous homes, was now at 46 East 9th Street, between University Place and Broadway, in a small, beautiful old brownstone with wonderful parquet floors. Martha's apartment was one flight up and comprised a long, narrow dance studio and her private little room with a bed, a telephone and her very simple belongings.

Bonnie was a 'gofer', someone always ready to take on any odd job. Because she was good in practical matters and picked up skills easily, with Martha's guidance she became quite good at cutting and sewing dance costumes. She quickly applied these skills to redesigning the official dance and drama costume worn by all the girls at the Playhouse School. She also learned how to make up her face and dress her hair to Graham's particularly demanding standards and began learning parts in Group works. Soon she was standing in for absent dancers in late night rehearsals. The twice-a-week 'arrangement' was quietly being augmented.

Nearly all dance studios held late afternoon and early evening beginner and intermediate classes to attract working people, and it was usually seven-thirty before Martha could begin Group rehearsals, which generally continued until eleven o'clock. All her dancers were girls, mostly in their twenties, who held only part-time jobs so that they could be on call during the hectic times before performances. For Bonnie and Dorothy, a rehearsal was usually followed by a late dinner with Martha and Louis, full of smiles and laughter, in some small Greenwich Village restaurant.

Martha was working on two new solos and a Group work for her December concert: *Dithyrambic* (Aaron Copland), *Serenade* (Arnold Schoenberg), and *Incantation* (Heitor Villa-Lobos). Towards the end of October she invited Bonnie to watch a rehearsal of *Primitive Mysteries*, her first dance that dealt with the universality of religious myth, a subject she would explore many times in her long career. That night Bonnie, transfixed, watched the three sections. *Hymn to the Virgin, Crucifixus* and *Hosannah*, danced by Graham and twelve girls. She found it "thrilling and glorious, simple and yet utterly beautiful." Afterward, the girls told her that it was the first time they had seen Martha at performance level in a Group rehearsal. Bonnie was deeply moved to think that Martha had done it for her. It made her all the more proud to be a part of all that was to come.

Graham soon again demonstrated her delight in winning people to her when two artists she greatly admired, but who had never seen her work, expressed their desire to watch a rehearsal of *Primitive Mysteries*. They were the English poet, Maurice Browne, and his brilliant wife, Ellen van Volkenberg, who together had directed one of America's first intimate, non-commercial theaters, the Chicago Little Theatre (1912–1917). Now both these artists were active in the drama department of the Cornish School. Instead of a rehearsal, Martha arranged for them to see her dances in a private performance at the Henry Street Playhouse.

Bonnie was there in her capacity as a gofer to help Martha change costumes, work the curtain and handle some of the backstage controls. The only mishap that occurred was when Louis asked her to raise the asbestos safety curtain. She began to pull on the rope, but it was so heavy she could not do it alone, so Louis joined in. Then the flautist Hugo Bergamasco also pitched in and the three heaved at the rope until they managed to get the curtain to the right height. Louis bent down to put a cleat in the pulley but fumbled it; the curtain came down with a tremendous thud while Bonnie, still holding tightly to the rope, went flying upward. Martha's ringing laughter could be heard even above Hugo's guffaws. "Somehow they got me down and we finally made it stay, but I have never seen Louis work so physically hard. He actually did a little manly sweating from bending so much!"

That night, seventeen-year old Bonnie saw Graham dance some of her finest works, for an audience of two. They included *Lamentation* (Zoltan

Kodaly, premiered in January, 1930), which she had previously seen in Seattle. She found it "as striking as ever; so fine and clear." She thought the Group in *Primitive Mysteries* was "outstanding and so direct," and the grim, powerful *Heretic* (premiered in April, 1929, danced to a revolutionary folk song of 10 bars repeated throughout the work), "more beautiful than I can say. It must be seen."

Then Martha danced solos Bonnie had never seen before. *Dolorosa* (Villa-Lobos, premiered in February, 1931) was "very intimately and beautifully danced." She loved *Harlequinade* (Ernst Toch, premiered in January, 1930), in which Martha waved her polka-dotted scarf as a symbol of all the tragedy and comedy in the world, and she thought that the two characters Graham created – the biting, brilliant Pessimist and the subtle Optimist – were "marvelous in their subtlety and brilliance." She described *Two Primitive Canticles* (Villa-Lobos, premiered in February, 1931), with its *Ave* and *Salve*, as "a work of astonishing simplicity."

After the performance Louis went out front to speak with the Brownes, who were thrilled with what they called "this new art." Their positive response elated Bonnie. She felt that Martha's work deserved supporters who would spread the message about her genius. She was sure the Brownes were the kind of people who followed up their words with action. In high spirits she and Dorothy packed up the costumes and went back to the Studio with Geordie Graham and Dini de Remer, Martha's rehearsal pianist and general secretary, and on to supper.

Herbert Gellendré, a former drama teacher at Cornish, had recently become the Playhouse School's head of drama. He taught the Stanislavsky approach to acting that he had learned as assistant to Richard Boleslawski, a former member of Stanislavsky's Moscow Art Theatre. Bonnie enjoyed Gellendré's classes very much, especially the assignments she shared with the captivating Geordie Graham, who came to the school for drama classes. Gellendré liked Bonnie's work and told her so. Both he and Mrs. Veazie, Bonnie's diction teacher, thought her voice was very good. Mrs. Veazie declared it had the stamp of Columbia University on it rather than the sound of Seattle, which was also Veazie's home town. By the following spring, after several successful stage appearances that showed off her acting ability, Bonnie was not sure whether she should concentrate on dance with Martha Graham or focus on a career as an actress. She felt that both teachers wanted to do their best for her, and her own indecisiveness made her very unhappy. Directly after an appearance in a drama production, final talks with Graham and Gellendré on this matter took place in the wings. The two masters then retired to the back of the theater to let Bonnie make her own decision. She chose Martha and dance: that was what she had come to New York for and where she felt her real interests lay.

All through this first year of new experiences, the pace of city life made it difficult for Bonnie to feel close to the Northwest she so loved and missed. Robin Hill seemed far away, and so did glorious Swede Hill where she rode her two horses, Black Bess and circus-trained Bright Eyes. To keep her in touch with the land, her father sent her books on Indian legends and medicine men's dances, and because she treasured them she shared them with Martha.

In her first weeks at the school, one of her overriding concerns was to obtain passes through her father's connections for the big November rodeo at Madison Square Garden. She invited Louis, but was not surprised when he said he was too busy. Dorothy and Geordie were more than pleased to join her and admire her favorite rodeo stars as they performed in the heart of Manhatten.

In long letters to her brothers, Bonnie advised them, with a maturity beyond her years, on their education and responsibilities, and reminded them how lucky they were to have such a wonderful home. She told Scott-E. (Scottie) that children in New York City did not have their own horses, nor did they have the natural wonders that surrounded him in the West. "In New York, people ride subways and elevators instead of horses."

Mr. Bird did not have the money for Bonnie to return to Seattle during the 1932 summer break, but she was not left on her own. Gellendré invited her to join his drama group, a collective of theatrically-skilled young people, many from Cornish, called the Repertory Playhouse Associates. It was based at Elm Lea, an arts-centered camp in Putney, Vermont. Bonnie taught dance and was Geordie Graham's assistant for *Corrido*, a dance work she created. The group, in which Geordie also proved a popular actress, spent eight weeks performing a variety of plays and dance-dramas. There was some trouble with the camp sponsors because of a play by e.e.cummings called *him*, which the gentle ladies decided had not been written in 'proper' English and was too raw. The local farmers were also on edge, unaccustomed as they were to having thespians on the loose and sometimes a bit tipsy late at night.

During that summer, Martha Graham and Louis Horst were visiting ancient ruins on the Yucatán Peninsula and the Pyramids of the Sun and Moon outside Mexico City, a project made possible by a Guggenheim fellowship which Martha had been awarded – the first dancer ever to be so honored. From her cruise ship, the *Morro Castle*, Martha wrote Bonnie long letters full of advice about little Alla, who, together with Mäd'l and Max, had been left in Bonnie's care.

1932–1933: A Balancing Act

Dorothy Bird became a full-time member of the Graham Group while Bonnie, in her second year at the Playhouse School, spent more and more time at the Studio learning all the Group works, sewing costumes and generally helping out. Because of their late night rehearsals the girls moved to 224 Sullivan Street on the south side of Washington Square, a short walk from the Studio.

Martha Graham's first concert of the season took place on Sunday, November 20th, at the Guild Theatre, and included three premieres. In her letters home, written with sensitivity and perception, Bonnie shared her impressions of Graham dancing at the height of her physical prowess.

Of the new opening dance, *Prelude* (Carlos Chávez), she wrote, "To this tumultuous flood of Chávez' chaotic music, Martha moved quickly, lightly, almost unconcernedly catching the changing tempi in amazingly dextrous foot rhythms. It was a frank, joyous greeting that finished as simply and startlingly as it began."

About the second premiere, *Dance Songs* (Imre Weisshaus), scored for flute, drum and baritone, she wrote, "It is an ingenious and exciting work. Of its four exquisitely danced solos, *Ceremonial* was like a sacred rite in which the earth, giver of great fruitfulness, was blessed. It was a sensitive and extremely stirring dance. *Morning Song* was full of exuberance and the joy of living, conveying the feeling of a clear, bright Indian morning. *Satyric Festival Song* was accomplished in the impudent, slightly mad style that is one of Martha's best, and *Song of Rapture* was serious and not at all in the usual sense of rapture. Formal in the beginning, it built logically to a beautifully controlled ecstasy that finished with simplicity." Bonnie also observed that Martha's style of dancing in this work had changed significantly. "It has become more positively lyric and pervaded by a great sense of clear, wakeful stillness."

The new work for the Group, *Chorus of Youth – Companions* (Horst), brought this response: "A rather unwieldy title, but an exquisite thing for which Louis has written superb music. The dance is quite delicate and sensitive in mood, reminiscent of *Adolescence* [Paul Hindemith, 1929] which we saw in Seattle. For me, it is one of the loveliest things Martha has done in this vein, despite the fact that she does not feel it is such a fine thing herself. She dressed the girls in white skirts, with solid bright red or blue tops with kerchiefs – almost like middy tops. Dorothy was very beautiful and danced extremely well. Everyone commented on her handsome blondness." Of *Primitive Mysteries* and *Dithyrambic*, she wrote, "These older works have grown clearer, stronger and more thrilling than ever."

When Bonnie was writing her observations about Graham's works, the art of the professional dance critic in America was still in its infancy. John Martin had begun writing about dance for *The New York Times* in 1927 and a year later became the first dance critic employed by a newspaper. At about the same time the New York *Herald Tribune* hired Mary Watkins as its dance critic. Dance reviews in almost all other newspapers were usually handled by music critics or sometimes even by sports columnists. The few magazines devoted to ballet hardly touched on modern dance. There were some people, however, who thought that this 'new art', especially that of Martha Graham, needed its own dance publicists. Starting in early 1934, Louis Horst, Winthrop Sargeant, Henry Gilfond, Ralph Taylor, Mary P. O'Donnell and others would write paeans and criticisms for *The Dance Observer*, a monthly magazine edited by Louis Horst that was committed exclusively to recording the achievements of modern dancers. Louis was a discerning writer, though always prejudiced in Graham's favor. Based on the premise that dance is a major art in the modern world, *The Dance Observer*'s dedicated writers began to bring a new awareness and appreciation of modern dance to a growing public.

After the Guild Theatre performance, Bonnie went back to the Studio with Martha and helped her repack her bags for a three-day tour to North Carolina and Virginia. On the way to the station Martha told Bonnie that she did not know how she could get through performances without her help, and a bit of luck, in that order. She wondered what she would do next year when Bonnie would be in the Group. Bonnie took her "sweet flattery" as just that, but was happy that her hard work was appreciated. She knew that the years ahead as a Group member would be hard, but she was even then looking to the distant future when she would start her own independent career in dance.

While Graham was away Bonnie stayed in Martha's small room and looked after the Studio. When Martha returned she told Bonnie that she was considering taking the house on Washington Square they had both looked at in September. Half of it or more would be Studio space and her own apartment, but there would be plenty of room for Bonnie and Dorothy to come and live with her. "She said that she knew of no one else she would like better to be with her. It would be grand."

A few days later Martha was off to Cleveland for the previews of *Lucrece*, André Obey's adaptation of Shakespeare's dramatic poem, *The Rape of Lucrece*, produced by the actress-manager, Katharine (Kit) Cornell. Graham had assisted Cornell and her husband, the director Guthrie McClintic, in setting the staging and the stylized movement. Under her guidance, Kit Cornell, who did not speak until the final scene of the first act, filled the stage with voluminous movement. The play opened at the Belasco Theatre in New York in January, 1933, and achieved a modest success. It also began a professional association and a deep friendship between these two great women of the American theater.

The last week of December, spent at Radio City Music Hall, was an unforgettable experience. Samuel L. Rothafel, 'Roxy', who already had one big New York theater, The Roxy, dreamt of building the largest, best-equipped theater in the United States in which to present the finest attractions from vaudeville and the concert world. Rockefeller money helped him realize his dream. On December 27, 1932, Radio City Music Hall, the huge, not quite finished, 6000 seat artdeco theater on Sixth Avenue at 50th Street, opened with a program that included Martha Graham and her Group. Perhaps Roxy remembered Martha from her early appearances as a Denishawn dancer at his theater in Los Angeles and thought she would provide a similar act. If so, he was in for a big surprise. Also featured in the Music Hall premiere were the German expressionist dancer and a Graham rival, Harald Kreutzberg, popular stage and film actor-dancer Ray Bolger, comedian W.C. Fields, opera singer Jan Peerce, and the trapeze artists 'The Flying Wallendas'. The Music Hall's own stage productions under Leon Leonidoff's supervision included a ballet of sixty dancers directed by Florence Rogge, Russell Markert's forty-eight precision dancers, the Roxyettes (later renamed the Rockettes), and an orchestra of one hundred.

Bonnie was surprised that Martha had agreed to perform in such an "undignified milieu." She was even more surprised when she found herself included among the dancers for *Choric Dance for an Antique Tragedy* (Horst), Graham's first Group work using ancient Greek subject matter.

Any part of the enormous stage of Radio City Music Hall could be lowered or raised quickly. With all the most modern stage gadgetry at his fingertips, the stage manager lived in utter terror of pressing the wrong button and plunging untold numbers of people to their deaths. He almost had a nervous breakdown and was not helped by Roxy's continuous hollering. A grand piano was lost during the chaos and by opening night it still had not been found. A section of the stage on which the piano stood had apparently been lowered during rehearsals, the piano had rolled off and people kept pushing it out of their way. It was eventually discovered a week later in the labyrinth of unfinished under-ground passages under Fifth Avenue.

The dress rehearsal lasted non-stop for two days and two nights and the gala opening night was a marathon performance that finished about one o'clock in the morning. Martha and the Group came on after mid-night. "The stage floor was still moving as I got to my place. Through a sliver of light coming from below I could see scores of performers and a horse from *Carmen*, the previous act, still walking around. They were on the lowered upstage section of the stage while we performed on the downstage area. I had to lie on my back, feet towards the audience, exactly where two interlocking blades of the stage came together and I could feel the restless floor underneath me just beginning to settle. It was a terrifying experience.

"Louis Horst was conducting. At the drum roll we sat up in second position, a rather startling effect; you didn't see us and then you did, but not in what would be called 'a ladylike position' even though we wore skirts. We filled the whole width of the stage with our dancing, but hardly 20 feet of its depth. Only a cloth curtain masked the huge drop onto the set below, making us very nervous when we had to move backwards upstage."

The press review Bonnie best remembered was by a sports writer sent to cover the big opening. He especially loved Martha's dances because the girls galloped over the stage at such a fantastic pace. In his column in *The New York Times,* John Martin put it more succinctly when he praised Graham for the volume of movement she had created on the huge stage.

Because Martha's technical demands were continually increasing, Bonnie observed that there were one or two girls in *Choric Dance* who could no longer keep up; however, she loved to watch Mary Rivoire, whose thrilling movement brought praise from Martha. She also immediately liked May O'Donnell, a new Group member and also a Westener.

The second night's performance was full of the comical mishaps in which film makers of the 1930s gloried. Getting ready for *Choric Dance,* the instrumentalists took their places in the pit on the lowered platform. On cue it began rising and as Louis Horst came into view his white hair glowed majestically in the dazzling light. He raised his baton and signaled for the first drum roll, but all was silent. The percussionist, having managed to survive the unending dress rehearsal and overlong opening night performance, had fallen asleep on his drums. Other misadventures included a violin that was held too near the edge of the platform and had its fingerboard chopped off on the way up.

The Music Hall extravaganza did not attract big audiences and Roxy admitted that his wonderful dream had become his swan song. Shortly after the opening he was 'out'; the reason given was a health problem requiring an operation. Graham thought that he had probably been thrown out earlier, when Rockefeller had threatened to withdraw funding, but because of his name he was kept on until the ballyhoo was over. Martha and the Group, as well as several other performers, were quickly taken off the program; nevertheless, she twice waited in the wings ready to go on with all the girls until the stage manager handed her a formal dismissal notice. It was very humiliating. Because Roxy was so highly regarded as a man of his word there were few written contracts, but Graham eventually got her full fee according to his original promise. Just two weeks after its opening, Radio City Music Hall became a theater premiering films on a program with sumptuous stage shows. Its special family Christmas show still features versions of Leonidoff's famous production from those early days, *The Living Nativity*.

With the excitement of working closely with Martha, Bonnie became impatient with her second-year studies at the Playhouse School, particularly the drama presentations. She made a proposal to the drama department that she appear with Geordie Graham in a production of Christa Winsloe's *Girls in Uniform*. She thought it was an exceptional play and felt confident she could act any of the roles; however, she lost her argument. Unshaken and always practical, she hurried back to the Studio to mend Martha's *Heretic* costume once again.

Agnes de Mille's ballet classes delighted her. She found de Mille "frank, but taciturn to the nth degree when anyone is the slightest bit raw; a worker, and witty. She is very nice to me, but cross if ever I am an inch off. It's wonderful to have discipline such as that. No mollycoddling. She knows so much about the history of ballet, the style and manner that go with each period, and where its place is in today's world of culture and art. She is one of Martha's greatest admirers, but nearly brains anyone who carelessly combines ballet technique with modern dance. They belong to two entirely different worlds: one, a highly developed code of gesture; the other, a code of life." De Mille was convinced that Bonnie would become a dancer and energetically argued the point with a visiting drama director who was positive she should be an actress. Much to Bonnie's disappointment, de Mille taught only one term; all her discreet lobbying could not bring de Mille back again.

During that year Bonnie studied voice and diction with the volatile Laura Elliott, whose former pupils included the leading actresses Katharine Cornell and Eugenie Leontovitch. Elliott had given up a promising operatic career because of psychologically-induced vocal difficulties. To understand her own problems and be of greater benefit to her students she studied the works of Sigmund Freud and other psychologists. It was through her work with Elliott that Bonnie began to acquire an understanding and appreciation of the delicate relationship between mind and body.

In her first Playhouse year Bonnie had declined to join Elliott's classes, having been warned off them by Dorothy's description of her freightening tantrums. But now she looked forward to these weekly classes, even if Elliott might fly off the handle, tear her hair and scream at a student. She especially liked the choric speech classes in which the students chose a particularly beautiful poem or one with a catchy rhyme and then built a musical approach to the poem's meaning, feeling and structure. She discovered a thrilling new dimension to poetry in these classes. Elliott also enrolled Bonnie in a choric speech class at Columbia University. The young student found herself the only participant who was not a teacher, did not have a degree and was under twenty years old. "If Laura Elliott decided you should do something, you did it!"

The goal of Elliott's teaching was to bring out the unique qualities of each individual through movement and voice. She kept Bonnie busy working on the role of Henrietta, Elizabeth Barretts' high-spirited younger sister in Rudolf Besier's *The Barretts of Wimpole Street*. Katharine Cornell had recently been enjoying a huge success in the leading role. At one point Elliott suggested that the drama department should feature Bonnie in her own play, as yet unwritten, about Mona Lisa. "A corn-fed Mona Lisa, say I," was Bonnie's droll remark, and she declined, ostensibly because of her heavy work load. Elliott became very excited when she felt that she had found her young student's true quality, and described Bonnie as "a visionary who brings her own Western lands with her wherever she goes."

The Playhouse students sometimes sang in the world-famous Dessoff Choir, under the personal direction of their singing teacher, Madame Margareth Dessoff, a woman Bonnie came to admire deeply. Her first awareness of what Hitler was up to came in January, 1933, after his appointment as Chancellor of Germany, when Madame Dessoff came to class in tears and apologized for being German. Bonnie was very moved. She was only just beginning to understand the impact of politics on people's lives.

Lectures on theater by Miss Irene provided a lighter side to the studies. By no stretch of the imagination was the kind lady a good public speaker; there were so many agonizing pauses filled with 'aahs' in each of her sentences that the students organized competitions whose winners, Bonnie often among them, counted the most aah-filled pauses in each lecture.

In January Graham began directing and choreographing the *Six Miracle Plays* (Horst) for the Stage Alliance, presented at the Guild Theatre on February 5th and 12th, 1933. "Martha asked me to watch rehearsals. The plays are a surprisingly charming and different comment on the Bible. They are in dance movement with the speakers off-stage, and Martha is the Virgin in all six ten-minute pieces. They are so simple and stunning. In one of the six, Geordie is the Magdalene and Dorothy is Luxuria, one

of the Seven Deadly Sins. Dorothy is very good in her small part. So is
Mary Rivoire as Salome. The Cornish School boys Ken Bostock and John
Harrington are in them, but they don't move very well and are having
a hard time. They don't seem to understand that motion creates emotion,
as well as emotion causing motion. The costumes are so lavish and
elaborate that there is a good deal of movement lost and Martha is on
the verge of a showdown with the costume designer, Natalie Hays-
Hammond, who is also one of the producers. Martha hates directing
plays, but she is being very good about it. She is unhappy because she
was roped into this project against her will. Poor darling, she is so tired
of contending with stubborn people when she wants to do her own
work."

Back at the Studio Bonnie was learning new Group dances Martha was
choreographing to complete a trilogy that included the Radio City Music
Hall piece. The whole work was called *Tragic Patterns: Three Choric Dances
for an Antique Greek Tragedy* (Horst) and was presented on February 20th
at the YMHA in Newark, New Jersey. *Chorus for Supplicants*, *Chorus for
Maenads*, and the earlier dance, now called *Chorus for Furies*, made
awesome technical demands on the girls.

Bonnie's Playhouse and Studio activities overlapped until they were
inseparable. While Graham was busy choreographing, Gertrude Shurr,
her professional assistant, often taught the Playhouse School classes. But
when Shurr took leave to have a nose operation, Bonnie was asked to fill
in for her. She was very proud of herself for surviving her own rigorous
school schedule and her Studio work on top of the extra teaching and
demonstrating.

Graham sometimes attended Playhouse drama classes and on one
occasion watched a classroom presentation of W. B. Yeat's poem, *The
Only Jealousy of Emer*. When it was over, and in front of the class, Martha
praised Bonnie's devastating power and straightforwardness, her ability
to create a monumental figure, and her simple but passionate use of her
hands.

Bonnie was in a state of elation until the next class, when Louis brought
her down to earth with a thump. He made her run endlessly in
circles – half time, double time, with pauses, with hands on hips or body
bent. Louis yelled. Bonnie had hysterics. The rest of the class withdrew
inside themselves.

When Martha returned at the end of February after a concert in Detroit,
she taught her first class in six weeks. "It was hard! She gave us one
combination that had leaps in a pivotal circle on march rhythms, a terrific
run in place and hopping turns. It was a strange happening – like the
tale of the ten little monkeys. First, Edith tore a gash in her foot on a tiny

piece of stone on the floor. She hobbled off and we swept the floor. Then Bernice got a terrible cut in her foot from heaven knows what. Then Lil, Ethel, Jane, Rose and I got terrific blisters. And then there were none. It was almost funny, but everyone is safe, doctored and bandaged. Poor Martha got so worried she didn't know what to do."

In March Graham was fighting off exhaustion and illness. "Martha gave two recitals and a concert with the Group within two weeks. The first was at Bennington College in Vermont, the second in New York City, and the third in Brooklyn. They were good and she danced well, but the audience in Brooklyn was dead. So are all the Brooklynites, I am told."

Bonnie was busier than ever with her performances for Louis. "Next Friday we are dancing some place on 106th Street. I am doing the everlasting *Lyric Gavotte* of mine, plus *Jazz Epigrams* (Kodaly), a Debussy, an authentic Sarabande and a Pavanne. Geordie can't come so I have to teach Ethel Butler the seven Kodaly dances. Tonight I'll finish the entire outline with her. Then comes the polishing and group work. It could be that I have to manage this entire concert as well as the costumes, which have yet to be done. Wow, but I love work – lots of it!"

Even though the already small number of new Broadway productions was getting smaller, in the spring of 1933 Bonnie was still able to see quality theatrical offerings from many different parts of the world, at affordable prices. Of a recital by Harald Kreutzberg she wrote: "He is surely an artist who has the power to thrill and excite through purely technical movement, but he doesn't have much to say that is meaningful." She wished her brother Scott-E. had been with her when she saw the *Teatro dei Piccoli*, Vittorio Podrecca's Italian marionette troupe that specialized in lampooning famous people. "I saw Sergei Rachmaninoff in the audience laugh at a satire on a concert pianist until tears fell. Louis, fat Louis, shook like jelly and embarrassed Martha by his guffaws." Bonnie delighted in the "exquisite perfection, delightful naïvité and gorgeous costumes" of Uday Shankar and his dancers. She saw Katharine Cornell in *Alien Corn* and thought it "not nearly as thrilling as *Lucrece*", and *Grand Hotel* with the Russian actress Eugenie Leontovitch – "a slapstick comedy chock full of laughs. I loved it for being so melodramatic and impossibly impossible. Leontovitch has the Russian method of broad comedy."

Martha's mother, Mrs. Homer N. Duffy, came to New York for a visit and Bonnie escorted her around the city. "She is a darling – old fashioned, very wise, gentle, homey and unlike Martha, whom she worries about. I doubt if she can see Martha as a great person. When Martha dances, Mrs. Duffy worries about her tiredness. Typical mother.

Bonnie at the family ranch, Robin Hill. Mrs. Bird is second from right. Photo: Bonnie Bird Collection.

She was shocked by Geordie, whom she has not seen in over two years. Mrs. Duffy remembered her as 'a babe in arms' when she left, and now she found her quite a sophisticated lady – long hair, dressed up, etc. She wants to take her home right away. I think she might, too."

At the conclusion of Bonnie's last year at the Neighborhood Playhouse School she went back to Seattle for the summer to be with her family, her horses and her much-missed open country. On her return to New York in September, 1933, she became a Group dancer and teacher with Martha Graham.

1933–1934: "Great Times are Coming!"

Instead of the talked-about house on Washington Square, by the spring of 1933 the Graham Studio had moved to 66 Fifth Avenue, between 12th and 13th Streets in Greenwich Village and Martha had taken an apartment around the corner at 29 West 12th Street.

The Studio was in a modest building that today is occupied by the Parsons School of Design. It was quite spacious and was greeted favorably. Happily, it did not have the usual intrusive support post in the middle of the room. Louis Horst also held courses there in Pre-Classic Dance Forms for Martha's students and Group members. Often during rehearsals mysterious voices rising from a foreign film cinema on the ground floor caused the girls to break into giggles. Ruth St. Denis and La Meri once had studios in this building, and Wigman-trained Tina Flade and Ruth Wilton were then teaching there. Mills College of Primary Education, a women's college, occupied several floors, and its teachers and students sometimes participated in the Graham classes.

Louis had his apartment at 63 East 11th Street – a big studio with a skylight and two little rooms at either end. Later on, while continuing to hold some of his courses there, he let it to Dorothy, Bonnie and Ethel Butler, another Group dancer, when his rotund body could no longer negotiate the many steps of its narrow, downward-tilted staircase. The girls often drew straws to see who would push the other two up these unfriendly stairs after a long rehearsal. Because it had no kitchen they used it only for sleeping and storing their clothes. Bonnie remembered once returning late at night and seeing Louis' huge bulk sitting at the piano, cigarette dangling from his mouth, eyes closed, unknowingly playing to a traumatized mouse near his feet. Early in 1934 it also became the official address of *The Dance Observer*.

When she began teaching at the Studio Bonnie earned four dollars for each of the lessons she gave to the Apprentice Group, the advanced students Graham had her eye on as future Group dancers. She was paid a total of twelve dollars a week and felt she was the highest paid assistant in New York. For each of Martha's concerts she earned five or ten dollars. Not without jealous objections from some of the other Group members, Martha selected her for various extra teaching assignments at the Playhouse School and Eve Le Gallienne's Civic Repertory Theatre on 14th Street, where she taught movement classes for actors. During the following year she also demonstrated and taught for Graham at Sarah Lawrence College in the nearby suburb of Bronxville.

Bonnie found some of the classes at the Playhouse especially difficult to teach. "The students know nothing about movement. They had a year with Tina Flade, just long enough to get mannerisms. I am expected to recreate them in ten lessons, so I will certainly give them hard workouts. Whether or not they have the guts to stand up under them I do not know!" Mrs. Morganthau tried to calm her ardor, but Bonnie felt she had to teach to Graham's high professional standards, regardless of whether the students were ready for such demands. Years later she would remember this episode as a perfect example of how not to teach.

Most of the Group members earned their living doing all kinds of tiring and tatty little jobs, mainly waitressing in vegetarian restaurants or working as artists' models. But the girls found strength through their joint efforts to solve financial problems, such as the time Martha did not have money for the rent and they all took on extra jobs so that they could lend her the money. Bonnie did not let her family know she modeled in the nude for Eugene Speicher and Walter Kuhn, both well-known American painters. Kuhn, whose subjects were mainly circus people, dressed the girls in amusing headdresses. He thought Bonnie terribly funny because she was a Westerner.

Guarding her every penny, Bonnie made her own clothes, which she described as being "clumsy in this era of fine tailoring." With the onset of bitter cold weather she put a warmer lining into her old winter coat rather than buy a new one. When all the banks were closed by the Federal Government for five days in March, 1934, and only those that were deemed 'good banks' were allowed to reopen, neither she nor Dorothy were much bothered because they had so very little money on deposit. But the long lines of desperate people on the pavement outside the banks remained deeply etched in her memory.

Always a little homesick for her beloved West, Bonnie treasured a newspaper photo her father sent her entitled, "Good headwork at the Issaquah Rodeo." It showed Strawberry Red Wall roping a galloping horse while standing on his head.

Bonnie taught, demonstrated and shaped her classes in the mold Martha established. When she began studying with Martha at Cornish, she consciously paralleled her feet in a dancing class for the first time and often afterward said that she did not turn her legs out again for several years. Graham was seeking the most economic use of movement to achieve a startling simplicity: when she stood with feet parallel, one slightly behind the other, and spiraled her back from the base of the spine, she captured not only the weight, but also the reality of an archaic Greek statue come to life.

Bonnie was fascinated by the way the technique changed as the choreography developed. Martha was not teaching because she wanted to create a technique. Teaching was a laboratory where she worked out the problems that arose in her choreographies. Each year the body of the work, pivoting around her new core concepts of 'release' and 'contraction', became more complex. Along with these came Graham's awareness of the power of the 'turnout'.

Martha's dance vocabulary began to use powerful transitional movements common to athletes but never before made the basis of a dance technique, the release and the contraction, which were exemplified in her solo, *Ekstasis: Two Lyric Fragments* (Lehman Engel), created in May, 1933. She often watched tennis matches with Louis, who had been a keen player in his youth, and she studied the players' movements. She observed that when gathering and focusing energy for the serve, the player first prepares the body's structure in which the whole musculature is fully committed to the action. She developed this in her dance technique as the release. The contraction, perceived as a concave, half circle between the base of the spine and the top of the neck, occurs at the moment the player prepares to hit the ball, and in the action of hitting all the focused energy of the body is expelled. The contraction and release allowed for an organic development of movement that led to a new lyricism in Graham's dances. But she recognized that this continuous reorganization of the body had nothing to do with conscious breathing. When the tennis ball is hit, the breath is expelled because of the action. The breath is the result of action, not its instigation. Release and contraction are not breath-initiated. She never talked about breath. When someone held their breath she would touch their chest to open up their body.

Martha's rediscovery of the turnout began with her 1931 solo, *Dithyrambic*, in which she used the broken rhythms of Copland's score in a relatively small movement vocabulary that traveled in space only because she repeatedly fell, rose, fell again, got up and moved on. For several years afterward she worked on finding out the technical secrets inherent in these movements. She continuously explored the recovery from the fall and the powerful use of the legs as they turned outward from the hips and brought into play the interaction of the strong thigh and pelvic muscles. As a consequence of her work on this dance she experienced for herself the value of the turnout, through which a new kind of ecstatic movement began to make itself manifest in her choreographies.

Graham's perceptions of what she was searching for and wanted to emphasize in a work-in-progress, such as the way the weight of the dancers' bodies was carried in *Mysteries*, could be shifted slightly according to the dancers she used to demonstrate the movement. The technique also varied to accommodate particular characteristics of key teachers or dancers. Bonnie saw a clear example of this two years after she had left the Group, when, during its 1939 West Coast tour, she observed that Ethel Butler had greatly influenced the basic body placement. Ethel had an unusually flexible body and tended to carry her upper back very high, almost backward, in an exaggerated, primitive way. She performed with enormous strength and could leap into the air with her chest parallel to the ceiling, which Martha liked very much. Bonnie observed that most of the Group had adopted Ethel's placement and were using it in a wide range of works that she herself had danced. But Martha soon saw that this carriage was causing lower back problems and within a few years it was dropped.

When Bonnie joined the Group modern dance concerts in New York City usually took place on Sundays, a fairly recent development. In the late 1920s, public entertainments on Sundays were still subject to each state's own 'Blue Laws', and in the Puritan traditions of the Founding Fathers Sunday theatrical presentations in New York were forbidden. Performances of music were permitted, however, but there were grey areas in the interpretation of the rules. Silent films accompanied by music enjoyed a big Sunday public, and when talkies started in 1927, Sunday showings continued. In 1924 the dance-mime Angna Enters was the first dance artist to rent a theater for a Sunday evening performance; Graham followed in 1926, Doris Humphrey and Charles Weidman in 1927, and afterward any dancer able to afford the reduced Sunday rental fee. The owners of the Guild Theatre on 52nd Street, for instance, were happy to rent their theater out for dance concerts on normally dark Sundays. The Schubert family's string of theaters, like many others, remained closed. Dancers were harassed when the Sabbath League tried to invoke the law against them and even Mary Wigman, in whose own country Sunday dance concerts had been popular for years, was brought to court by a religious fanatic after her first American performance on a Sunday in New York City in December, 1930. In answer to the judge's question as to whether or not she had danced, a policeman testified that she had only interpreted the music, and since there was no law against the interpretation of music on Sunday the case was dropped. Wigman was vastly amused by this experience.[1] The fight to have dance performances on Sundays was finally won in 1932 by the Concert Dancers League of New York City, an organization set up by the dancers themselves with the prime purpose of fighting for their legal rights.

Organizations ranging from trade unions to women's clubs provided Graham with venues for her many out-of-town engagements. But because it was difficult and expensive to find a suitable theater with a good stage for dance, her New York City concerts numbered only four or five a year. A New York concert might cost her about $860, more than a third of which was for the theater rental.[2]

For Graham, a Sunday performance meant lighting rehearsals late on Saturday night after the theater's show was struck and early the following morning. She often gave a matinee as well as an evening performance so there was very little time to work. She did her own lighting because she could not afford to hire anyone else. Except for summer premieres under the auspices of Bennington College from 1935, lit by Arch Lauterer, and a set of New York premieres lit by Philip Stapp in 1939, it was not until 1943 that the lighting genius, Jean Rosenthal, a former Playhouse student, became Graham's specialist lighting designer, as well as one of her most sensitive collaborators.

For Bonnie, a long Saturday night spent frantically sewing up costumes until exhaustion overtook her usually preceded an early Sunday morning lighting rehearsal. Martha frequently changed her mind about costumes a day or two before a premiere, threw them out and started creating new ones. Sometimes the last stitching was going on backstage at curtain time. With two performances on the same day nerves were stretched to break- ing point. Time and again the costumes were completely redesigned fol- lowing a premiere. Only after Bonnie left the Group in 1937 did Martha hire the designer, Edythe Gilfond, to take on all this responsiblity.

Modern dance concerts were usually performed in front of simple black plush curtains. When Graham experimented with minimal sets there were sometimes disagreements with the stagehands about whether the dancers themselves should move certain pieces on and off the stage. In later years Graham and her designers created extraordinary pieces that could be carried, rolled, unrolled or pushed onto the stage by the dancers in the act of dancing. These were classified as stage props so she did not have to hassle with the stagehands' union. It was a practical and eco- nomical solution to what might otherwise have been an expensive undertaking.

From the autumn of 1933 Bonnie's daily life consisted of teaching, rehearsing and performing, all of which she loved, and sewing costumes. Though a good seamstress, she did not enjoy being used in this way. There were also difficulties with several of the other girls, as often happens when a group of sensitive artists work long hours closely together. Ailes Gilmore, a Group member from 1930 to 1933, advised Bonnie to keep herself to herself, trusting only her friends Dorothy, Sophie [Maslow] and Lily [Mehlman].

Martha was often ill. In October, with a season full of solo performances ahead of her, she lost her voice. "She has to give a concert tomorrow night in Colgate College in upstate New York and has only been able to practice about twice. She is as fit to dance for those football fans as to go up into the stratosphere. We have to go back and help her fix costumes tonight."

Bonnie was very nervous before her first performance as a regular Group member on the 19th of November, 1933, at the Guild Theatre. "I am working hard on *Primitive Mysteries*. Have a part in a back line, which is fun. I am with May, Dorothy and all the girls. It's like the wind, huge and strong. Have to perfect the *Choric* dances. They terrify me."

The house was sold out. The program also featured Martha's new solos, *Dance Prelude*, a dance of greeting, (Nikolas Lopatnikoff), and

Frenetic Rhythms, whose *Three Dances of Possession – Wonder, Renunciation,* and *Action* (Wallingford Riegger) represented categories of obsession. She also danced *Dithyrambic* with Aaron Copland at the piano. The critics and audience went wild with delight. In a later review of *Frenetic Rhythms* critic Ralph Taylor wrote in *The Dance Observer,* "This mature creation provides ample display for Miss Graham's virtuosity as a dancer. Hers was a superb exhibition."[3] And several years later Mary P. O'Donnell wrote in the same magazine, "*Frenetic Rhythms,* no longer startling in its space concept, continues to hold its enormous popularity with audiences of every type. From the very first, onlookers have cherished it with devotion."[4]

The concert was a success and Bonnie was pleased that she had danced well. The pressure was off and the strain over for at least a short while. It was time for a change of pace and who but Martha knew that better? She took Dorothy and Bonnie to a performance of a Wagner opera at the Metropolitan Opera House. It was the first time Bonnie had ever seen a grand opera, and to add to the magic of the occasion they sat in Mrs. Morgenthau's box. More from astonishment than merely as a remembrance token, Bonnie kept her $60 ticket stub.

During the Christmas season Martha and Louis took the two girls to midnight supper after a rehearsal and talked and teased about everything in general and nothing in particular. For one thing, Prohibition, which had come into law in 1917, had officially ended on the fifth of December throughout the whole of the United States. "Martha suddenly got the bright idea of taking us to some new tap room to have our first real cocktail. She wants to do it this week. She laughed when Louis said, 'Well now, maybe our daughters are a bit young'. But she promised to take care. You would think we were still in rompers."

On New Year's Eve they gathered at Martha's apartment. Champagne made everybody dreamy. With Bonnie at her side, Martha read aloud from a book of Navajo legends, while Dorothy curled up on the rug in front of the fireplace and Louis sank deeper and deeper into the couch. Afterward everyone acted a bit silly.

The new year saw the arrival in New York for the first time of René Blum and Colonel de Basil's Ballet Russe de Monte Carlo. With the indomitable impresario Sol Hurok watching over its reception, the company opened at the St. James Theatre to artistic acclaim. Its repertoire of Diaghilev ballets and new works by George Balanchine and Leonide Massine were danced by the exotic prima ballerina Alexandra Danilova and the eye-catching 'baby ballerinas' Irina Baronova, Tamara Toumanova and Tatiana Riabouchinska. Even though Hurok lost a great deal of money on this first season, over the succeeding years he brought the company back for longer seasons and more extensive tours. It soon became a popular money-maker.

"The Ballet Russe de Monte Carlo arrived today. They are sensational and make more difficult the recognition of American dancers by their own country. Perhaps the effects of their visit will have worn off by February 18th and 25th, the dates for our next concerts in New York. Let's hope so. Martha is helping us costume and set our own dances for Friday. She is wonderful!"

Bonnie was referring to one of a series of special evening programs in which promising choreographers in the Group showed their own dances. Louis had persuaded Martha to let their pieces be performed at the Studio. He offered advice while Martha, acting as a 'general supervisor', often tore the dances to pieces, expecting the young choreographers to rework them until the promise she felt within them was fulfilled. For Bonnie, her help was positive and inspiring.

The day before Graham's February 18th solo concert the girls were busy sewing costumes for her two new dances: *Transitions*, which included *Prologue, Theater Piece No. 1 – Sarabande, Theater Piece No. 2 – Pantomime*, and *Epilogue (Engel)*; and *Phantasy* (Schoenberg). That night Martha became very ill and was in terrible pain. Bonnie and Dorothy stayed with her and by three o'clock in the morning she began to feel better.

With daylight came a hectic time, beginning with a lighting rehearsal. "I had to hold up or put on all Martha's costumes while she lit them from out front. It took hours but was fun. Martha felt low and nervous all day and the girls still had to finish sewing her costumes and tights. They ran crazy right up to the minute she went on. Well, it was a thrilling experience. Wonderous is the word for it. Martha danced superbly. It was her first New York solo concert in several years. The audience rose in waves of bravos and were warm and enthusiastic long afterward. We all went to an Italian restaurant and dined on homely scrambled eggs. Martha was tired beyond knowledge so we took her back to her apartment and put her to bed and wended our happy, tired way home.

"Martha's *Transitions* is amazing. Its dances are like Japanese Noh plays. The action is carried by words and acting as far as possible, but there comes a time when words are insufficient. Then the actors must dance the meaning and the audience understands. Martha used the voice of a boy soprano for accompaniment in the *Sarabande*. No other voice could have had more compassion and yet have been so impersonal and pure. It stirred the depths. Critics who did not favor Martha before now turned tail and raved. John Martin said Martha had never danced better. She did not feel that was true, but you never can tell about such things."

The Dance Observer's Ralph Taylor wrote of the *Sarabande*, "With perfect control and clear intention, the pre-classic dance of Renaissance aristocracy was wracked and distorted to the utmost, projecting a peculiar implication of emotional overtones. Against a background of the sterile, time-beating reiteration 'un, deux, trois', the dead form expanded and grew monstrously, as if feeding horribly on its own lack of inner compulsion and necessity."[5] This dance became one of Graham's most frequently performed solos.

"The day following Martha's solo performance was devoted to furious struggles with one of the two new Group dances, *Celebration*. It is by far the most difficult, technical, virtuoso piece of choreography Martha has done for the Group. We literally sweated blood through rehearsals. The dance lasts about eight minutes, but for me it is eight minutes of the most amazing feats in the air. It winded me so in rehearsals that I ached all over and felt as if I were being consumed by fire. My throat was parched and my lungs burned, but gradually I learned how to sustain it. Perfection is ever yet to be attained."

"On Saturday, February 24th, we worked all day and night on costumes. Martha had been fitting costumes continuously for over twelve hours and was worn out. Sunday I held up the blue and black costumes on stage in the light for her and afterward we rehearsed. It was terrifying. I had become accustomed to the spacing in the Studio, focusing for balance on certain places. The floor there is smooth and sprung, but the Guild's stage is full of cracks and screw holes and is laid over stone, which means it has no give, so we had to use every extra bit of strength to gain elevation. On the Studio floor we soared, but so high it threw us off rhythm. How we had to work! But it was a great success. The house was completely sold out and over one hundred were turned away, and this on a raging, stormy night. The other new Group work, *Four Casual Developments*, with Dorothy [Bird], Sophie [Maslow] and Anna [Sokolow], was very lovely and successful. They were all so beautiful."

Four Casual Developments (Henry Cowell) was a satiric piece about innocent Victorian maidens, undoubtedly drawn from Graham's own adolescent experiences. *Celebration* (Horst), a remarkable tour de force of technical virtuosity to a score for trumpet and drums, was the first dance in which Graham let her Group fill the stage with airborne exuberance. Sensational jumps carried the dancers away from a center point into smaller, contrapuntal groupings, with only a short middle section on the floor. It sparkled with joy and the audience loved it. In the Group were Bonnie Bird, Dorothy Bird, Ethel Butler, Louise Creston, Lil Liandre, Marie Marchowsky, Sophie Maslow, Lily Mehlman, May O'Donnell, Lillian Ray, Ethel Rudi, Lillian Shapero, Gertrude Shurr and Anna Sokolow.

Bonnie's letters during March were an almost daily account of that hectic month.

Wednesday, March 7th: "We gave a second Studio concert that was quite good. We sold out, turning away over thirty people on the promise that we repeat it."

Thursday, March 8th: "We repeated the Studio concert to over one hundred people. The audience was very serious. It was composed mostly of men, who are a very exacting audience."

Friday, March 9th: "We danced at the New School for Social Research, or rather demonstrated the technique and Martha lectured. It was interesting. People did not heckle as is their wont at these affairs."

A series of lecture-demonstrations on dance had been taking place at The New School for Social Research on West 12th Street since it had opened in 1931. Composer and faculty member Henry Cowell had first suggested the idea to Graham and Doris Humphrey. They agreed to participate and asked John Martin to organize and lead the programs. It was for this series that Graham began developing the lecture-demonstration as an art form to explain her dance technique and its motivations to the general public. Spanning eight years, these programs played a major role in building modern dance audiences in New York City.

Saturday, March 10th: "My choreographic masterpiece, ironically called *The Death of Tradition*, was quite well received. At least the audience was convulsed with laughter and my costume designs were like nobody knows what. Reminded me of necromancers of fantastic legend. The whole thing resembled a satire on a funeral procession. Martha liked it and so did the audience. People were terribly surprised to discover, as somebody said, 'that side of my imagination'." [On November 25, 1934, Bonnie's piece was performed in a concert given by the Workers' Dance League at the Civic Repertory Theatre. It was slapstick and good fun and received not only hearty applause, but also a mention in *The Dance Observer.*[6]]

March 11th: "Tomorrow night we go to Toronto for two days. Dancing at the Massey Hall on March 13th. We are doing six dances and, more amazing yet, seven girls are going. It was such a surprise to discover how hard I have to work! I am also dancing *Bacchanale*, which has the reputation of being just about the most difficult dance to do outside of *Celebration*. Martha has been very nice to me. She is making me wear her handsome tweed coat to Toronto in case it is extremely cold."

March 12th: "More rehearsals. Costume fittings that went haywire because Martha started reminiscing about her friendship with Rouben Marmoulian, Garbo's latest so the papers say. He was director at the Eastman School in Rochester when Martha was there. According to her, Marmoulian is a very magnetic and poetic man with definite hypnotic powers. We are ready to leave for Toronto tonight, with our woolens."

March 15th: "The concert in Toronto was quite an experience! The house was about the size of Carnegie Hall. It wasn't sold out, but the audience was warm in the restrained 'British' manner. Martha had a cold so we did not have a rehearsal on stage. I had never done three of the dances outside the Studio, so I was terrified. The ground cloth was gritty and loose, there was very little lighting equipment and we had plush drapes rising about six feet up from the floor which were attached to dirty tan-colored hangings from there on up. Outside of these minor tragedies, we were well fixed. The audience was so shy and naïve that they didn't know when to laugh. They remained stoney through some of the wildest antics. In *Four Casual Developments* the girls all but winked at them to let them know they could smile if they wished. The critics were a riot. One, in a heroic attempt to describe *Heretic*, said, in effect, that Martha, 'in one of her white, true-like creations, pleaded and begged for mercy from the group, which relentlessly depicted the attitudes of galvanized stupidity'. How strange we must seem to them. Toronto is not much of a city even if it is supposed to be the Queen City of Canada, but it was fun going there. I only wish I could have kept on going right to the Pacific Coast."

March 19th: "This week we began work on a new dance to be done on April 17th with the Pan-American Association of Composers. It will be entirely different from anything Martha has done before. It will be more theatrical, with other people collaborating on costumes, lights and music. It is going to be terribly difficult, though no worse than the agonies of *Celebration*, which are something!"

April 1st: "Last night we had a concert at the Washington Irving High School on 16th Street and it was packed in spite of the pouring rain. Martha danced very well and the audience was enthusiastic. The Group thought they danced well, but we were told otherwise. Ailes said we looked awful, so I fear we have more trouble in the offing. We have another Studio concert on the fourth of April."

Bonnie had become good friends with Ailes Gilmore, the strikingly beautiful and refined daughter of a Japanese father, but possessed with the wit, humor and impulsiveness of her Irish mother. She often came to performances and the girls took her critical evaluations of their dancing seriously. Ailes lived at the Hotel des Artistes on West 67th Street off Central Park. Her brother, the young sculptor, Isamu Noguchi, who was soon to begin a life-long collaboration with Graham designing startlingly spare, symbolic sets and props, often spent hours there exchanging ideas with his friend, the eccentric architect-inventor genius, Buckminster Fuller. Fuller had just designed and built his Dymaxion car for the Buick automobile company – a five-seater on three wheels – and he took Bonnie for a ride in it. She found that "the crazy car could turn on a nickel." His concept of modern living included a house in the air supported on a hundred-foot column. It would be air-conditioned, automated, and fire and burglar proof. "He is mad enough to have the quality of greatness," she wrote.

One night after a Studio performance Bonnie and Dorothy were waiting for the elevator when Louis came bursting out of the Studio and asked them to meet Martha and him at the Jumble Shop Taproom. "It was the most beautiful snowy night, so gentle it seemed as if a great caressing hand had succeeded in hushing this noisy, tumultuous city. Dorothy and I walked around Washington Square and then to the nearby Taproom. The walls were covered with drawings and paintings and a great fire roared in the hearth. The whole atmosphere was mellow and pleasant. Louis was in a good humor and Martha told such drole tales. It was one of the nicest evenings this year." It was at the restaurant in the Jumble Shop, with its friendly, relaxed atmosphere, that the four often celebrated Martha's May birthday together.

By mid-April rehearsals were climaxing for what was the second concert of a subscription series given under the auspices of the Pan American Association of Composers at the Alvin Theatre. It featured Martha's new dance, *Intégrales*, subtitled *Shapes of Ancestral Wonder* (Edgard Varèse). The proposed costume collaboration with the architect-designer Frederick Kiesler failed utterly when the girls demonstrated that they were unable to move in his close-fitting rectangles of material that went from head to foot and had only a small circular hole at eye level to see through. Martha threw them out and designed new ones. The dance was full of leaps, runs and jumps – "fifty or so in one place, and breathtakingly fast turns. I don't see how we can last out." Graham used the stage more freely than in any of her previous dances while maintaining the strong structure and growing emotional intensity characteristic of her work. Although severely tested by the rhythmic intricacies of Varèse's music, the technical precision of the Group was highly praised. *The Dance Observer's* Winthrop Sargeant wrote, "With this work, the American dance has reached a new high point."[7] The program included *Four Casual Developments, Ekstasis, Primitive Mysteries, Two Primitive Canticles* and *Frenetic Rhythms*, along with orchestral interludes. The concert was sold out.

Bonnie was exalted by Martha's triumph. In a letter to her family she showed herself as an inspired prophetess, a willing martyr, and a modest supplicant: "Last Sunday's concert was a tremendous success. Martha won an audience unaccustomed to dancing and they gave her a huge ovation. They stood and cheered. By the end, some of the pedagogues of the classical arts who have been more than cool toward her came to thank her and extol her greatness. John Martin was warm in his enthusiasm. We were told that the Group had never danced so well. *Intégrales* was a tremendous success in spite of a rotten conductor and all kinds of troubles. Martha's greatness lies in her dancing, her driving energy and her uncompromising will. Hers is not a personal ambition urging itself on to be satisfied, but the burning force of one whose inherent qualities are those of a genius. I know you believe in her because I do, but believe me, great times are coming! A new American culture is being born and is manifesting itself not only in the dance, but in all the arts. Martha is the first leader of the band now and will continue on as such. We are the pioneers, as you once said so truly. The way is hard and mean at times. It takes great sacrifice and self discipline, for we are our own best critics and believers. I do not wish to sound like a wordful schoolgirl, but these are the things I feel deeply and haven't the power yet to phrase properly."

Bonnie knew she was in a critical phase of her career, but if she could make the most of these valuable, formative years they would most certainly lead her to a life of her own in dance that would be, in her words near the end of this letter, "radiant, strong and perfect."

Even though she would have liked to have gone home for the summer, interesting plans were taking shape that made Bonnie realize she was "one of the luckiest girls in the world, being so close to one of the greatest dancers in the world today and one of the greatest in the history of dance."

"Martha is not going West this year. She is scheduled to teach in July at Bennington College in Vermont. Louis will be teaching there also, but for a longer time. Martha, in the strictist confidence, has been given a sum of money to carry out her plans for the summer. She has asked Dorothy and me to spend the time with her in New England. She wants to buy a car which I am to drive so that we can get around the countryside. She plans for us to give some small concerts of our own dances for several groups around New England, so we must work on them consistently."

From its inauguration in 1932, Bennington College had offered a Bachelor of Arts degree with a concentration in dance. The series of events leading to a dance program started during the last building phase of the college, when it was found that there was no money left to erect and equip a gymnasium. A suggestion by the college president's wife, who knew of Martha Graham, that dance classes might replace athletics, was taken up. Graham's advice was sought about a head for the program and she

Bonnie as a young member of the Martha Graham Dance Group.
Photo: Paul Hansen (Bonnie Bird Collection at the Laban Centre).

recommended Martha Hill, a former Graham student and early Group member (1929–1931), who, since 1930, had been teaching at New York University's School of Physical Education (PE). Apart from Wisconsin University, it was the only academic institution in America that offered a graduate major in dance. Hill agreed to became part-time head of the Bennington dance program while still continuing at New York University.

In the spring of 1933, at the low point of the Depression, Bennington's president, Robert D. Leigh, started investigating ideas on how the college could cover its expenses during the summer months. It was Martha Hill who set forth and developed the idea of an experimental modern dance summer school. She quickly gained the active support of John Martin. On the day of Bonnie's first concert as a member of the Graham Group in November, 1933, he prepared his *New York Times* readers for the first stage of a support structure for modern dance in America by outlining its difficult situation, with particular emphasis on the public and private support that European modern dancers were receiving. He had already agreed to lecture at Bennington without fee and publicize the school in his Sunday column.

The first Bennington School of the Dance took place from July 7th to August 18th, 1934. Organized through academic channels, the six-week session drew its student body mainly from university and college PE departments. The hundred or so students were all women and mostly PE teachers. On the staff were Martha Hill, her colleague Mary Josephine Shelly as administrative director, Gregory Tucker, teacher of music for dancers, Bessie Schönberg, a former Graham Group member (1929–1931) as Hill's assistant, and Norman and Ruth Lloyd as accompanists. The visiting faculty included John Martin and Louis Horst and the four major creative dance artists: Martha Graham, Doris Humphrey, Charles Weidman, and Hanya Holm, with their assistants and accompanists.

Graham, assisted by Dorothy Bird, was the first of the four to give a week of technique classes, followed by a solo recital. May O'Donnell and Dini de Remer assisted Louis Horst's course, 'Music Related to Movement'. He shared the final presentation with Hanya Holm and Martha Hill and their students. Martha Hill gave courses in teaching methods, fundamental techniques and dance composition while other faculty members led discussions on current events, physics, American painting and modern poetry. Sculpture and painting exhibitions and film showings were also on offer. John Martin's lectures on dance history and criticism concluded with a symposium on modern dance. In his *New York Times* column he praised the school for having "succeeded beyond the hopes of its most ardent well-wishers toward building a sounder and more vital art."[8]

That first summer proved so successful that the program was expanded each summer from 1935 to 1938. In 1939 the Bennington School of Dance took place at Mills College in Oakland, California, returning to Vermont for the summers of 1940 and 1941 as the Bennington School of the Arts. From 1935, Graham, Humphrey, Weidman and Holm and their companies were featured in six-week residencies of concentrated creative work. The 'Big Four', as they came to be called, created 16 of the 42 works presented over six Bennington Festivals. (There was no festival at Mills College.)

Bennington created its own legend. The hundreds of participants who came from all over America carried their newly discovered cause, "... physical education's own dance, its own art"[9] back to their campuses and studios, which in turn became part of a national network of sponsors for modern dance performances. Only a short time after John Martin had first made public the "precarious predicament" of American dance, a national support structure was in the making.

The saga of Snake Hill Barn began with Martha's friend, Edith J. R. Isaacs, the brilliant, wealthy founder-editor of *Theatre Arts Monthly*. Because Edith Isaacs believed that the arts were an important educational and social force, she actively supported and publicized the work of the Lewisohn sisters. She took Martha under her wing from the early days of the Neighborhood Playhouse School, inviting her to her famous salons and seeing to it that Graham's works were reviewed in her magazine. While the Bennington Summer School actually involved Martha for only one week, Edith Isaacs arranged for her to get a much needed rest away from the pressures of the city by renting a charming, small, converted New England barn in Connecticut for her use during the whole of the summer. It was called Snake Hill Barn. After holding the Studio's first June Course, four weeks of intensive classes, Martha, Louis, Dorothy and Bonnie set off for the country.

Snake Hill Barn, in Highbridge, about ten miles north of Stamford, was built partly on stilts on sloping ground. It is still there, a typical barn of that area. Bonnie was intrigued with its many doors and windows. Inside was a quaint balcony that connected the two tiny bedrooms under the eaves where Martha and Louis slept. Everybody bumped their heads on the low timbers as they went in and out of these rooms all summer long. There was a stone fireplace that shot up right through the middle of the house and one entire wall was lined with hundreds of books. "There are shelves, cubbyholes and concealed drawers everywhere for hiding things from oneself, crazy carved chests to fall over, two astonishingly long tables, and built-in floor cupboards that double as benches whose lids tilt up, turning them into deep wells large enough to hold someone." At some time in the past an enclosed front porch had been added that was just wide enough to accommodate the two couches where the girls slept.

The house was surrounded by a lovely meadow that was very private except for the foxes, skunks, woodchucks and deer that wandered around and through it. To one side was a small wood with a brook that ran deep enough to bathe in if the mosquitoes could be endured. The climate was almost tropical. Rain storms with thunder and lightning often shook the little barn to its foundations and increased the already unbearable humidity. "Everything is continually green. There is so much vegetation it almost stifles you. This country is gracious, but not spacious. For that reason I miss the West with an awful ache."

Life's saving grace at Snake Hill Barn, thanks to the generosity of Edith Isaacs, was a second-hand 1928 Model A Ford touring car that cost $75. Bonnie had searched for it while plans for the summer were being finalized. A local garage in South Norwalk checked it over and pronounced it a good buy. The Model A had a canvas top that could be rolled back on a fine day and if it rained side windows made of mica could easily be snapped into place. It looked "very much like an insolent hen about to ruffle her tail feathers" and was accordingly christened 'Tookee, the Tin Chicken.' Without Tookee, everyone at Snake Hill Barn would have been hopelessly isolated because there was neither a telephone nor a bus service. Bonnie was the only one of the barn four who knew how to drive a car or fix a spare tire. She skillfully drove her passengers more than 6400 miles that summer, often with the canvas top rolled down, her head scarf fluttering in the breeze, wearing a train engineer's denim jacket she had bought second-hand for twenty-five cents.

Life at the barn was not all roses. Believing himself to be a totally urban person, Louis disliked country life in any form. He was silent and disapproving, which made Bonnie so nervous that it was all she could do to keep from having hysterics. He was only able to tolerate life at the barn by listening at full volume to the huge supply of Sibelius records he had brought with him. The interior walls were so thin they began to quiver.

Martha was made miserable by the realization of her mistake in attempting to be domestic for most of the summer, and also by having to contend with a short visit by her mother and her second husband, Homer M. Duffy, who had driven all the way from Santa Barbara to be with her. Bonnie was upset to find Mrs. Duffy a difficult person who was continually dissatisfied. She found Mr. Duffy "a fussy Rotarian type, stubborn and loquacious." She finally concluded that Martha loved them only because they were family, but they really did exhaust her. "They can be very sweet when they try, which is wrong because people should not have to try." To get away from it all the girls moved to nearby South Norwalk for a week.

At the start of the Bennington session Bonnie delivered Louis to the campus high on a hill just north of the old town of Bennington. He was lodged in Jenning's House, a white clapboard New England Colonial building, in a suite with pale green, frilly, organdy curtains. "For Louis!" was Bonnie's disbelieving comment. That dark afternoon she drove the 150 miles back to Highbridge through torrential rain and noted that Tookee had already clocked up 3000 miles in four weeks of gadding about.

Mr. and Mrs. Duffy drove Martha and Dorothy to Bennington a few days later. "I thought I was going, but I have to stay at the barn, teach my two evenings of classes in New York and do odd jobs. I was disappointed because I very much wanted to go. We didn't have enough money to manage it, among other things. Since Dorothy was the official assistant she went. Martha said she might have to send me a hurry call because they might need me, being as how there are so many students registered to learn something of her technique in a week. If Martha knows what her name is by the end of the week it will be a wonder. She is teaching three batches of 30 students daily in one-and-a-half-hour classes. That is worse than her schedule at Cornish was. However, I am going up to see the recital she is giving there."

While everyone was away, Anita Alvarez, still a student at Washington Irving High School, stayed with Bonnie at the barn. Anita was just beginning intensive study with Martha and Bonnie thought that she looked and moved like the beautiful Mary Rivoire. Anita soon joined the Group and, like Dorothy Bird and other Group members, her subsequent career took her successfully into Broadway musicals.

On Friday, July 20th, after teaching four-and-a-half hours, Martha finished her Bennington week with a performance on the tiny stage of the 150-seat College Theatre in the Commons Building. Although Graham's energy had been sapped by her heavy schedule, Bonnie wrote home that she had danced superbly. With Louis at the piano, her two-hour program, with only one intermission, offered *Dance Prelude, Lamentation, Dithyrambic, Satyric Festival Song, Exstasis, Primitive Canticles,* the *Sarabande* from *Transitions, Frenetic Rhythms* and *Harlequinade.*

After the recital, Bonnie, with Dorothy, drove Martha to Putney where she joined Mr. and Mrs. Duffy for a short tour of Vermont and Massachusetts. The girls headed back to Snake Hill Barn, leaving Louis at Bennington for the duration of the summer session.

All summer long Bonnie drove the fifty mile round trip from the barn to New York City twice a week to teach evening classes at the Studio. Although the small number of transient students would never make professional dancers, Bonnie was continually fascinated by these young people who moved with such a strange beauty. Martha and Dorothy often accompanied her on the journey, and Martha sometimes remained at the Studio for a few days to work quietly on dances for the coming season.

The soothing summer quiet at Snake Hill Barn was once again torn asunder when Geordie Graham and her boyfriend, the arts writer, Winthrop Sargeant, along with his brother, Emmet, came for a short visit. Sargeant had first become acquainted with the Graham sisters when he played the violin for Martha's 1926 debut recital. The trio's visit severely tested the limits of the cramped barn's role as a peaceful retreat. "Martha is sitting next to me, in a lather about her fuddled bank account; Geordie on the other side, fussing over a jigsaw puzzle; Winthrop upstairs scrawling his articles for the *Saturday Evening Post*; Dorothy deep in a book; and Mäd'l about to bring forth a litter. We are very peaceful though. This is the kind of seething and boiling that doesn't make any noise because everyone is so problemed over one thing or another. Simplicity is sometimes very complex..."

Usually the barn was a quiet haven for reading, working, being generally domestic if only casually so, and the base from which Bonnie took Martha and Dorothy for long rides along the winding New England roads. According to Bonnie's recollections, however, the modest program of events sometimes took on theatrical proportions in Martha's hands.

The barn did have electricity, but water for bathing and washing in the big 'Saturday-nite tub' had to be heated on a tiny propane-fired stove. Graham liked to be left alone in the early mornings, so while the girls slept she got up and made tea or coffee, set the bath water to heat, cleared away the rug from in front of the fireplace and began her workout there in the tiny space that went clear up to the roof. Although the polished timber floor was full of uncomfortable knotholes, this small area was the strongest and safest part of the building. If Martha moved two or three feet to either side she was underneath the dangerously low balcony that led to the bedrooms. She had found a working space, high but very narrow, and Bonnie speculated that it was from this time that her technique began to use the turnout. "We had used our legs in parallel position for several years, employing some turnout but not emphasizing it. Martha was reworking *Dythyrambic* in her morning workouts at the barn and it was my notion that because the space was so narrow she didn't have more than two alternatives to the recovery from the backfall. She either had to turn out and rise, or remain in parallel position and stay on the floor!" This may have been an over-simplification of the early use of the turnout in the Graham technique, but one based on Bonnie's daily observation from the front porch.

"Dorothy and I started our morning class by doing stretches on the porch railing. We synchronized our warm-up to follow one sequence behind Martha's because the porch was very narrow and there was no space for the standing work. We would begin our technique class on the porch floor when we could see that Martha had nearly finished doing her own floor work, including her continuous work on the back-fall, in front of the fireplace. After her standing work and while she was jumping and finishing off with a few combinations we would move in behind her for our own standing work. Then she would disappear around the corner – there were no doors in the barn except for the loo – and take her little bath with the water she had cooked while Dorothy and I were still doing our jumps on the safe floor in front of the fireplace."

Afterward, Graham usually sat in the garden and read the books Louis had found for her. She read a great deal and was always searching for new ideas. During that summer she was very interested in problems relating to the anatomy of pain. She was enormously influenced by two contemporary German graphic artists and sculptors, Käthe Kollwitz and Ernst Barlach, whose work was deeply affected by their experiences during the First World War.

In dance classes she often talked about watching people's feet, about how a person's foot curls in pain, anguish or despair. Her dance, *Lamentation*, based on pain and how the body communicates emotion, made a very deep impression on Bonnie because its serious subject matter was seldom dealt with in dance. Graham was all about plunging into reality and examining it. This was very important to understanding her work and was part of the great attraction she had for young people who, growing up during the Depression, were deeply concerned with its effects on the world immediately around them.

The Depression was not the only disaster to tear at the heart of the nation. Vast areas of the Midwest – Wyoming, Nebraska, Colorado, Kansas, Oklahoma, Texas and New Mexico – were being reduced to desert by years of poor farming methods, erosion and drought. Spread by high winds, huge dust clouds brought ruin and starvation to farming families in this 'Dust Bowl'. In June, 1934, Congress voted six billion dollars in aid for the farmers in stricken areas, but it was too late to stop thousands from migrating to the West Coast in search of jobs. Countless numbers of unemployed were already there and the situation was made worse by widespread strikes for better living and working conditions. By July the chaos in San Francisco led to the imposition of martial law.

Bonnie wanted the workers to hold out for their rights, but at the same time the realization that so many people would be made even more miserable upset her. The news from Seattle was not good. Because daily necessities were in short supply she wanted to send her family a crate of food, but the railroads were on strike. She wished she could give Tookee to her mother to help her get through her long days spent working in the medical relief program for the unemployed and, as president of the King County PTA, her strenuous battles to keep Seattle's schools open.

It was seven one morning when a young, ambitious Fuller Brush salesman, seeking customers in the back of the beyond, rang the bell on the front porch where the girls slept. Bonnie had already opened the door when Martha suddenly appeared, panic-stricken for the girls' safety, and the unlucky man was quickly dispatched. Almost immediately she took the girls off to a 'five-and-dime' to buy a strong door lock. Not finding one, she bought instead a dozen catches that resembled hooks and eyes – one part flipped down and was noisily secured by the other. With these she 'seamed' the whole door. If the girls wanted to go out, all twelve locks had to be clicked open. To lock the door afterward, all twelve had to be banged shut. Relieving themselves out-of-doors in the still of the night was quite a noisy performance.

Louis did not return to Snake Hill Barn because Ruth Page asked him to accompany her in a concert in Chicago. At the end of the Bennington summer session Bonnie picked him up and drove him to Albany, New York, where he boarded a Chicago-bound train.

The three women continued their summer at the barn without him. Martha, who appreciated good food but did not know how to create it, usually made supper. She was a kitchen comedienne whose humor and theories about good cooking were the real stuff of her simple concoctions. Her idea of 'Italian style' green beans was to pour olive oil over them after they had been partially cooked. The girls ate her creations out of a sense of duty. Afterward they usually piled into Tookee for a long drive with the top down. They never went out in pouring rain, however, because a big hole in the canvas still needed a patch job. They all enjoyed getting purposefully lost and discovering new roads. These evening drives often opened up interesting conversations about America, the differences in its Western and Eastern topography and their feelings about the land. Martha enjoyed playing the role of mother-teacher in these lovely, relaxed, family-like evenings. She discussed relationships, marriage and a great many other things in a maternal and caring way. And she also talked a great deal about her own feelings on art. It was during these trips that she would say things like "one must never stop growing" or "as soon as you think you have discovered something and you choose to settle for that bit of knowledge or perfection, it is the beginning of the end." She would parallel her ideas about constant change and the dynamics of growth with the function of art. These chats along quiet New England country roads were a way for Martha to sound out her ideas.

The summer mixed work and play. Alexander (Sandy) Calder had recently returned to the States after living in Paris for several years and was staying in a nearby barn with his wife and two young daughters. Influenced by Mondrian's theory of color and Miró's forms, he was creating hanging, floating mobiles – dynamic shapes on wire tendrils that danced through space – and was becoming a leading figure in the school of sculptors who worked in metal.

Sandy came over to Snake Hill Barn to experiment with two giant mobiles for a work that Martha was to create the following summer for the first Bennington Festival. His mobiles were to be controlled by the dancers themselves and the first experiments took place in the field in back of the barn. There, Bonnie and Dorothy worked with Calder to discover the movement possibilities of these flying forms made of lightweight wire covered with stretched fabric.

The afternoon rehearsals started as each girl shinned up a tree where a pulley had been suspended from a strong branch. Each put a long rope through the pulley and tied one end of it around her wrist. Down on the ground Sandy tied the other end of each rope to one of his big mobiles. Returning to earth, the girls used their arm movements to control the flight of these forms in varying ways and at different speeds. Sandy, with his bubbling enthusiasm and childlike sense of wonder and play, made the rehearsals endlessly good fun.

Edgard Varèse, the composer of *Intégrales*, was also summering nearby with his wife. They were living in a houseboat, built by Leopold Stokowsky for his children, which was moored out on a newly created lake. Its flat roof was encircled with marvelously carved wooden animals, so it was called 'The Ark'. Bonnie loved to see Varèse, a big Burgundian Frenchman, pedalling his water bike out to it with his friend Sandy Calder splashing close behind. Varèse's wife was a wonderful cook and evenings at The Ark were full of good food and gaiety.

On another occasion, Martha and the two girls dressed in their best finery for a party in the orchard of Edith Isaacs' home in Stamford. Among the guests was the tiny Russian actress, Maria Ouspenskaya, whom Bonnie admired for the character roles she played in Hollywood films as well as her teaching of the Stanislavsky method. "We were immensely enriched in New York and on the West Coast at this time by many of the Russian exiles who had come to the United States via Paris and China."

Under Martha's caring eye, Bonnie was quickly becoming a young lady who accustomed herself with grace and ease to cosmopolitan settings.

1934–1935: "Opening the door on a new and shining world"

The fresh air and relaxing country diversions of New England were soon forgotten amid relentless rehearsals for two November concerts a week apart and two plays for which Graham created the dances.

A few days before the first concert on November 4, 1934, Martha sprained her ankle and it was postponed for a week, but she recovered quickly and was at the top of her form for both performances. Two premieres were the fruits of her quiet summer. *Dance in Four Parts* (George Antheil) was a twenty minute solo comprising *Quest, Derision, Dream*, and *Sportive Tragedy*. Each dance contained six emotionally related moods in which she created the dance motifs through the exploration of pantomimic symbols. The two dances of the second premiere, *American Provincials* (Horst), were given their titles by Bonnie: *Act of Piety*, "... this caustic brew, mother-liquor of worm-wood and acid"[1] and *Act of Judgement*, "... the veritable lashing of the tongues of dance, which, speaking in terms of movement and movement only, forms the elemental wrath of the dancer."[2] Over the course of the two performances Bonnie danced in *American Provincials, Celebration, Primitive Mysteries* and *A Chorus for Furies*. "The audience almost brought down the roof with its loud huzzas."[3] Louis Horst drew his own special set of cheers at the final curtain.[4]

Edith Isaacs had a wide range of contacts as editor of *Theatre Arts Monthly*. She kept Graham informed of the latest important theater developments and introduced her to leading theatrical personalities, some of whom invited her to work with them in legitimate theater during the 1934–1935 season. Making dances for Broadway productions was no longer the domain of music hall artists such as Albertina Rasch, but these jobs were scarce because the number of new productions steadily dwindled after the Wall Street Crash. Thanks to the repeal of Prohibition, vaudeville had begun a process of rejuvenation and by early 1934 nightclubs and floor shows were making a comeback. Broadway producers hoped that quality productions would provide an incentive for audiences to return to the theater.[5]

Anna Sokolow and Bonnie were Graham's assistants for a new Maxwell Anderson play, *Valley Forge*, which tried to make a dramatic hero of George Washington. The play, for which Martha made only a minuet, opened in Washington, D.C., on November 26th. As rehearsals climaxed, Bonnie reached her own conclusions about the production: Anderson's play was mediocre and so was John Houseman's direction. She considered the whole production mismanaged by the Theatre Guild Company and was not surprised when it quickly closed.

Having worked closely with Martha in the staging of *Lucrece*, Katharine Cornell asked Graham to choreograph the dances for her company's production of *Romeo and Juliet*, to be directed by her husband, Guthrie McClintic. Kit Cornell was an elegant woman who was aware that at times she could appear somewhat clumsy. She welcomed Martha's help with movement, as well as her advice on her costumes and the way she dressed her hair.

Martha asked Bonnie to assist her in teaching and rehearsing the dances and released her from the Group for the production's out-of-town tour before the New York City opening on December 20th. Graham devised stunning dances for the ballroom scene on a set of varying levels and steps that covered much of the stage.

Because Cornell was tall, the men in the cast had to be over six feet so that she could look like a fourteen-year old. Basil Rathbone, the British actor, played Romeo, a choice many people thought odd because he was not the Romeo type. Bonnie discovered that he was an enthusiastic balletomane: "I don't think he had a great deal of truck with modern dance, but he liked Martha," she later recalled. The Hollywood movie star, Brian Aherne, also British, six feet four inches tall and extremely attractive, played Mercutio; Lord Capulet was played by an actor from Salt Lake City who bore a fine Mormon first name, Moroni Olsen; Lady Capulet was played by the British actress, Brenda Forbes; Tybalt by the startling young actor, Orson Wells; and Edith Evans (not yet a Dame of the Order of the British Empire) played the Nurse.

During rehearsals Bonnie took every opportunity to watch Guthrie McClintic at work. Both of them had attended the same Seattle high school and he was pleased to learn that she knew the speech teacher and the school vice-principal, his greatest supporters there with whom he was still in touch. But Bonnie was surprised by the amateurish way McClintic demonstrated the moves he wanted. She asked Edith Evans what he was up to. "Watch him," Evans said. "He asks us to do very unsettling things, and he demonstrates so badly that it makes you feel you could do it very, very much better. It is a very interesting device."

Bonnie soon discovered that many of the actors in the lesser roles were Playhouse graduates who got jobs in serious productions because of the high regard directors had for Graham's unique movement training.

"Martha's interaction with actors and directors was very important to her," Bonnie recollected. "Perhaps that was one of the determining factors in the development of her particular art of theater. Her concern was for the variety of visual impacts that expressed her particular point of view through a dance structure. Martha's teaching has always made very practical references to the theater."

Bonnie took her work very seriously. She was tough on company members and her reaction to sloppy work was fiery. She did not think twice about bossing any of the actors around, including Brian Aherne and Brenda Forbes. In return she took a great deal of friendly teasing from them. To keep herself in shape she warmed up on stage every morning before rehearsals and was soon joined by cast members, some of whom had been her fellow students at the Playhouse. As their numbers increased she even modified her training to accommodate them. Basil Rathbone often came in early to observe her classes.

During the Buffalo and Detroit segment of the out-of-town tour Bonnie watched performances nightly and afterward gave the company movement notes. Katharine Cornell asked her for notes, too. "I went to her dressing room and gave her my notes on staging details as well as interpretation. It was very clear that she had the greatness and simplicity to welcome this response from me. She is quite a remarkable woman." Bonnie was paid twenty-five dollars a week, inclusive of expenses, which she thought a princely sum for "doing nothing more than rehearsing the dances and watching from out front."

Cleveland, however, was a big surprise. When Bonnie arrived at the theater the stage manager told her to put on a page's costume. The only short people in the play were the pages and one of them was ill. A bet had already started among the cast that Bonnie would get in somebody's way in the opening crowd scene, something she was always fussing about. Being a good player she took on the challenge and got into the costume. She was positive she knew all the moves, but she quickly discovered that things were quite different on stage. At the very moment she walked into the scene Moroni Olsen came dashing on as Lord Capulet to stop the street fighting. With a sudden movement the big actor picked her up by the scruff of the neck, lifted her out of his way and set her down with a harmless thump. After the curtain fell she tried hard to defend herself from being teased by the gleeful cast, when suddenly silence descended. Guthrie McClintic, who was supposed to have been in New York, strode on stage. "Keep that business in!" he said with delight. From then on it was incorporated into the production. That evening Brian Aherne told Bonnie that if he had known it was to be her first night he would have sent her a telegram; Edith Evans said she would have sent her a summons.

At the New York opening the company received huge ovations. On New Year's Eve Bonnie went back to see them and was touched by their warm welcome. Afterward she joined Martha, recovering from a month of illness bordering on pneumonia, and Louis and Dorothy. Together they toasted in the New Year with egg nog and scrambled eggs.

A short time into the new year Edith Evans had to return to England because of her husband's illness. Brenda Forbes took over the Nurse's role and twenty-year old Bonnie was asked to play Lady Capulet for the two weeks it would take to work in an understudy. It was not a big part and she knew the dances well and could easily handle the beautiful, heavily-padded costumes. In the ballroom scene she danced with Brian Aherne, who enjoyed making her furious by stepping on her train. Once, at the end of the first act, he danced her into the wings as usual, but a stagehand had forgotten to position the platform steps and they both fell off into space, ending on the floor in a great heap of padded costumes.

Bonnie remained good friends with Katharine Cornell and many of the cast. She was proud to have worked with such a company of distinguished people and wrote home, "I think they liked me. I was not rude or harsh. I am thankful for my good breeding, for they were people of quality. I do not say these things with my nose in the air, for I realize the value of good breeding."

She last visited Katharine Cornell many years later on Martha's Vineyard, shortly before her death. Cornell was very frail, but her memory was excellent. She always considered that her productions had created an atmosphere of family kinship among the cast members, something she felt was very important for each actor's personal satisfaction and success.

Martha's new Group work, *Course* (Antheil), full of youthful vitality and optimism, was in its final stages of preparation for the premiere on February 10th. Louis Horst was not able to get his hands on the orchestral score until 5 p.m. on the evening before the concert. At four o'clock the following morning, the girls were still fitting costumes because Martha had thrown out the first set; they were too sophisticated for the effect she wanted. Bonnie got to bed at 5:30 a.m., but was in the theater at nine o'clock for the lighting rehearsal and more sewing. Louis spent the day rewriting what he described as the worst jumble of orchestration he had ever seen. Because Bonnie's dance with May and Lil was rhythmically very intricate she grew more and more nervous as performance time approached. Martha was sick with worry when she was finally able to watch the whole work from out front. She was sure it would be a failure. All in all, everyone was convinced they had a complete fiasco on their hands.

The house was sold out long before curtain time – an unprecedented occurrence. The audience was a *Who's Who* of the theater world: Katharine Cornell, John Martin, Brian Aherne, Noel Coward, Edith Isaacs, George Balanchine, Lincoln Kirstein, the strip-tease artiste Sally Rand (she had recently been paired with Graham in an 'Impossible Interview' in *Vanity Fair*), Doris Humphrey, Charles Weidman and the art critic James Johnson Sweeney. When the curtain went up on Martha there was thunderous applause, something that had never happened before. She caught her audience off guard with "an unexpected playfulness and frivolity"[6] in her new opening solo, *Praeludium* (Paul Nordoff), and they received it enthusiastically. Brian Aherne, who had sent Bonnie a "Put your best foot forward" telegram, disliked the concert and made ugly remarks. "Although he is brilliant, gutsy, virile and not without charm, nobody likes him very much," Bonnie wrote.

In his review of *Course*, Henry Gilfond wrote, "Rarely has a dance ended so brilliantly, in such swift moving patterns, urgently gathering energies in its momentum. The curtain moved slowly down from its moorings, the running circle stiffened its tempo, feet trip-hammered out their contagious, swifter rhythms, and the audience, caught in the pull and the pulse, the beat of the dance, found voice and shouted out its approval. Martha Graham has been perhaps more profoundly moving, but never before more exciting; the dance comes closer home, and the response is a spontaneous greeting.

"This is perhaps the most thoroughly human composition Martha Graham has yet presented. Miss Graham (*One in Red*) set the tempo of the composition in a running, light prelude introducing the first impulsive rush of the Group across the stage – lifting, elemental, strident vigor. *Three in Green* (Bonnie Bird, Lil Liandre, May O'Donnell) took up the hurried pace in a grouping of spreading leaps and runs. A second rush across the stage was prelude to the andante, *Two in Blue* (Dorothy Bird, Sophie Maslow), and the third sweep set the frame for *Two in Red* (Lily Mehlman, Anna Sokolow), a closer, tighter movement to maintain the pace for the last thrust of the Group, a repetition of the three segment themes, and the final sustained circular current that moved everything before it in the climax of an urgent, overwhelming statement.

"The Group worked admirably. The young dancers caught the spirit and moved with it in the slow phrases as well as in the more exciting, swifter movements, never more sure, more positive. Of Martha Graham one speaks in superlatives…. Of *Course*, it may be said, nothing was more evident than a buoyant optimism in youth, in the rebirth of all that is strong and urgent, racing through the course which is all living."[7] Thirteen years later, Graham would create its sister dance, *Diversion of Angels* (Norman Dello Joio) for a new generation of admirers.

After the performance Bonnie went to dinner with Muriel Stuart, a teacher at Lincoln Kirstein's School of American Ballet. Kirstein was striving to understand modern dance's creative use of American themes that portrayed and magnified the native character and feeling for the land. He was very interested in what Graham was up to because he wanted his European-influenced American Ballet Company, for which George Balanchine was choreographer, to find its own American character. At Kirstein's request, Muriel Stuart had begun studying with Graham and Horst.

Bonnie adored Muriel's vitality and chattiness. Even though she was hardly ten years older than Bonnie, Stuart had already enjoyed a long dance career. Her training began with Anna Pavlova and Enrico Cecchetti at Ivy House in London when she was eight years old. Later she also studied Indian dance with Uday Shankar and German modern dance with Harald Kreutzberg. She danced with Pavlova for ten years before opening her own school in San Francisco in 1927. Many teachers from the West Coast had studied with her, including Caird Leslie, who had often asked her for additional material to teach to his Cornish students.

During mid-February Bonnie was busy preparing a lecture-demonstration for Louis for the New School for Social Research. As usual, she was in almost every dance. Among the works was a difficult duet with Ethel Butler in seven-eighths meter. It caused her great agony because Louis continually yelled at her, but her determination not to give up pulled her through. A good performance of *Jazz Epigram*, a work for six dancers from her Playhouse days, made her feel better.

The concert and Louis' lecture-demonstration exhausted Bonnie. Her way of relaxing was to watch others perform. She enjoyed seeing *Noah*, a charming Biblical fantasy by André Obey, for which Anna Sokolow had created the dances and Louis Horst the music, which she thought "perfect and delicate." Pierre Fresnay was its star, and Geordie Graham was also in the cast. Bonnie went standing room to see an English play, *Escape Me Never*, with Elizabeth Bergner. She was thrilled by Bergner, "the tiniest, most porcelain-like creature I have ever seen, who possesses an incomparable technique that radiates power, style and simplicity." She saw Harald Kreutzberg, whom she had last seen in concert in 1933, at the Guild Theatre. "Even though his old dances were as provocative as ever, his new dances were hollow and mostly pantomime. But he is poetry to watch moving. I have never seen a man move as he does. His dancing delighted and pleased me as gay entertainment, but left me with nothing. I met him at a reception after his concert. He is a little man with a shiny bald head and great charm. Frances Hawkins is managing him.

She says he is naïve and bumptious. He is crazy about Martha and they get along very well together."

On a Saturday afternoon near the end of February, the Group danced for PE teachers, drama teachers and students attending a day of lectures on dance at Columbia University Teachers' College. Rehearsals with Martha and Louis began at nine in the morning. At two o'clock the girls demonstrated Louis' work and then gave a small recital with Martha which finished around six o'clock. They danced in a great, barn-like gymnasium, with no lighting, curtains or illusion of theater. The eight hundred strong audience sat directly in front of them and at the end yelled their heads off in delight. Afterward Bonnie felt even more exhausted than usual.

Between the lows and highs of exhaustion and exhilaration she went to see a dance debut that she found very depressing. In the intermission John Martin came back to her seat and they talked about his job, Pavlova, debates, technique and *Romeo and Juliet*. She liked and respected this tall, knowledgeable, carrot-topped and moustached gentleman who was giving modern dance and Martha Graham so much support. Afterward she wrote, "I have chosen the hardest and most dangerous profession in the world; the most dangerous because it is so easy to be wrong and almost impossible to be right." On a more positive and less frustrating note, she took comfort in the knowledge that she was trained to believe that nothing was impossible, provided she had the will to stick it out.

Miss Aunt Nellie arrived in New York in March and contacted the Studio during her gallivanting around town. Bonnie met up with her at a tea attended by many past and present Cornish School teachers and students, including the painter Mark Tobey, long associated with Cornish as a teacher. "Aunt Nellie says I am too grown up and she doesn't like my hair, but she thinks I am still beautiful."

Miss Cornish told Bonnie that she was proud of her performance with the Group at Washington Irving High School. She also saw one of only three special performances at the Imperial Theatre of Archibald MacLeish's leftist political statement, *Panic*, for which Martha had devised extraordinary crowd scenes. This was one of the few times Graham associated herself with a left-wing theater production. Bonnie managed to see a rehearsal and found Martha's work striking, but she also thought that producing dances for theater productions was no longer important for Graham's future direction.

Bonnie also learned that Miss Cornish had asked Graham to teach during the next Cornish summer session, but that was not possible because plans for the coming summer's dance program and production series at Bennington were already in the advanced stages. They were so exciting that Bennington was being referred to as 'Salzberg in America'.

A few days before *Panic*'s premiere, Martha went off on a two-week solo tour to Illinois, Missouri, Ohio and Nebraska. In a letter to Bonnie from Rockford, Illinois, she wrote, "Audiences slightly stunned but valiant. The college dancers here are of the 'follow through' school, if you know what I mean [overbearing sentimentality]. Louis is so embarrassed by them. We must suit the middle-class minds who like their thrills and emotional moments to be safe, but permit their longing, yearning bodies shocking moments of spent passion."

The Group gave their last Guild Theatre concert of the season on April 28th. The new work was *Perspectives* (Horst), comprising *Frontier* and *Marching Song*, for which Isamu Noguchi created his first stage set for Graham. Bonnie felt that everything went brilliantly and that the Group had danced *Marching Song* as if they were possessed. "Martha's new solo, *Frontier*, was sensational. It is so American and so beautiful, and the first time she has employed real decor. She used about a hundred feet of cheesecloth to make the rope we braided. It took five of us to do it. Stunningly effective. It gave such a feeling of perspective and wide-openness to the stage. I have been working very hard to project a new quality clearly across the footlights. I am still a long way from perfect but am improving. The trio in *Course* went very well."

On April 30th Bonnie celebrated her 21st birthday. "Martha was a darling. She blessed me with good wishes for the future." Muriel Stuart, with whom Bonnie was staying and "having too much fun to worry about the extra travel costs," gave her a fine string sweater. At the end of demonstrating for the six o'clock class the students warmly congratulated her. At the hospital where she had been receiving treatment for a peculiar swelling in her cheek, the doctors were astonished to discover she was 21, not 17 as they had thought. Miss Cornish's recent comment that she was "still untouched by the city" seemed to confirm what Laura Elliott had said about Bonnie carrying her Western lands with her wherever she went.

Demonstrating for classes had become more and more difficult as the technique kept on changing and developing. Bonnie was worn out and felt as if her joints were made of wood and strung together on thread. She was looking forward to a break to catch her breath before the June Course and Bennington, after which she planned to go home for a short spell. She was hoping that Aunt Nellie would invite her to teach at Cornish and to this end Martha helped her draft a letter of proposal that also gave her Graham's authorization to teach her technique. Because

Welland Lathrop was scheduled to teach during the weeks Bonnie had proposed, Miss Cornish suggested that she and Dorothy open the season at Cornish in a concert of their own works. The girls were delighted. Further good news arrived from the P.E. Department of the University of Washington, whose campus was near Cornish; Bonnie was invited to teach for a month. Frances Hawkins, who had recently set up her own independent management and was acting as agent for Graham as well as for many of the upcoming young modern dancers, provided professional advice on settling contractual terms.

About this time Bonnie heard from her mother that the Cornish School might slip out of Aunt Nellie's hands. The problem lay with the board of directors, a group of businessmen brought in to inject much-needed money into the school. Instead, they insisted that it should pay its own way. Miss Cornish maintained that making money was not the prime function of an arts school and that the arts needed financial support. Her on-going battle received active support from Bonnie's mother, a fighter for the maintenance of high educational standards in Seattle.

By early May Bonnie was homesick for the West. She waxed sentimental when she went for walks in the small parks around Washington Square, soaking up the vibrant colors of spring flowers, or was awakened by the music of a dawn chorus. She had a great longing to breathe fresh, clean air and to be able to see for more than a city block.

While Martha was away recovering her strength at Katharine Cornell's country home, Bonnie and Dorothy went to South Norwalk where Tookee wintered to get her into condition for the coming months "with paint, glass and trinkets." Bonnie was ecstatic when Cornell invited Louis, Dorothy and her to join Martha at her home in Sneden's Landing, on the Hudson River north of Nyack. There was nothing that could be so welcome as a change of scene before the Studio's hectic June Course. "What an impulsive, affectionate creature Kit Cornell is, and with the vitality and energy of a strong, healthy animal." Cornell soon left with her husband for Bavaria, her favorite retreat. While she was away Anna, her German housekeeper and cook, delighted everyone, especially Louis, with her magnificent apple strudels.

During an idyllic fortnight Bonnie drove Martha and Dorothy the eighteen miles from Sneden's Landing into New York City twice a week for classes and rehearsals. It was so much fun to be adventuring again that she would not have minded driving fifty each way. In one of her many letters over that summer to her Aunt Grace van Dijk Bird in Bakersfield, California, she wrote, "At this moment life feels so full – like Van Gogh's grapes that could burst from the canvas they are so ripe and rich. I am sitting by a glowing fire in one of the most beautiful rooms

Bonnie, Martha Graham, Tookee the Tin Chicken and dogs at Sneden's Landing, 1935.
Photo: Bonnie Bird Collection at the Laban Centre.

I've ever been in. This whole house is pervaded by an air of peace and rest, a clean luxury, an atmosphere of well-being and an understanding of the art of living. It is Aladdin's Palace and I am absorbing sun and more sun, deeply breathing air filled with the smells of earth and becoming quite intoxicated with this bucolic release after the intense pent-up-ness of a long winter. Martha is resting up for the long three-month siege ahead. It is going to be a hectic summer.

"The house is a remodeled and enlarged revolutionary relic, all white inside and out, with a tremendous fireplace. No definite style, not set in any period, just the most livable arrangement I have ever seen. There are vases of flowering dogwood, lilacs and tulips of every color in all the corners of the rooms. No cars come near, no trains, no highways; a boat comes every hour or so from Dobbs Ferry across the Hudson. A long walk through the untouched, pungent woods and you are in Italy – a patio of stone is overhung with wistaria, carpeted with violets and set at the base of a high waterfall that breaks into a crystal spray half way down. Uneven rock gardens are cushioned with bleeding hearts and moss, and trilliums grow in the woods while the goofy Dutchman's pants career crazily near the water's edge and dogwood and Japanese maple march side by side; colors sing glad, gay songs in this, the spring of the year. It's exciting! There is such a passion in living, just living!

Martha Graham, Bonnie, Dini de Remer and her husband in Kit Cornell's garden at Sneden's Landing. Photo: Bonnie Bird Collection at the Laban Centre.

"This rest and new stimulus should lubricate our souls for the months to follow. I wish we could stay beyond the first of June, but there will be classes every day except Sunday and commuting would be tiring and throw me off balance for dancing, so we will probably return to town soon, much against our hearts' desire."

The intensive June Course quickly put Bonnie back into harness. She taught and rehearsed in the melting New York heat six days a week from nine in the morning until midnight. She became hoarse from making corrections, laced with philosophy, which she described in a letter to Aunt Grace, such as "Shame, shame, you banged your knee. You know very well that the most sacred joint in a dancer's body is the knee. You should never, under any circumstances, throw your weight on the knee. Where is your control?" or "You must not be romantic, emotional or sentimental in your technique. Your technique is a cold, clear science – the science of movement. It is the pure, complete, physical functioning of your whole body. The dance? That is another thing. There you are at liberty to do as you please, to dramatize and project your ideas. Your technique is your springboard. You must have that first and foremost, otherwise it's as if you play on a violin that's not tuned." She sometimes felt so frayed at the edges she was sure she would go under. "But then,

I never did rely on edges. It's the center of things I care about. We are ruthless and deep cutting, even with ourselves. I should say even more with ourselves. But that is as it should be. Discipline is a bitter but effective pill."

Early in July Tookee the Tin Chicken arrived for her six-week stay on the Bennington campus, Louis beside Bonnie, Martha and Dorothy squeezed together in the back seat with hat boxes and over-stuffed bags on their laps. Bulging suitcases were precariously strapped to the back of the car. "The colonial buildings stand in the golden sun, whitewashed and green trimmed. I have a wonderful room overlooking a large lawn, a common, around which all the buildings are arranged. We have our own studio in addition to the large studios and the theater in the Commons Building where most of the teaching and rehearsing takes place."

Student numbers were well up from the preceding year. Among the participants were Muriel Stuart and Hanya Holm-trained Jane Dudley,

Louis Horst, with Bonnie and Dorothy Bird on his left, Bennington College, 1935. Photo: Bonnie Bird Collection at the Laban Centre.

both of whom studied with Graham and appeared in the new work she created using summer students. Welland Lathrop, head of dance at Cornish, was also there. The faculty was larger, with special guests teaching two-week courses, and there were also many more concerts, lectures, discussions, exhibitions and film showings than the previous year. Among the many events, Louis presented the 12 Group members, on campus for the whole session, in formal presentations of dances from his Pre-Classic and Modern Forms courses, and members of the New Dance League, a propaganda-motivated alliance of modern dancers, presented *An Evening of Revolutionary Dance.*[8] For Graham, the climax to her Bennington summer was to be a premiere involving her Group and a large number of selected students, given as a "Workshop Production."

Bonnie's working day started at eight o'clock in the morning with a lecture by John Martin. At nine-thirty she participated in, or demonstrated for, the main Graham class. This was followed by a practice session for the same students with either Bonnie or Dorothy teaching. There were about forty people in this class and Bonnie, at 21, was teaching heads of departments from all over America. They were eager and they never complained, but to compensate for having such a young person order them around there was much good-humored leg pulling. Muriel Stuart, for one, playfully crossed her eyes whenever Bonnie approached her to make a correction. A master class and rehearsals for the Group followed. From three to six o'clock Bonnie and Dorothy led practice sessions for the Workshop participants, 50 hopeful students of whom 24 were to be chosen to perform. From eight in the evening everyone rehearsed together under Martha's direction. Bonnie somehow also found time to appear in Louis' classroom demonstrations and concert presentations and rehearse with Dorothy for the September Cornish concert.

The technique Martha was developing continued to amaze Bonnie. For one thing, she was asked to perform jumps that she was sure even boys who were stronger and physically better prepared could not do. "We are not man, woman nor child when we dance; we are creatures of mass, weight and air. Our technique is beyond the real. We are like a new race – people who are sure and strong in their convictions. How thrilling it is to discover a truth for yourself – it is like opening the door on a new and shining world."

Her most difficult hour and a half of the day was John Martin's early morning lecture in the College Theatre, with the whole summer school in attendance. He spoke on dance history, the subject of the book he was working on. He was not a brilliant speaker, but following Martha's wishes everyone in the Group attended his sessions; it was both a good thing for them to learn more about the history of their art and politically important to show their support for him.

John began on the raised stage, with the students sitting on the floor below or propped up against the walls. Finding the distance between them uncomfortable, he soon moved down among them and sat at a table. Many of the students were so stiff they could hardly walk, and some began bringing in inflatable swimming rings to sit on, hoping to ease the pain in their tortured backs and bottoms. Often arriving a little late, they would slide down the walls and land heavily on their rings, forcing the air out in sudden, suggestive wooshes that ruptured the thread of Martin's thought for a few embarrassing seconds. Bonnie said these incidents must have been the worst part of the summer for this very correct gentleman.

But she found that John also had a genial side. She liked him best over the faculty breakfast table, especially when he and Louis got into friendly arguments over whether Gilbert and Sullivan operettas would live longer than Strauss waltzes, both men spontaneously illustrating their claims with impromptu singing. John even succeeded in persuading Graham to let him sit in on her rehearsals so that he could observe the creative process. Even though she had never allowed anybody except Louis to be present – sometimes blasting even him right out of the room – she let John watch, but she was visibly distressed by his presence.

Bonnie got to know and like the Wigman-trained dancer Tina Flade, head of dance at Mills College in Oakland, California. Flade had only three years previously given her first American concert. At Bennington, she was subsituting for Hanya Holm, who was herself teaching the summer course at Mills. Bonnie found Tina's recital in the second week of July very moving, in places thrilling, particularly her solo to the plucked strings of a piano, *Dance in the Early Morning* (Henry Cowell). Tina admitted to being as much influenced by Graham as by her new environment. Bonnie sincerely hoped she would meet up with her soon again.

When Doris Humphrey arrived for her two-week residency, Bonnie wrote, "It is going to require quite a bit of diplomacy to keep from putting our hands in hot coals and causing any tension in feeling because Doris is an extremely difficult and hard person with an artificially sweet manner. She is, I think, cold and bitter. It is very unfortunate because it is spoiling her choreography and undermining her dancing. I am going to be as tactful as possible, which is a bit of a chore because I'm pretty bluntly honest. It will be good for me though."

At the beginning of August she saw Doris Humphrey and Charles Weidman and their 17-member Concert Group in a performance that included *New Dance*, a work Bonnie thought "a very definite upward state – it was very interesting both musically and choreographically, but it did not move one very much." John Martin, however, immediately hailed it as a masterpiece.

For the Workshop Program, Martha created *Panorama*, a work using her Group and the 24 selected summer course students, with Louis as musical director, a score specially composed by Norman Lloyd, and sets and lighting by Arch Lauterer. Alexander Calder, in his first dance collaboration, created the mobiles.

Because her dances evolved during rehearsals, Martha did not want the dancers to be influenced in advance by any emotional ideas, so she told them nothing about the new work. Motion came first; out of that came emotion. But there were many students who needed emotional stimulation to enable them to function as dancers. Bonnie found some of them so helpless and undisciplined that they hardly at all resembled her ideal of real dancers. "But they are learning the rigors of this chosen life daily and experiencing the absolute devotion and concentration that is essential to become a truly great artist; there can be nothing else allowed to stand in the way. In that sense, the dancer is an extremely selfish individual, but she is selfish to herself, too, denying herself any indulgences, no matter how small, that will in any degree interfere with her work. And that is what they have had a taste of. How they rebel at first! They hate the kind of regimentation that is necessary for the functioning of the group as a group.

"We have had our difficulties this summer and there have been times when feelings ran so high that a blowup was certain. Martha has been in a state several times. The big problems are the strain of choreographing a work in six weeks for 36 dancers, many of whom are strangers unaccustomed to working with her and by no means an extension of her own body and mind, as her sensitive Group is, and making them really move and dance. Nevertheless, it has been a terribly valuable experience. We have had ideal working conditions, no financial worries and everything taken care of so that our entire focus can be on the dance. Mary Jo Shelly and Martha Hill are remarkable – they have seen this whole thing through. It is entirely without backing and run on its own capital."

Among Tookee's inestimable uses, the greatest was its service as an escape valve. Before production problems closed in, the old Model A with Bonnie at the wheel often took Martha, Louis and Dorothy out for drives in the Vermont hills. Louis was reading up on the history of the Battle of Bennington in the American Revolution and the quartet spent hours in the countryside deep into the night or at weekends with an excited Louis plotting out what skirmish had taken place where and when. Along the way they all developed a great affection for this part of America.

The touring car also served other purposes. One day Martha wanted to buy a bottle of rum, but Vermont was a 'dry' state. Even though Prohibition had been repealed, it was left up to each state to make its own decision about whether it was going to allow liquor sales. Massachusetts, next door, was not dry, and Williamstown, about 14 miles away, had a liquor store. "We drove off for a bottle late one afternoon in the worst rainstorm you can imagine," Bonnie remembered. "We had to fit the side windows in to keep the rain out. All bundled up we arrived in Williamstown and bought her bottle of rum. For the return journey the three of us, with Martha in the middle, crowded into the front seat to keep warm. As we drove along I noticed a bulge in the roof canvas over us, exactly where I had made a repair with bits of tape and tar-like stuff. Without thinking I pushed it, and water came gushing through a hole and right down Martha's neck. Well, she had a great sense of humor about it. She said she thought she could take care of anything if she could get back and have a nice hot toddy."

Soon the time came to costume the new work. As was her usual practice, Martha designed a model of the costume she wanted on the well-made body of a Group dancer. Bonnie, with three girls to assist her, was in charge of cutting, fitting and sewing. By setting up an assembly line she quickly finished making all the costumes, only to discover to her great dismay that, with 36 bodies of all shapes and sizes, they did not look the same on everyone. Martha was furious when she saw them. She hated them. "I remember her holding a skirt to her waist and saying, 'Now look, look at this skirt!' and I hastily answered, 'Martha, I did cross the two panels one inch below the navel, exactly as you instructed, but not everyone's navel is in the same place!' She thought I was being insolent and she fired me. That was nothing new. I got thrown out of the Group quite regularly. I was so tired I just left the room and went for a long walk. I meant to walk back to New York but I was going in the wrong direction. Pretty soon I heard someone coming up behind me. It was Frances Hawkins. She walked along with me in silence. Half in tears I turned to her and said, 'Frances, tell me, how do you work with her?' After a long while she answered, 'Well, whenever she talks about anything artistic, I listen. If she talks about anything else, I don't listen.' I decided the problem between us did not have to do with anything artistic. Martha was mad at me because she thought I was being insolent. Of course she took me back into the Group by early evening because she needed me. This type of thing happened often. Martha would get furious with you and you were *persona non grata* for a while until she calmed

down or Louis would tell her to come off it. During the rehearsal that
night Martha ripped up one costume after another and designed new
ones. The entire 36 had to be made over again the very next day. We
finally finished them, but I don't even remember what they looked like."[9]

"It seemed to me almost a compulsion with Martha to keep changing
things up to the last minute," Bonnie recollected. "It became a tradition.
When I first had my own company on the West Coast I did the same
thing until I suddenly realized it was a lot of nonsense. It wasn't necessary
and usually didn't improve things. Our concentration should have been
on the dancing itself. I can remember falling asleep alongside her on a
pile of costumes the night before a concert. We were often dancing on
our nerves. The situation improved as we gradually developed a store
of costumes and performed pieces over a longer period of time. Then we
could really concentrate on dancing."

Arch Lauterer liked designing sets for dancers because their needs often
led him in creatively new directions. For *Panorama* he redesigned the
interior space of the Vermont State Armory in the old town of Bennington
where the performances took place, incorporating the small stage and
building an open, three-tiered set on the Armory floor itself.

Sandy Calder's three giant mobiles, modified versions of those Bonnie
and Dorothy had rehearsed with the previous summer, were put to the
test. May O'Donnell joined the two girls as one of the 'Three Fates', the
name they themselves gave to their roles because their movement
generally determined how these freely dancing shapes flew. White ropes
attached to the mobiles went up into the rafters and through pulleys; the
rope ends were then bound around each girl's wrists so that their arm
movements could control the mobiles as the girls passed each other
laterally across the stage, their hips almost touching. It took long and
exacting rehearsals to come to an accommodation with these aerial
partners.

During the rehearsals there were also experiments that did not succeed.
For one section of the dance Calder had invented a huge, jointed,
scissor-like 'lightning' device that was placed up on the balcony at the
back of the stage. Ideally its joints were supposed to stretch out along
the balcony in a sideways, jack-in-the-box-like explosion when Bonnie
stepped on a lever, but in rehearsal its force was so great that she was
nearly thrown off the balcony. It was abandoned.

The situation grew more and more hectic with upsets over the music
and the compounding problems of a world premiere using summer
course students. For peace and quiet Bonnie often worked with Arch
Lauterer on the theater lighting until the small hours of the morning.
Tookee's midnight rides among the fragrant hills were a thing of the past.

Panorama was performed in the Armory on August 14th and 15th. The program opened with *Celebration*, followed by *Sarabande*, *Frontier* and the Workshop premiere, *Panorama*, a dance presenting a broad overview of American history. Its three sections were: *Theme of Dedication*, based on the fanatic intensity of the Puritan fathers; *Imperial Theme*, which focused on slavery, superstition and fear in the American South; and *Popular Theme*, which showed a people with an awakening social consciousness in the contemporary scene. Members of the Martha Graham Dance Group were Anita Alvarez, Bonnie Bird, Dorothy Bird, Ethel Butler, Lil Liandre, Maria Marchowsky, Sophie Maslow, Lily Mehlman, May O'Donnell, Florence Schneider, Gertrude Shurr and Anna Sokolow. Among the summer students who participated were Miriam Blecher, Nadia Chilkovsky, Jane Dudley, Merle Hirsch, Helen Priest, Muriel Stuart, Theadora Wiesner and Marian Van Tuyl.

For all its high hopes and hard work, *Panorama* was not a success. John Martin's review had some kind words, but the gist of his comments was that it was not up to Graham's high standard of excellence. Martha had taken a tremendous risk by agreeing to use students dancers, with the result that the quality of her work had been greatly impaired. Her artistic vision had also been frustrated by the very nature of Sandy's freely revolving mobiles. Bonnie thought that the mobiles had been accepted by the audience, "causing neither furor nor great praise because they were an integral part of the dance." Ideally, Martha had wanted the sections of each slightly different mobile to begin revolving slowly on the way down; instead, all the parts had sprung to life almost immediately and had remained in constant motion. This aspect had been beyond the control of the dancers manipulating them. After much thought she concluded that the mobiles should have been employed as complete entities in themselves, which is how she handled them six months later in *Horizon*.

Panorama pleased very few and least of all Martha, who was deeply hurt by the adverse criticism. Visitors were never again allowed into rehearsals and *Panorama* was never again performed in its entirety. A short while after the premiere, the 'Three Fates' received gifts of jewellery made by Sandy Calder. Bonnie's was a beautiful bird.

The day after the last performance, Bonnie drove Martha to Peterboro, New Hampshire, for a recital at the Town Hall and by Monday afternoon she had deposited Tookee with Aunt Kay in South Norwalk. Soon she would be on her way to Seattle – but not before she went to the Neighborhood Playhouse, saw her doctor, took the dogs to Long Island, got the trunks back to the Studio and said goodbye to many friends. With one hundred dollars her father had sent she was able to pay her dentist's bill, buy a train ticket home and still have some money left for daily expenses.

Bonnie's four weeks of teaching at the University of Washington had been arranged through its Extension Division by Nelle Fisher, a former Cornish classmate, who was about to leave for New York to study at the Neighborhood Playhouse. Bonnie was to receive a commission of ninety per cent of the receipts. In the meantime, Miss Cornish responded positively to a suggestion from Welland Lathrop, undoubtedly impressed by her teaching at Bennington, that she give a two-week course for Cornish students as soon as the school reopened in mid-September.

With large classes of PE teachers, professional dancers and students, Bonnie's courses were not only financially successful, but also, as she had hoped, generated a great deal of interest in Martha's work. For relaxation she rode a little, but she spent most of her free time making up for two years of lost sleep.

1935–1936: "A Delicate Receiving Instrument"

On her return to New York weariness and signs of rebellion took hold of Bonnie as she was again thrown into the pressures of life as a Graham dancer and teacher. Early morning classes for a private pupil, "my prize dumbbell," started many days off badly. Demonstrating and teaching at Sarah Lawrence, a women's college in the wealthy northern suburb of Bronxville, did not please her either. Two days a week she left the city at noon to work with students who she felt were probably the worst Martha ever had to teach. "They are supposed to be the standard-bearers, the future mothers of fine men, but they have no guts. They are jellyfish!"

Returning to the great marbled halls of Grand Central Station she would hurry downtown to the Studio to teach yet another class, followed by a long rehearsal late into the night. Then home to laundry and bed. "This is a dancer's day. How unglamorous, how unromantic. The funny notion that people have about dancers, that life is all joy and a bed of roses! Oh well, let them enjoy their illusion and keep it. One is a bit weary of being bruised for far too long, but then that makes the high times all the more wonderful. This letter sounds as if I am blue, and I have been, but it is over now. I was low over my work and had a bad temper streak which I was not even aware of until Martha scolded me severely. It hurt plenty and I am not sure what she meant, but I'll try to be better. I have been working extremely hard and my technique has improved, but sometimes I get terribly confused about what is what. I have my eye on the future and I am not afraid of work, although I am tired of it. Fame is a most unnourishing, useless, unstable sort of thing. It is only the knowledge within yourself that you are building something and increasing your dimensions as a person that keeps you from giving up. Everyone has spells; I can't get by without an occasional one. Well now, it is off my chest and I am smiling again."

The first of two November performances a week apart was quickly sold out. There was no Group premiere, but Martha showed two new solos: *Formal Dance* (David Diamond), subsequently retitled *Praeludium No. 2,* and *Imperial Gesture* (Engel). The audience, packed with celebrities, shouted waves of bravos. The critics were enthusiastic, although Bonnie thought Martin's review too reserved. "John Martin can never be made to remember that he was given to live as well as to intellectualize."

Dorothy Bird did not take part in these concerts because she was in hospital with a serious mastoid infection. Her absence meant even more cast changes in *Course,* as Anita Alvarez was already standing in for Anna Sokolow who had been given leave to choreograph; so May O'Donnell took over for Dorothy while a very nervous Bonnie danced in May's place. After the performance Bonnie received many compliments; her spirits soared and she began to feel that her hard work was at last bearing fruit.

During the week leading up to the second concert, Bonnie felt more exhausted, depressed and ill than she had ever thought possible. By Thursday the reason became obvious; her left cheek was swollen, burning and hard as a rock. By Saturday morning the swelling had increased considerably. With the concert on Sunday and no Dorothy or Anna, Martha was in a panic. Bonnie described her condition over the phone to one of the Group's doctors, Anny Kulka, who immediately held a consultation with her colleagues at New York Hospital, "then came flying down to see me, hurrying her daughter Maidi so much the poor girl nearly threw up her lunch. Dr. Anny was so nervous she was cross as a bear and scared the daylights out of me. She was relieved after examining me because she had thought from my description that the swelling was larger, but she could not diagnose it as an allergic condition. She made me get out and walk and walk for two hours in the cold air because it acted as a cold compress on my face. Then I had to report to Dr. Ernst Kulka, her husband. He gave me such a huge injection containing calcium gluconate that for a couple of minutes I thought I would burn up." With her face wrapped up like "a mumps case" the Kulkas carted her off to their home in Bayside, Long Island. Bonnie was missing the orchestra rehearsal, but they would not hear of her rehearsing if she were to dance at all on Sunday night.

Although in pain, she was enchanted by Dr. Kulka as he entertained her at the grand piano in his beautiful home. Exhibiting his native Viennese fervor for the music of Richard Strauss, he performed the entire opera *Ariade auf Naxos*, familiarizing her with each of the motifs as he played. When Martha had sprained her ankle he had also entertained her at the piano, but with lively renditions of Viennese waltzes. He and Anny spoke German much of the time and they laughed a great deal. In her depressed mood Bonnie found it refreshing to be with people who could laugh; it was so like being with her own family and so much fun. "That night was the best thing that happened to me in ages. I really appreciated it. It was the right medicine, too, because by Sunday noon the swelling was considerably reduced and they let me go on stage."

After the performance friends told her that the Group had danced even better than the week before. "Martha has been working very hard on us to have less strain when we dance. We have learned to be more gracious – at least to look like we enjoy dancing, not by smiling and grinning, but by looking less cross and pained. It has not been easy because sternness has become a habit. Dignity is not sternness; it is pride and reticence and good taste and manners. I am finding new feelings as a dancer and performer. There has also been a noticeable change in all the girls, which is what we have wanted. Oh, we shall startle the world with our new frankness some day not so long away!"

Rehearsals continued with Martha for a December lecture-demonstration at the New School for Social Research and for Louis' lecture series beginning at Sarah Lawrence College, for which Bonnie made two new solos – a gavotte and a study in dissonance. During this period Louis' gifts were in much demand: in the space of two weeks he played for Berta Ochsner, German dancer Yvonne Georgie, and Martha's solo concert in Buffalo. "He became so tired and nervous he promptly got a cold, so we have had to wait on him hand and foot. He demands it. If he does not get it he makes life so complicated that it is easier to please him. I had a riotous time getting him a set of underwear. The giggling shopgirl nearly choked when I said I wanted size 50. In awed tones she asked me, 'Is it for your husband?'

"Louis has been awfully nice about all our recent difficulties. He is a generous, sweet man, ever wise and learned and everlastingly provoking; a great person – one of the greatest in the history of dance for criticism, knowledge and music. No one writes for the dance like Louis – he seems to know and feel everything the dancer does. He has everything for the dance except the figure. He is just this side of 235 pounds and going strong."

On December 11th, Martha and the Group danced at the Brooklyn Academy of Music. Bonnie found it very tough going and had to push hard to cover the huge stage.

A sold-out Carnegie Hall concert followed on December 15th. It was a fund-raising event under the auspices of International Labor Defence, an organization set up to pay the legal costs of defending labor leaders and others accused of being leftists. Graham, Humphrey, Weidman and Tamiris and their groups were appearing together for the first time since the Dance Repertory Theatre season of 1931.[1] It was Bonnie's debut performance at Carnegie Hall and it turned into quite a special event for her. For several days Martha had been in a poor state of health because of a stomach bug and Bonnie had been nursing her, with Dr. Kulka in constant attendance. "On the night of the concert I put Martha's makeup on in the kitchen and finally, at the last possible minute, Dr. Kulka said he thought it would not be taking too much of a chance if she danced and returned to bed immediately afterward. So I bundled her into a taxi and we flew to the theater where I climbed into my costume for *Celebration*. The curtain was being held as I dashed on. It all went very well except for Lil Liandre who displaced a vertebra in her lower back right at the beginning of the work. She was in great agony but covered it up so well that no one knew anything had happened until the curtain came down. We carried her upstairs and called the doctor while Martha was on stage with *Imperial Gesture*. In *Course*, the last work of our section of the program, Lil, Marie Marchowsky and I had a very important trio which came immediately after Martha's opening solo. There was no one to fill in for Lil, so I had to do both of her solo parts as well as mine. What a strange way to make one's debut at Carnegie Hall; practically alone, doing a dance that you have almost improvised. In all that space I felt like a small bug held under the fascinated gaze of thousands of pairs of eyes. Strangely enough, I was not scared, but calm and sure – more than I ever had been in my life. The applause was relieving. People were not uneasy and no one had noticed any discrepancies in the Group numbers. Afterward we took Lil home and phoned Dr. Wisenthal again. It was late but he came."

Martha had four doctors in readiness for the girls: the orthopedists Dr. Leo Mayer and the brusque but charming Viennese, Dr. Alfred Wiesenthal, and for general health problems the Doctors Ernst and Anny Kulka. Dr. Wiesenthal charged his wealthy clients twenty-five dollars for a consultation, with the actual treatment "costing the earth." He charged the girls just five dollars, and that included even the most expensive spinal injections.

Bonnie thought that Dorothy Bird was a very special and beautiful person and felt sure that Martha loved her more than any of the other girls. When Dorothy's ear had healed completely she returned to their Sullivan Street apartment a few days before Christmas. Martha joined them there for a farewell dinner for Dorothy's mother, who had been staying with Bonnie all through her daughter's illness. Afterward, Martha accompanied them to the station where they put Mrs. Bird on a homeward-bound train. "Martha, in one of her magical story-telling moods, told tales about the Indians and the people of the Southwest, of how the primitives love the Madonna because she is one of them – a mother and a woman who loved and received love in return. Martha has such a wonderous naïveté that comes from deep in her when she tells these stories. Many of them are reflections from her childhood – vivid, real and utterly engrossing."

On Christmas morning Bonnie spent hours practicing and criticizing herself for her inability to handle the trick ropes her father had sent her. "When I was a child I used to get into such a state trying to control these ropes that I would cry. I still do. I am more severe with myself than ever, though I think with application I might become a good trick roper." That evening she went off with Dorothy to open presents at Martha's. The next day she wrapped up the ropes and sent them to the two Kulka children, Peter and Maidi, who delighted in stories, games and customs of the American West.

After a short rehearsal the following Saturday evening, Bonnie went to the Kulka's in Long Island for the night. While the doctor played excerpts from *Tristan and Isolde* she taught the children some of the rope tricks she knew. In the living room stood a beautifully decorated Christmas tree hung with fruit and curios in the Austrian fashion. Weighing down a branch was a shiny packet for Bonnie, an exquisite set of antique silver Austrian folk costume buttons. The next morning they all went ice-skating until Bonnie left for an afternoon rehearsal. New Year's Eve was spent performing at the dreary Venice Theater on 58th street. Thankfully its gloom was soon forgotten in a lively house party that followed.

In mid-January Martha and Louis left for a recital at Rollins College in Winterpark, Florida, leaving Bonnie to teach Martha's classes and look after the Studio. "Annie Russell, the famous old actress who was presenting her, died the day before she arrived, so the performance on January 17th became a memorial. The following morning Martha had to attend the funeral. Two other concerts scheduled in the South fell through, one because the auditorium had burned down a week before she arrived. So that little episode was not good."

In late January Ballets Jooss[2] came to the Metropolitan Opera House. Bonnie saw her former teacher, Louise Solberg, along with fellow Cornish students Eddie Harrington and Bethene Miller, perform in Jooss' anti-war ballet, *The Green Table*, which had won first prize at the 1932 Grand Concours International de Chorégraphie, and *Ball in Old Vienna*. Louis found both ballets *déjà vu*. "The movies do this kind of thing better," he wrote.[3] Bonnie agreed with him and wrote home, "What ideal working conditions they have: Dartington Hall, a vast estate, at their disposal, an outdoor theater, their accommodation and board taken care of and a small but adequate salary for each to cover extras so that their entire concentration and time can be devoted to the dance. But what comes out of it? Some of the most trite and dated concoctions imaginable because Jooss is the choreographer. His choreographies are well executed, mind you, but twenty years too late for the dance of today. They are just slick, not made of flesh and blood. If only they had someone at the head of their organization who had something to say. Of the three from Cornish, Louise has improved the most technically, but she is pale at her best."

"Martha has been struggling with new ideas and new works. So much was tried before the right things were found. In the birth of a dance she almost hates us because she is trying to get her ideas out properly, even as a mother must almost curse her child during labor. That very baptism of pain strengthens the bond between the creator and the creation. But the dances are not her greatest worry: Martha now wants to use Sandy Calder's mobiles as visual preludes, having the same relationship to the dance as an overture has to an opera. An overture sets a mood and creates a certain condition before the opera begins. She wants Calder's mobiles to give the stage a greater sense of space to release the mind's eye – as well as the physical eye – to a new dimension.

"The new work is called *Horizons*. Louis has written the open and serene music which has a plastique, lyric beauty. The first part of the suite is to do with the period of the early settlers in America. Next year there will be two other sections: one to deal with the period of conflicts, such as the civil war, and the other to be of today, the now.

"The first concert on February 23rd did not have sufficient technical rehearsal. The Guild Theatre was occupied so we could only have it on Sunday, the day of the concert. The stagehands were nervous, the pauses too long and the lighting was not careful enough – it became too bright on the mobiles and lost the sense of space. Also, Martha was not pleased with the costumes for the first dance.

"The dances themselves went well. The first of *Horizons'* four dances is called *Migration*. It is exactly that. The Group does it alone. It is pervaded with the same serenity as Martha's *Morning Song* [from Dance

Songs, 1932, Weisshaus]. It is a reaching out for new lands. It has that loose, wandering, yet holding-back feeling integrated within it. The whole thing is so calm that difficult technical feats seem as nothing, they are so smooth and absorbed in the whole. The second dance, *Dominion*, subtitled *Sanctified Power*, is about the church and its converts in the new lands. The third is Martha's solo, *Building Motif* (we call it *Song*), the most sensitive and delicate of her solos that I have seen. She is a woman at once tender, strong and so human, rich in wisdom from experience, and a rare genius. The fourth, *Dance of Rejoicing*, is a Group dance of thanksgiving in gladness of possession of a new land. It is a very youthful and gay dance, built on old dance forms and rhythms. *Horizons* is really an exciting first part for a potential ballet of Americana. The second performance went much better. We were all less tired and things ran better because we had learned much through the experience of the preceding Sunday."

The consensus among the critics was that although Martha was broadening her theatrical scope this work did not contain much of her strong inventiveness. Martha, once more dissatisfied with Calder's mobiles, never again collaborated with him. Despite the criticisms, Bonnie felt that the confused beginnings would be clarified with time. "In a year they will be eating their words. They always have." Bonnie's prophecy came true in 1938, when, fulfilling the promise of *Panorama* and *Horizons*, Graham created the best of her Americana Group works, *American Document*.

The Group's concert season ended soon afterward with a performance to a large, new audience in Orange, New Jersey. "Very enthusiastic, though quite surprised," Bonnie wrote. In preparation for Graham's first national solo tour, *Time Magazine* ran a feature article about her in its March 9th issue. "Good for publicity because it is read by such vast numbers of businessmen who have no time for art until it breaks into *Time*, when they pay a little attention and are provoked into wondering what it is all about."

Graham's 1936 six-week tour started in Michigan on March 15th. Five days later she was in Seattle. Bonnie had written her mother, "You positively have to see Martha. She is very sincere and real and very much wants to see and talk with you. Louis will probably succeed in making some very neat remarks. He always likes to appear formidable. His weaknesses are stamps, dachshunds and steak tartar. Martha likes to see people backstage, so all of you go back. She knows you all very well. Also, she won't mind if you aren't arrayed in the 'Astor' manner. Frances Hawkins will probably be with her. She is a grand person, highly strung, but very kind. She comes from Denver, has a great sense of humor, and loves and knows horses." A follow-up letter included two dollars from the girls for a corsage for Martha. In an unusual gesture that Bonnie felt was a tiny but wonderful tribute to Dorothy and herself, Martha wore their orchids after the concert.

The Bird family, Mother, Father, Bill and Scott-E., turned out in force to see Martha and Louis, not only in Seattle, but again in Tacoma on March 24th, where she was also greeted enthusiastically. At a reception given at the Cornish School Louis fell sound asleep over his tea. "He goes to the most important gatherings in New York and does the same thing. He dislikes anything that is formal. I have a feeling you made a hit with him. He adores having someone appreciate his music, though he may snort if complimented. He has the heart of a generous, spoiled child. Don't be too sure Louis was sound asleep. He pulls the wool over our eyes all the time, pretending to be in a deep sleep in rehearsals and never missing a single mistake.

"I have heard marvelous reports about the tour and am so glad Martha is being appreciated so much on the Coast. The two L.A. concerts in April are already sold out, according to Lincoln Kirstein who just flew back. We howled over a review that said, 'Martha's art is as different as your next year's hat'."

From San Francisco Frances Hawkins wrote that Martha and Louis were having substantial success and there was a great deal of interest and enthusiasm everywhere. Louis wrote the girls not to expect any further communication, but that he still loved them. He also gave them instructions about articles for *The Dance Observer*, which had become their special charge while he was away.

Classes at the Studio were going exceptionally well. There were now daily classes for beginner and intermediate/advanced students and twice-weekly rehearsals with the Auxiliary Group – advanced students who were learning some of the most difficult dances, such as *Mysteries* and *Celebration*. Bonnie was pleased to find promising material among these girls.

During Martha's absence, Muriel Stuart gave the Group ballet lessons. Her classes, particularly designed for the Graham dancers, were full of difficult elevation exercises. "I am so stiff I can hardly waddle, but then that is a chronic state with us old lady dancers. Muriel has discovered a new set of our muscles to make stiff. She is probably the only person who, with her ballet background and open-mindedness, could or would teach us ballet. She has studied Martha's work for over a year and finds it as difficult as we find ballet technique. One thing our schools have in common is sincere, disciplined work. Much is similar in the techniques – the basic fundamentals are, in most instances, identical. After all, they govern the functioning of the same instrument. The ballet, to me, is limited because it is two-dimensional, a technique of the extremities, with the torso held in a rigid, unchanging, straight way. Martha's work uses the legs and arms, yes, but also the torso – not as a hinge, but as a source of controlled, strong impetus, giving vitality and a new kind of lyric action to the legs and arms."

With the first hint of warmer weather, Bonnie's longing for change and open space increased. She liked to imagine the Group having its headquarters in a large house and studio in the country, but since she knew this was never to be she escaped to those city pleasures she could still, only just, afford. She heard the 15-year old violinist, Ruggiero Ricci, went standing room for Toscanini's all-Wagnerian program with the New York Philharmonic in which Kirsten Flagstad and Lauritz Melchoir sang *Tristan und Isolde*, and had a good seat for Katharine Cornell's St. Joan. "Slow is the experience of all deep fountains; long do they have to wait until they know what has fallen into their depths. With these rare experiences shall I grow to my fullness. May I always have the power to keep myself a delicate receiving instrument."

She did not join Martha for the June Course, nor for her two weeks at Bennington in July. Instead, Bonnie had arranged a summer of teaching on the West Coast. She would start with a well-paid (one hundred dollars) two-week course at the University of Washington, concurrent with a week's teaching at Cornish. Then she would go on to Los Angeles for a six-week course for Norma Gould, Ted Shawn's early *thé dansant* partner. Her father arranged for her to pick up a new car from a Detroit automobile factory and drive it west, a cheap method of delivering both car and driver to the Coast. On June 10th, Bonnie, along with Geordie Graham on her way to see her mother in Santa Barbara, and Winthrop Sargeant in search of the peace and quiet he needed to write a book, headed out on a 2 a.m. Detroit-bound Greyhound bus, and from there the long drive to her own special lands.

1936–1937: Leaving Martha: "New York Was Not My Milieu"

In October Mr. Bird telephoned Bonnie to say that the family ranch had been sold. "It is a clean break and a new life in Seattle," she wrote, "a fresh exploration that will be much more interesting for having lived in the country. Robin Hill, for all its beauty and dearness, was a white elephant amid the increasingly changing interests of the family." Soon it would become Bonnie's turn for a break with the past and new undertakings for the future.

The two Guild Theatre concerts at the end of December featured Martha's new forty-minute work, *Chronicle* (Wallingford Riegger), with sets by Isamu Noguchi. "The first performance was a madhouse. On the day before opening Ethel Butler tore a muscle in her right calf – not severely, but enough to incapacitate her for several weeks. This meant hurried readjustment for most of the dancers. I had to change places in three dances in *Chronicle* which made me frightfully nervous as I had rehearsed my own place for months and suddenly I had to appear for someone else with only one rehearsal. The first concert did not go so well. The music was extremely difficult, the musicians were not steady, and because of the difficulties of shifting decor the pauses between numbers were too long, which caused the audience to shout to the rafters. On top of everything, we were all so physically exhausted that we were pushing and using all the nervous energy we had left. All those were bad things. We rehearsed furiously all Christmas week and on second showing things went smoothly. The audience was magnificent and very responsive."

The program also included *Celebration, Frontier, Primitive Canticles* and *Primitive Mysteries*. *Chronicle*, Graham's most ambitious undertaking to date, was a composition on a grand scale that made huge demands on the soloist and the Group. It was divided into two parts: *Dances Before Catastrophe*, including *Spectre-1914* and *Masque*, and *Dances After Catastrophe*, with *Steps in the Street, Tragic Holiday – In Memoriam*, and *Prelude to Action*.

From *The Dance Observer*, January, 1937, unsigned: "The composition is a vibrant commentary on war and its destruction, not *a* war or *the* war, although the program indicates a 1914 derivation, but the looming horror of a universal catastrophe and moral breakup.

"In *Spectre-1914*, with a red, white and black banner stretching across the stage, Miss Graham appears as a solo figure in a black and red costume so designed that its employment becomes part of the action. The colors suggest blood and desolation; rivers of blood which are spread at the whim of an impersonally mad figure who sits playing with the destiny of nations. In *Masque*, a similar figure is shown treading the staid traditional measures of society's dance, unnoticed among the conservative members who are all dressed in the same optimistic shade of yellow.

"*Steps in the Street* is the aftermath, the mental and moral turbulence which follows a great national or international upheaval, danced in the solo part with great distinction by May O'Donnell, and *Tragic Holiday* is a solemn representation of the kind of futile observance which, in spite of flags and monuments, cannot replace the values its prelude has torn away. *Prelude to Action* is a swift and brief exposition of the movement towards the future. Costumed in white, decisive and terse, the dancers in it move with one accord away from the shambles of the past into a new beginning..."

The composer-philosopher Dane Rudhyar differentiated between propaganda as intellectually learned doctrine and art based on the artist's personal experience. American modern dance in the service of propaganda had lost its way, but the horrors of the raging Spanish Civil War profoundly moved many artists to espouse it as their personal cause and create masterpieces. Graham's *Chronicle*, followed within a year by *Immediate Tragedy* and *Deep Song*, were her intensely felt, well thought-out personal statements about injustice and war. These same themes, felt ever more keenly by Bonnie as she matured as an artist, were to influence her own creative work.

With intensive rehearsals in the week between the two concerts, Bonnie could not shop for gifts until Christmas eve. She did not have enough money to post them until the following week. "This is deeply humiliating to me because you are my family most loved to whom my thoughts and wishes go. My salary begins again soon. I am happy and well fed, so please don't worry about me; I don't need any money."

On Christmas Day the Kulkas awaited Bonnie's arrival before lighting the candles on their tree and singing carols. Their present to her was an Austrian dirndl costume – a white dotted-swiss organdy blouse with puffed sleeves, a black velvet bodice and a red skirt covered with small white flowers. Her antique silver buttons soon found their true home. In the evening Bonnie joined Louis, Frances Hawkins, Ethel Butler and Dorothy at Martha's for a champagne toast. Bonnie's gift from Martha and Louis was a fine Picasso print.

Bonnie was going to leave Martha. She knew instinctively that she had to do it and had thought long and hard about it. One reason was that she did not like New York. She felt she did not belong in the huge, impersonal metropolis. More important to her was the complex question she had been asking herself for several years: Where did Martha leave off and the real Bonnie begin? At late family-like dinners in little Village restaurants with Martha and Louis, other artists often joined their table and made fascinating observations about the art and dance worlds outside the sacred enclosure of the Graham Studio. Bonnie wanted to escape and adventure for herself, even though it saddened her to think of leaving a second beloved family. From their first years at the Playhouse she and Dorothy had been a kind of surrogate family for Martha, who in her own way had also fulfilled their need for family. They identified strongly and emotionally with her. Although their daily life with her included doing many of the Studio chores, the "donkey work" as Bonnie called it, it was all part of the privilege of knowing Martha, of being close to her, of being cared for by her.

But the period of initiation was coming to an end and Bonnie wanted to do her own work, even if it took a long time. Looking back on her decision to leave the city that was the focal point for American modern dance, she said, "I also knew that I had to have the right to be half-baked and not get killed in the process. New York was not my milieu."

Because Martha spent a great deal of time carefully training her dancers it was hard for her to lose them. Bonnie had seen her anger when some of them left. When Lillian Shapero, Mary Rivoire and others left the Group there were a great many painful scenes that distressed everyone. Although Bonnie was anxious not to let this happen she was at a loss to know how to avoid it. She had great admiration for Anna Sokolow and Sophie Maslow who were both beginning to develop as independent choreographers while still remaining in the Group. But they, too, experienced times of great ambivalence towards Martha because of her attitude about what they were doing.

Boyfriends were another big problem. Who wanted to take a girl out to dinner when she finished rehearsal at eleven at night? Martha did not want the girls to have gentlemen callers and managed to scotch many relationships. Bonnie always prayed she would get to the Studio phone first if she were expecting a call from a prospective date, otherwise Martha, with great finesse, quickly dispatched her young cavalier; by the time Bonnie was handed the phone she had already been undone. Thus were Martha's girls 'protected'.

The solution presented itself as if on cue. For two years Miss Cornish had been suggesting to Martha that the West Coast was ready for a first-rate teacher of Graham technique. When Welland Lathrop made known his plans to leave Cornish at the end of the 1937 school year, it was the opening that both Miss Aunt Nellie and Bonnie needed. With understanding and goodwill, Martha agreed to release her from the Group for a year.

Meanwhile the season continued with preparations for the first transcontinental tour of the United States by Martha Graham and her Dance Group. Studio classes were left in the hands of Jane Dudley. The six-week tour, beginning the 13th of March, was made possible by the devoted following Graham had built up over the years, especially by the many dance and physical education teachers who had been her Bennington students. They had also been among the sponsors of Martha's 1936 solo tour, in which many concerts took place in what Harald Kreutzberg aptly named 'The Gymnasium Circuit' – college gymnasia transformed into very basic but functional theaters.

As the time for the Group's departure neared, Bonnie snatched a few moments to write a diary-like account home. "Preparations: Only two concerts and two demonstrations to occupy our time. Chaos has reigned for weeks; packing done into the wee hours of the morning; tired, sleepy laughter; Martha dancing fragments from *Tanagra Figurine* upon unearthing the costume and reminiscing about tours in her Denishawn days, with chuckles over old photographs; telephone in a constant buzz; doors wearing thin from knocks; everyone babbling at once; Martha swamped with questions; Sandy Calder telephoning adieu – leaving for Paris with his wife Louisa, mobiles, stabiles and all; rehearsals impossible in all the confusion; packing of trunks even as the moving men wheel them away. Finally a semblance of peace. Alla happy in new home. So to leave-taking: Penn Station, 10:30 a.m., Black Diamond to Chicago, information desk the stamping ground. How 'vogue' the Group looks. Nina Fonaroff [unable to make the tour because of an arm injury] writing an ingenious document on Scottish dancing from Duncan to Graham, illustrated edition; Charlotte Chandler [one of Bonnie's private students who had once entranced her by wearing a glass hat] holding forth in grand gestures and bestowing a gardenia and a lovely poem on each girl; Frances Hawkins counting her chickens as best she could; husbands too sad to show up; mothers resigned to releasing their young ones."

Before they left, Martha felt it essential to advise her "wildcats from New York" about their behavior on tour because she wanted her girls to be respected as fine dance artists. She began the road code with the pronouncement that they were to leave the railroad washrooms spic and span.

Only a few major cities and several small, scattered places were interested in having the Graham Group. They averaged three major performances a week, often with big distances separating each concert. The popular lecture-demonstrations, however, kept the girls busy. The company of fifteen (12 Group dancers, Martha, Louis and Frances Hawkins) began their journey through America in Madison, Wisconsin, then went south to Chicago, Illinois, before traveling west to Billings, Montana; Vancouver, British Columbia; and Tacoma and Seattle, Washington. Heading south along the California coast they stopped in San Francisco, Carmel, Santa Barbara and Los Angeles before turning east to Denton, Texas, and Tallahassee, Florida. From there they went north to Lynchburg, Virginia, finally finishing in Pittsburgh, Pennsylvania. During the tour the good word spread and impresarios in the major cities were impressed enough to offer Graham their support for her next tour.

The Graham Group's first national tour, March/April 1937. Graham top right. Photo: Bonnie Bird Collection.

In Chicago the Group was registered at the same hotel as the Ballet Russe de Monte Carlo, whose stars were David Lichine, Tatiana Riabouchinska and Tamara Toumanova. Most of the taxis there were on strike and so the girls, in a demonstration of their left-wing convictions, supported the strikers by not using strike-breaking taxis. In the bitter cold, wearing their practical low-heeled shoes and one-button coats, they carried their suitcases the long distance from the station to the hotel. They all had rooms on the same floor and the hotel help, curious about what they did, concluded that these unglamorous, athletic creatures must be members of a female softball team. When they learned that they were dancers one of the surprised maids said, "But you are not really like dancers. We have dancers here and they leave their mink coats on the floor and their liquor bottles in the waste baskets. One of them has just tried to commit suicide because her lover rejected her." Bonnie found it all "too Russian."

The Chicago Auditorium stage was vast and the dressing rooms cold. The program included the recently recostumed *Tragic Patterns*. "Martha insisted that we wear headbands across the middle of our foreheads," Bonnie remembered. "We felt absolutely silly wearing them and there followed a typically unsuccessful attempt to use Group power. Trying with humor to dissuade her, we all put the headbands on and trouped into her huge, bare dressing room in a stylish parody of an Egyptian chorus. Martha would have none of it and roasted us right out of the room. We rarely won those battles with her. Anyway, the dance didn't last much longer in the repertoire."

After the performance in Billings, Montana, Group left-wingers organized a special pilgrimage to Butte, home of the troubled, labor-intensive Anaconda Copper Mines. They wanted to show their solidarity with the cause of the miners. Bonnie, untroubled by any strongly-held political views, went along to enjoy the camaraderie and see the sights.

The performances in Vancouver, Tacoma and Seattle were surprisingly well-received. "Seattle has awakened a little. I should say that some of Seattle is wide-eyed and not going to allow the slow-eyed ones to cheat them out of a cultural advantage."

At the close of the first concert at the San Francisco Opera House a tiny lady came dashing backstage. Still in tears from the stirring performance, Charlotte Mack asked for Bonnie. Mrs. Mack, the aunt of Bonnie's private student Charlotte Chandler, had met her future husband Adolph, a poor immigrant to America who eventually became head of Imperial Oil, while she was acting as a lady's companion on a camel trek in the Sahara. In their home on Knob Hill she had assembled a priceless collection of rare paintings, among them Picassos, Braques, Kandinskys and Klees. She had exquisite taste. She also collected the works of contemporary American painters and helped bring young artists to the attention of the West Coast. Their first meeting began a long friendship. Years later Bonnie's children also fell under her spell and 'adopted' her as their grandmother.

"The concerts in San Francisco were hard," Bonnie wrote home. The audience was responsive on the first night, and when we did *Chronicles* at the second performance three nights later they were wildly excited. In the days between, a few of us participated in lecture-demonstrations at Stanford University in Palo Alto. The Carmel concert was warmly received. The stage at Sunset High School was small, so the cast numbers were reduced. Carmel is a delightful spot. I walked barefoot on the white sands and felt so peaceful for a while. Santa Barbara, Martha's home town, was fun. The house was very full and the audience excited; they sent flowers over the footlights and all. This year they took Martha to their hearts, even if they didn't always understand. The reception Martha's mother gave was sumptuous and fun."

While in Los Angeles the Group visited the RKO Studios to watch a shooting of *New Faces of 1937* in which the eighteen-year old tap dancer, Ann Miller, featured. "After our concert, Louise Palmer, Frances Farmer, John Biel, Martha Ray, Paulette Goddard and many other famous film

Group members at play. Anna Sokolow supported aloft by Bonnie (center). Sophie Maslow seen at rear. Photo: Bonnie Bird Collection.

stars came backstage. Neutra, the famous architect, and his wife also came back. I was thrilled he remembered me. Better yet, I like his work. He is a wonderful, rare man. Aunt Grace came, too. She was very excited."

Grace Van Dyke Bird was another woman in the family who excelled in the field of education. In 1917 she had been hired as a teacher at Bakersfield, California, High School, and from 1920 to 1950 was Dean of Bakersfield Junior College, the first woman to hold this post. Aunt Grace had a reputation for being an extremely good letter writer and was the recipient of Bonnie's most carefully written letters. She was impressed enough with the Graham concert in Los Angeles to arrange for her college to sponsor a visit by the Group during its second nationwide tour in the spring of 1939.

"Last Saturday I went to Santa Barbara to visit Martha's mother and stayed overnight. They have a lovely old home, huge and roomy, whose interior is decorated in rich tones of wood, as in the bold, simple, fireplace mantels. Lizzie Pendergast, who was Martha's nurse, is an ancient Irish woman who kissed me profusely because I am one of Martha's girls, and so I am Lizzie's, too. Lizzie even sang me a bit of an old song about the moon and did me a jig. On Sunday she went off to the mission decked out in a green and tan flowered chiffon arrangement and a floppy hat. She seems a bit balmy, but she is a dear. Mrs. Duffy misses her daughters so very much. She appears very sad and lonely. She is not an active person and, although kindly, is inclined to enjoy moping a bit. She is hard on others, but worse on herself. It destroys her."

In Denton, Texas, the heat and humidity in the auditorium of the State College for Women were unbearable. The girls' costumes became so drenched in perspiration that they had to rip them off during a fast change. Immediately after the performance a little man came barrelling backstage. Arriving breathless in the midst of the Group, he anxiously asked, "What's your signal system? What's your signal system?" No one knew what he meant. "I am a football coach. If I can learn your signal system I can wipe out any other team! I have never seen people cross each other at such speeds without collisions!" When Bonnie told him there was no secret system – just counting and knowing where they were going – he was very disappointed.

The following day was free and the Group set out for New Orleans. During the train journey each girl mended her costume as best she could. Charlotte Chandler was at the station to meet Bonnie and Dorothy and take them sightseeing and to her aunt's farm. She arranged for two handsome, wealthy young Southern gentlemen to take them to dinner at Antoine's, an experience never forgotten by the boyfriend-starved girls.

On the way to Tallahassee, Florida's state capital, Bonnie was watching the poor shanty dwellers who lived in the marshes outside the city waving at the train. Suddenly their faces froze. There was a jolt and the engine and two of the front cars began to fall over. Steam was gushing out in all directions as she glimpsed the driver jump free of his cab. Word went around that the one-track line had been sabotaged. No one was seriously hurt, but all the costumes were in the overturned forward freight car. A short train was called in from Tallahassee and the Group and their retrieved gear were taken on board first. The train reversed all the way to Tallahassee. They arrived just in time for their concert at the college auditorium.

From the old Governor's Mansion Bonnie wrote, "I am on the porch of an old southern mansion, a real one, with huge 30-foot pillars on the front portico, tremendous oaks and magnolias dripping with smokey, Spanish moss, and stubby palm plants for shrubbery. The main street of this sleepy town comes right up to the gate. Write to me. I am going to be 23 in Pittsburgh!"

Bonnie left New York in June to teach an expanded course of six weeks at the University of Washington, with Dr. Anny Kulka, her daughter and one of their European friends in tow. Shortly afterward Barbara Morgan made a series of photographs of Graham's dances, some of which later appeared in Morgan's famous book, *Martha Graham: Sixteen Dances in Photographs*. Bonnie always regretted her absence from these photo sessions in which others filled in for her in famous, now lost works from those early, history-making years when she danced with Martha Graham.

7

RUMBLES IN THE WEST

Slowly and with much labor

Bonnie's apprenticeship was over. After five years of intensive, gruelling, exciting study and top-level professional work, at the age of 23 she felt ready to make her mark as a dancer, teacher and choreographer on her own stamping ground.

In the fecund dance world of America a generation later – one that she helped to create – an infrastructure of government and private organizations and associations would be in place to aid dancers and companies with information, advice and grants. But in 1937 there was little indication of the new order for which John Martin and others had been lobbying, especially on the West Coast. It would be many years before dance was to receive recognition as a major performing art.

Bonnie's second, popular summer session at the University of Washington (U.W.) opened up a useful network with West Coast dance educators, academics and students. Work at Cornish, however, started off on the wrong foot. Miss Cornish was in serious dispute with her board of directors. She had considered resigning, but decided there was still a battle or two left in her. Too much in-fighting at the top and too many budget cuts had demoralized and disorganized the staff. The school had not followed Bonnie's suggestion to advertise itself as having the only authorized teacher of Graham technique on the entire West Coast, nor had it capitalized on the success of her courses at U.W., and there had been no publicity for her potentially popular and lucrative courses for children and teenagers. She was very disappointed with the small number of dance students; only five were enrolled as dance majors. Nevertheless, she was determined to make a success and over the following months developed the five into a reasonably professional group. Along the way she found that three of them had considerable talent.

One was a tall, lanky, eighteen-year old named Mercier (Merce) Cunningham. Merce had recently entered Cornish as a drama major, but he quickly locked horns with the head of drama, Alexander Koiransky, of the Moscow Art Theatre, who was contemptuous of any form of contemporary art. Koiransky hated modern dance and seemed to enjoy

Merce Cunningham in *Skinny Structures*. Photo: Bonnie Bird Collection.

creating petty problems in co-productions with Bonnie. She found him a humorless, unspeakable bore and thought that Miss Cornish had made a bad move in appointing him drama director. Koiransky constantly poured scorn on Merce for getting excited about dance classes. After three months Merce dropped drama as his major and shifted to dance, beginning a career that was to span three-score years of startling artistic achievement.

Another was Syvilla Fort, one of the few Negro students in the school. Her mother worked as a housekeeper at Cornish to pay the tuition fees. She was in the third of her four-year dance training course while also attending U.W. Syvilla developed into a fine dancer–choreographer and later became a principal teacher for the eminent exponent of the dance traditions of the Caribbean and Africa, Katherine Dunham. The third talented dance major was Canadian-born Dorothy Herrmann, who also became a professional dancer.

Because Bonnie's productions combined dance and drama they attracted quite a few other male drama majors into her classes. In 1938 she was able to use as many men as women in her productions, the same year that a male dancer first appeared with Martha Graham.

Tall, gentle, Lincolnesque Ralph Gilbert was Bonnie's first composer-accompanist. Having worked with Welland Laythrop he was strongly

Bonnie Bird in her solo *The Judgement*, a sarabande, Cornish School, 1938. Photo: Bonnie Bird Collection.

influenced by the musical introspection of Central European dance. In the initial stages of their work together Bonnie gave him important clues to American modern dance through her composition classes based on Louis Horst's Pre-Classic and Modern Forms courses. With Gilbert she choreographed and presented many student pieces as well as solos for herself. At the end of the year he gathered up his courage and went to New York City, where he became an accompanist at the Graham Studio and composed for the new generation of young choreographers, among them Erick Hawkins, Iris Mabry and Nina Fonaroff.

Professional dance performances in Seattle were few, but included a well-received recital by Harald Kreutzberg in January and a visit in March by the Humphrey-Weidman Company. Of a talk by Romola Nijinsky, Bonnie wrote to Frances Hawkins: "She gave an uninformed lecture not equal to that of a first-year Louis student." An exhibition of paintings by *Der Blaue Reiter* artists Lyonel Feininger and Alexej von Jawlensky drew this telling comment from her: "Things do come here, but slowly and with much labor."

Towards the end of the year a small book, *Martha Graham, Dancer*, appeared. With exquisite photographs, it was a paean to Graham by the dance publicist, Merle Armitage. Louis wrote Bonnie asking her to "plug the book a bit for your old admirer who is annoying you now." Enthusiastically describing its reception on the local dance scene, Bonnie wrote Frances, "It has created a sensation in Seattle."

Within six months of having left the Graham Group, Bonnie revised her plans for the future. She realized that anything she hoped to accomplish would come to nothing unless she stuck to her new work for several years. "My day is full with teaching and rehearsing," she wrote Frances. "I expected I would have to start reconstruction from the bottom up, but I never realized how barren the bottom could be. Things are gradually breaking and I think I am slowly succeeding in bringing out a keen and intelligent interest in the work for about the healthiest and most alive people in town. At least there is much curiosity." Her plans were undoubtedly tempered by having met the man she was to marry.

During the previous summer Mary Aid de Vries, head of the PE dance department at U.W., had decided that Bonnie ought to meet some eligible young men. She and her husband gave a party on their boat to which Bonnie and two carefully chosen bachelor professors from the psychology department were invited. One had never been married; the other, Ralph Gundlach, was divorced and had a seven-year old daughter. The party was in full swing when Bonnie was introduced to Ralph while he was in the middle of winning a dare by hanging upside-down over the side of the boat by his knees, his head almost in the water, sipping a drink. In the short time before their next meeting Ralph had decided that dance was a very interesting subject. He enthused other U.W. psychology, philosophy and art professors and their wives and persuaded Bonnie to teach a Wednesday evening movement class for them. The classes were based on easily managed sports and natural movement themes and they all enjoyed themselves. Ralph later vowed that this was how he wooed her.

Ralph Gundlach was a social psychologist and an active member of many liberal-thinking organizations whose aims were to promote social welfare. They ranged from teachers' and consumers' unions to anti-fascist groups on the cutting edge of state and international politics. Ralph soon asked Bonnie to participate in a fund-raising evening for the Seattle branch of the Medical Bureau to Aid Spanish Democracy which he had helped form and of which he was chairman. The Bureau provided medical backup for the International Brigade's Abraham Lincoln Battalion fighting in the Spanish Civil War. The battalion was made up of Americans who backed the elected Leftist Popular Front government, supported by the Soviet Union, against the onslaught of General Franco's nationalist forces, backed by Hitler's tanks, guns and bombers.

Although Bonnie had participated in a politically-inspired fund-raising performance as a Graham Group member, she had little political awareness. But the ferocity of the Spanish Civil War aroused emotions and focused thought and action, stirring writers, painters and dancers to make their personal statements about war through their art. From her repertoire of brilliant anti-war solos, Martha Graham also performed for a Medical Bureau fund-raising program in New York called *Dances for Spain*. Now Bonnie's own career was taking her into areas of political involvement she had seldom thought about.

For the event she arranged a floor show that could fit into the living rooms of Ralph and two other professors who had built connected homes as an architectual experiment in creating cheaper houses. Ralph had built his seven-room home for $2500, including $50 for the land. Three more professors bought neighboring lots and together the six created a charming little close on a dead-end street almost in the middle of Seattle.

Merce, Syvilla and Dorothy devised their own dances in an amusing spoof called *Skinny Structures*, which wandered successfully through the three linked houses. Merce's witty hotel bellboy was a takeoff on a character in a popular national cigarette advertisement. He performed his brief number dressed in shorts and a smart bellboy's hat made out of the same red and white polka-dotted material from which Bonnie made all the costumes. Syvilla did a whimsical version of *The Good Ship Lollipop*, and Dorothy portrayed a sinuous street walker.

Syvilla Fort, Merce Cunningham and Dorothy Herrmann in *Skinny Structures*, Cornish School, 1938. Photo: Bonnie Bird Collection.

During this episode Bonnie and Ralph began seeing each other regularly and by spring they had decided to marry. Ralph was six feet tall, blond and good looking, with a great sense of humor. He was born in Kansas City, Missouri, on June 17, 1902. His father soon moved the family to Idaho where he was a lawyer for the Rocky Mountain silver miners. Ralph attended U.W. where he took his bachelor's degree in political science and his master's degree in psychology. At university he was a star basketball player. He was also an excellent mountain climber and swimmer and spent his summers working his way through college as a Rocky Mountains lookout. From his mother, who had a trained voice, he acquired a great love of music and sang in the university choral and madrigal groups. He took his doctorate at the University of Illinois in Urbana on the subject of prisons.

Ralph had taught at U.W. since 1927 and was a well-liked and highly-respected professor. He was a man of endless curiosity and enthusiasm, whose special interest, social psychology, involved him in the study of race relations, labor management and propaganda. "He was a fighter for civil rights before civil rights was ever defined as an issue," Bonnie said. He had been a champion of the 1934 waterfront strikers and of Harry Bridges, the radicalist father of the trade union movement on the West Coast who helped bring about many fair-work practices. He was a great admirer of the social psychologist, Kurt Lewin (1890–1947), whose work provided valuable insight into group behaviour and how it might be modified. In 1936 he joined with Lewin in founding the Society for the Psychological Study of Social Issues. The dean of U.W.'s Psychology Department, however, insisted that studies in these areas came under the Sociology Department; Ralph was advised to limit his teaching to recognized areas of psychology.

In early May, 1938, Bonnie and Ralph organized a Medical Bureau fund-raising performance at Seattle's Worth Theatre. The U.W. Chorus sang, the Seattle Repertory Playhouse presented a one-act play, and Bonnie created a thirty-minute dance for her Cornish students with Ralph Gilbert improvising at the piano from a cue sheet. Her *Dance for Spain* was a statement of support from American youth to the youth of Spain. Aspects of Spanish history – military repression (a group dance) and Church corruption (Bonnie's solo) – formed the first two parts, and the group concluded the dance with a celebration of youth.

On the lookout for activities by organizations they suspected of being communist fronts, the local newspapers did their best to sabotage the Medical Aid event by printing the wrong date and misquoting or losing advance publicity. The result was a half-full auditorium. Despite this setback Bonnie and Ralph felt they had won a moral victory. Their elation, however, soon turned to sadness with the news that Franco's nationalist forces had won Catalonia. The Spanish Civil War was over. Survivors of the Lincoln Battalion would soon be returning home.

The Depression was still biting hard, so there was nothing fancy about the wedding on May 19, 1938. Bonnie was not only taking on a husband, but also a new family, as Ralph's daughter and mother both lived in his home. Having discovered a Thursday in their heavy teaching schedules when they were both free at mid-day, they drove out to Everett, a small town north of Seattle, and found a judge in the courthouse who would marry them. Ralph had forgotten a ring, but they did find two people to stand in as witnesses. Afterward, one of the witnesses told a newspaper about their marriage and that evening they were accosted by a photographer while on their way to the tenth anniversary celebration of the Seattle Repertory Playhouse. Ralph knew the paper was pestering him because of his Medical Bureau association and he deeply resented this intrusion into his private life. Both he and Bonnie refused to answer any questions. The next morning's edition carried a front-page picture of the newly-married couple looking very distressed as they hurried to their car. Trying for maximum shock appeal, the caption read, "Psychology professor elopes with dancer!"

Unaware of the newspaper report, Bonnie was teaching her dance majors in a studio adjacent to Miss Aunt Nellie's private top-floor apartment when the door burst open and an excited Miss Cornish came rushing in. She had always run Bonnie's life, so how could she get married without telling Aunt Nellie? Then Miss Cornish broke into smiles and tears and hugged and congratulated her. In the afternoon the students took Bonnie out for a picnic celebration while Ralph taught his classes.

Bonnie sent Martha a telegram soon afterward. Long before her marriage, she knew that she could not go back as a member of the Graham Group. Working with a genius had not been easy; Bonnie was just beginning to understand who she was and where Martha stopped. She needed time. A protracted leave of absence was arranged; the door to continued good relations remained open.

While Ralph taught in Seattle Bonnie went to Mills College in Oakland, California, across the bay from San Francisco, to teach a two-week summer course in Graham technique. Merce, as her assistant, and Dorothy Herrmann went along with her. There Bonnie renewed her friendship with Tina Flade, who was teaching dance and composition. Bonnie's new colleagues were Lester Horton, teacher and choreographer, and Lou Harrison, accompanist and composer. In a letter to Frances Hawkins, she wrote, "I rather hold my breath as to the outcome of this venture. It seems awfully hodgepodge to me." It was during this summer, nevertheless, that the first of two short films was made of Bonnie performing segments of the Graham Technique. The films have become an invaluable piece of American dance history.[1]

Lester Horton had already made a name for himself in Los Angeles with his own company. For the course workshop he produced *Conquest* (Harrison), based on a Mexican myth, in which both Merce and Dorothy danced. Horton had not seen much modern dance, but he had taught at Norma Gould's Los Angeles studio where he had observed the work of the German modern dancers and the occasional classes in Graham or Humphrey technique. When still in his early twenties he had become an expert on North American Indian dances, and had also been greatly influenced by Japanese theater and Michio Ito's oriental approach to the Dalcroze system. "It was his special gift to look at any form of dance and take from it," Bonnie remembered. "Lester was one of those extraordinary people with a torso of India rubber. He did not have a dancer's body; he was stocky and not particularly good looking. He had, however, an amazing sense of rhythm and a keen eye for shaping movement and he was also a fine costume designer with a flair for the theatrical. He kept his dancers going with night club work, industrial shows, films and anything that came along. Some fine dancer-choreographers developed through their work with him, including Bela Lewitzky, Alvin Ailey and Joyce Trisler."

"Horton was developing a very tough, demanding technique that resembled the Graham technique in its class progression from floor exercises to standing, running and Graham-like falls. He was developing it on Bela's body. She always used a terrifyingly high energy level and could do almost anything. The problem was that once the technique was set it did not go on expanding and growing. It over-stretched and over-strained the body. Bela, however, using her sensibilities as a dancer, adapted and modified the technique."

Bonnie, newly married to university professor and surrounded by his friends and colleagues – people of high accomplishment and academic brilliance, was hungry to know more about the world outside the narrow confines of dance. Her teaching schedule at Mills allowed her to participate in classes in American culture at the nearby University of California at Berkeley conducted by Eduard B. Lindeman, a philosopher she greatly admired. Three years earlier, when Lindeman was head of the Whitney Foundation in New York City and his daughter was Bonnie's student, he had led a forum on modern dance and taken his students to watch rehearsals at the Graham Studio. Now he asked Bonnie to present a demonstration of modern dance and give a talk to the class. After Mills ended she continued studying with him, staying in San Francisco with Charlotte Mack, where she slept in a room with a Paul Klee painting. Years later she revisited masterpieces from Mrs. Mack's collection in museums all over America.

Ralph and Bonnie took a belated camping honeymoon in New Mexico to see the Indian ceremonial dances at the Galop Festival. During this time Martha Graham arrived in Santa Barbara after the Bennington premiere of *American Document*, her first Group work featuring a male dancer, Erick Hawkins.[2] Graham asked Bonnie to bring her new husband to the Duffy home on their way back to Seattle so that she might meet him. Soon after their arrival, Martha, with a hint of mystery, announced she was going to Los Angeles and would be leaving early the next morning.

After Mr. and Mrs. Duffy retired for the night the three sat talking in the study. "Martha was quite taken with Ralph, an accomplished flirt, especially when she discovered that he was a psychologist," Bonnie said. "But her state of euphoria astonished me. She was full of romantic notions about love and its healing effects. The implication of her rhapsodizing was that she was in love, but the questions she asked Ralph were very curious. I didn't put the whole story together at once, but the sum of it was that the power of a woman's love could redirect and heal an aberration in the partner. It dawned on me slowly that Martha knew that the person she had fallen in love with was homosexual, but she had already brought about an extraordinary change in this person and was terribly excited about it. Being a polite and properly brought-up girl, it didn't even occur to me to ask her who he was. At five o'clock the next morning she came in to kiss us goodbye before leaving to catch the train for Los Angeles. She was clearly all aflutter and looked very stimulated and wonderful. It wasn't until the following summer that I learned that the man in question was Erick Hawkins."

Bonnie asked Lou Harrison to be her accompanist for her second year at Cornish, but, having committed himself to composing as well as dancing, he was not available. However, he suggested a young composer, John Cage, who was looking for a job. By the start of the term John and his wife Xenia, the daughter of the head of the Russian Orthodox Church in Alaska, had settled into a large old house converted into apartments just down the hill from the Cornish School.

Cage's arrival brought a new stimulus to Bonnie's work. At the New School for Social Research he had been a student of Henry Cowell, a prolific composer especially popular with dancers. Cowell was seeking to extend the range of rhythms, harmonies and workable sounds from conventional Western instruments through his studies of Oriental, primitive and American folk cultures. His open mind, radical musical thinking and exploration of new forms and musical materials influenced John Cage, and his inventive manipulation of the tonal and resonant qualities of the piano undoubtedly played a part in Cage's later experimentation with the instrument.

For a short period John studied counterpoint in California with Arnold Schoenberg, the Austrian composer. Schoenberg had evolved the 12-tone system, up to that time the most radical innovation in Western music. John's musical outlook was broadened by this experience, despite Schoenberg's opinion that his work showed no feeling for harmony or melody. New ideas emanating from Germany's Bauhaus School, whose methods had been breaking down the separation between disciplines and forging closer links between artists and machines, appealed to John's inventive skills and imagination. He delighted in creating unusual sound textures with whatever was at hand, whether traditional, natural or mechanical.

While Merce Cunningham and Dorothy Herrmann were in their second year at Cornish, Syvilla Fort was preparing for graduation. With Bonnie as adviser, she was given the responsibility of producing a whole program of her own choreography that would also involve an original score by Cage. Syvilla asked John to compose the music for a solo, *Bacchanale*, which had startled Bonnie on its first showing because of its oriental, Dionysian quality. John felt that the strange percussive sounds of the gamelan orchestra, a new interest of his, would be right for the dance. Bonnie thought he was joking; there was nothing even resembling a gamelan orchestra on the West Coast of the United States at the time. Even if there had been they could not have afforded it. She asked him to find another solution. John, in his inventor's mode, experimented by inserting nuts, bolts, pieces of paper and other objects between the strings and under the dampers of a piano, turning the instrument into a one-man percussion orchestra sounding strangely gamelan-like. He called his practical answer to Bonnie's request for another solution the 'prepared piano'. It featured in many more of his works.

What interested John most at that time was percussion, but not as played by jazz or classical symphony musicians using standard instruments. He wanted to extend his knowledge about any materials that would make a sound when hit. Bonnie recalled: "I remember arriving to give a workshop someplace with John and remarking that there was no piano. John's immediate reaction was to 'play the room' using sticks to hit radiators, window sills, walls, anything, while he counted or stamped on the floor. I loved his response to the challenge." When he played for Bonnie's Graham classes he treated the piano mainly as a percussive instrument. She was accustomed to this because accompanists at the Graham Studio had used the piano in this way. Dini de Remer was called 'Dini One-Note' because she always started class with just one repeatedly hammered note. John only came close to what might be called a melodic line when he used chord clusters over a percussive left hand.

Imaginary Landscape, the first in a series of Cage compositions using this title, grew out of his and Bonnie's search for new ideas and sounds. One day while teaching her dance majors Bonnie was describing the beauty of the arm as it rises upwards, giving shape not only to itself but also to the space around it. Suddenly she turned to John and said, "I wonder if an arm would be really beautiful if it were separated from the body?" A new work was underway.

At the same time, Ralph, always keenly involved in Bonnie's activities as well as his own wide-ranging research, was exploring sound. He brought home several 78-rpm recordings made by the Bell Telephone's research division identifying pure tones. One entire record was devoted to the sound of a pure middle C. Bonnie was fascinated. Then John discovered he could obtain unusual sliding tones by increasing or decreasing the speed of the turntable. At the Cornish School Radio Studio

The first *Imaginary Landscape*, Cornish School, 1939. Merce Cunningham on left. Photo: Bonnie Bird Collection.

he used the records to build the basic sounds for the first recording of *Imaginary Landscape*. To these he added further layers of sound with a cymbal and by covering a two-by-four-inch piece of wood with cloth and 'playing' the piano by rocking the wood on the keys.

Bonnie had three triangles constructed, one with a truncated top angle. They were free-standing, covered with black cloth and large enough to hide a dancer's body. For Merce there was a six-foot rectangle with a step behind it so that his head could appear over the top. Staged in front of black curtains, arms and legs seemed to wander in space when the traingles moved around. Only Merce's head was visible when it traveled down the side of the rectangle almost to the floor.

John's totally arhythmic score had an eerie quality. At first it was difficult for a choreographer accustomed to structures and counts, but Bonnie met the challenge by identifying specific sound cues and choreographing movement phrases having their own independent rhythms between the cues. This way of choreographing was light years away from the accepted methods of the day, as was John's sound accompaniment. The student dancers revelled in these new adventures; Merce carried this experience into many of the works he later created for his own company.

Many musicians were in the audience for the spring concert in May. During the intermission they heatedly debated what instruments John had used for *Imaginary Landscape,* but could not think of any that were not conventional. Their general consensus was that much of the composition was purely melodic. John was delighted.

Cage also worked with Bonnie at the Bush School where Joan, Ralph's daughter, was a student. There, the eight-to ten-year olds were required to take dance classes and Bonnie had to struggle to find ways to hold their interest. She and John decided to focus on a production, something neither had ever attempted before with youngsters. They quickly discovered that once children knew their goal was a performance the impossible could be accomplished. For the spring festival Bonnie staged a Mexican fiesta, with musical accompaniment by the students on instruments they had made under John's direction.

Teaching dance to children was a new development for Bonnie, and she quickly understood that she knew little about child psychology. She read everything she could get her hands on and often asked Ralph for advice. While he was no teacher of young people, he did have enormous understanding and seemingly endless resources. Over the following years one of the main strands of Bonnie's career was teaching dance to a wide age range of youngsters with varing abilities and disabilities and, from these experiences, passing on her methods to student teachers through special courses.

During the school year Bonnie and John produced an interrelated arts series in the Cornish Theatre through which they hoped to enliven the once inspiring, now insipid, Friday night instrumental programs. The novelist Nancy Wilson Ross, an expert on the work of the Bauhaus artists, wrote her first major paper, *The Symbols of Modern Art,* for the opening program. Next came a talk by Mark Tobey, along with an exhibition of his paintings, etchings and water colors. John Cage presented the first of several concerts devoted entirely to percussion works in December, 1938.[3] To prepare for these performances he wrote to many contemporary composers, among them Virgil Thomson, Henry Cowell, Lou Harrison, William Russell, a puppeteer who worked with percussion instruments, and Ray Green, who had recently composed *American Document* for Martha Graham. Scores began filtering back from composers who had forgotten they had ever written for percussion. Some of the instruments they asked for were quite unusual, like the jawbone of an ass which had to be hit hard to make the teeth clatter, and a bull-roarer, a struck gong whose vibrations slowly died while it was being dipped into a bucket of water. In many cases John and the students had to make the instruments.

Ray Green based his *3 Inventories of Casey Jones* for pop bottles, bottle with marbles, drums, cymbals, gong and piano on a popular folk song.

3 *Inventories of Casey Jones*, Cornish School, 1938. Merce Cunningham, Bonnie Bird, Syvilla Fort and Dorothy Herrmann. Photo: Bonnie Bird Collection.

His whimsical rendition so charmed Bonnie that she created a dance to it, but one inspired by a recent working man's version of the Casey legend that had a sly political twist. In this account, Casey was a company fellow who, having driven his famous engine too fast around a bend and crashed, found himself in 'the other place' instead of heaven because he was not a union man. Bonnie, Merce, Syvilla and Dorothy danced this tongue-in-cheek piece in a set designed by Xenia Cage.

Bonnie and John sent out fliers that doubled as programs, printed on cheap, narrow, printers' leftover strips. Because John wanted them to have a contemporary look only lower-case letters were used. That startled some people, but a listing of the instruments intrigued many more who were curious about the different ways percussive sounds could be created. A few were incensed that the program was limited to percussion, but exactly for this reason there was much interest from young composers who were in the first stages of breaking into new creative territory – just the kind of people John wanted to meet.

Bonnie could sense a great deal of unease as the large audience began to take their seats. Then a series of absurd events started to unfold. Sitting with the dancers at the back of the theater, she observed a tall, bizarre-looking young man in weird clothes enter, followed by a group of other young men also in outlandish gear. One of her students told her that the leader was a former Mark Tobey student, Morris Graves, still a relatively unknown painter working for the Works Progress Administration. He and his group of artistic rebels had decided that the Friday night programs at Cornish were too stuffy and should include more experimental work. Graves had arrived on the back of a cut-down car, sitting in an over-stuffed armchair. With mock ceremony his followers had unrolled a filthy red carpet for him to walk on to the theater entrance. Once inside they settled into a row in front of Bonnie and noisily began shelling peanuts. An incensed spectator turned around in his seat as the curtain rose and gave Morris a dirty look which he answered by peering back through a lorgnette fitted with a false eyeball. The audience was so annoyed by his behaviour that they turned all their antagonism against Graves and his group and gave John Cage a very sympathetic reception. In his boyish and ingenuous way John spoke briefly about the program, how he had obtained the music and how the instruments were assembled. He was already beginning to establish his controversial credo of sound as music and challenge modern Western musical cultures and the belief that music was only what the music establishment decided it was. Then the five student percussionists began playing. They were neatly dressed in black trousers, white shirts with the sleeves rolled up, and black ties. They did not wear black jackets, which was already a departure from tradition. As unusual as the audience may have found the sounds they accepted them without too much difficulty, especially the strongly rhymic pieces. What actually broke their concentration occured during a long silence half way through a score when Morris Graves rose suddenly and proclaimed, "Jesus in the everywhere!"

Mrs. Beck, a well-known harpist of imposing proportions who presided over the Friday night concerts, decided that this young man had to be ejected from the theater. During the intermission two strong men from the school faculty approached Graves, who lay down on the floor in front of them and obligingly made himself rigid so that they could lift him. As they carried him horizontally past Mrs. Beck, he looked up from under her ample bosom and said, "Good evening, Mrs. Beck. Very interesting evening." Later, during Bonnie's lively version of *Casey Jones* he re-entered the auditorium through the second story balcony, only to come to the realization that he had misread the program listings and wasted his rebellion. He had, however, honestly attempted to show that he shared in John and Bonnie's belief that Cornish needed a dusting, and eventually they became good friends.

Merce Cunningham, like the other dance majors, worked closely with Bonnie and created many of his own choreographies. He thrived in John's wonderfully imaginative classes in rhythm and enjoyed displaying his awesome rhythmic ability playing several instruments in the percussion concerts. He was, however, a moody student; he often infuriated Bonnie by disappearing during rehearsal periods for a whole evening or even a couple of days. When Miss Cornish was told that he was not eating lunch in the small basement cafeteria she asked Bonnie to find out what the problem was. Bonnie discovered that he was saving up his lunch money to buy a pair of shoes that had caught his fancy. When eventually he proudly wore them for her, she had to take care not to let on that they were the funniest shoes she had even seen. To Merce these shoes, with their white leather uppers dotted with holes the size of quarters, a zipper up the front and thick crepe soles, were a great prize and clearly worth a couple weeks' lunches.

In March Bonnie produced *A Hilarious Dance Concert*, her answer to those who held that modern dance had no sense of humor. Except for *Skinny Structures*, she choreographed the whole program. In addition to *Three Inventories of Casey Jones* and *Imaginary Landscape*, it included solos for herself: *Contemporary Challenge* (Chávez), and *Of a Tender Age: Timid Yearning, Nevertheless*, and *Reckless Merriment* (Gyorgy Kosa), a humorous comment on adolescent naïveté. The concert had great success and was repeated twice.

Bonnie Bird in *Of a Tender Age*, Cornish School, 1939. Photo: Phyllis A. Dearborn (Bonnie Bird Collection).

Her big group work was her staging of Jean Cocteau's 1921 satiric pastische on human behavior, *Marriage at the Eiffel Tower*.[4] The scenario begins with a wedding breakfast taking place on the second level of the Eiffel Tower. A photographer is about to take a picture of the breakfast, but out of his camera pop beasts and beings Cocteau wished to satirize: an ostrich; a hunter; a manager; a photographer; a bride; a bridesmaid; a girl on a bicycle; a mother-in-law; a Trouville bathing beauty; an art dealer; and a general (Merce) who makes speeches full of hot air. Cocteau used the device of two 'phonograph' voices (Bonnie and Ralph) commenting on the stage action while making funny remarks to one another.

The piece accommodates different composers with ease. John composed several sections and asked Henry Cowell and George McKay each to write two others. Unfortunately, when John contacted Cowell about *Marriage* he was in San Quentin Penitentiary near San Francisco serving a four-year sentence on an morals charge involving young men. Bonnie maintained the charge was trumped-up by a local women's club. John and Bonnie traveled down the coast to talk with him and he agreed to write the opening and closing music. He sent them about twenty possible motifs from which they chose three or four, returning them with a description of the events on stage and suggestions about their length. Cowell then composed a selection of pieces from which a final choice was made. Written for piano and the percussion instruments the students could handle, the piece left space for incorporating whatever instrumental players might be available. "There is nothing very serious about the music," he wrote Bonnie, "but I think it will amuse everyone. Thanking you again for thinking of me..."[5]

After the performance he again wrote Bonnie. "Your letter today presented the performance with an astonishing realism to me and I feel as though I had witnessed and heard it. I really think it must have been a wonderful occasion and hope that maybe it will be repeated not only there but elsewhere. Have you ever thought of trying to bring it down to this vicinity? I am delighted that you liked the opener and the finale. I feel highly recompensed by the conviction that I have helped to make Seattle sizzle with modernity. Do let me know, too, about how the new percussion piece sounds in rehearsal. Martha gave a recital here [in the San Francisco area] which was even more enjoyed than usual. Folks here seemed to think her work showed new and finer qualities. She did my *Deep Song*, which was enthusiastically received, so I am told."

Bonnie's deep love of the Pacific Northwest nurtured her creative work. The sounds of the wind, the storms and the sea, the songs of the birds, the mists and fogs, the wheat fields, grasslands and sand dunes, the gigantic Douglas firs and sequoias, the earthquakes and glaciers, and, not

least, the dances of the indigenous peoples, all played a significant role
in inspiring her.

A late spring weekend might find her camping on the seashore with
her students, studying the shapes of driftwood or digging for long-necked
clams. A winter outing to observe tribal ceremonial dances was initiated
by one of her students, Joyce Wike, a young anthropologist, whose special
interest lay in studying the native peoples of the Northwest. Joyce had
been adopted by the Swinamish, inhabitants of an island in the Puget
Sound, and lived with them for two years while she filmed and notated
their dances. To verify that her personal notation was readable and
therefore a valid record, Bonnie's students reconstructed the dances from
her notes.

Tribes came from all over Washington State and British Columbia for
the ceremonial dances, supposedly celebrating the signing of a treaty
with the white man but actually the observance of the Winter Solstice.
They performed for the general public in a great cedar-wood longhouse,
a building about 150 feet long and 30 feet high. Bonnie clearly remembered the public relations program of singing and dancing they put on
for the Chamber of Commerce and their guests in which they did the
butterfly and other dances belonging to the Plains Indians. Although
these dances had nothing whatsoever to do with their own traditions,
they were popular displays for these occasions. Then, once the strangers
had gone, friends were invited to a place under the stars where they
did their own spirit dances. One of Merce Cunningham's first professional choreographies, *Totem Ancestor*, carried remembrances of this
experience.

Bonnie's work was spurred on by her belief that she had a personal
mission to raise the status and importance of modern dance in the
public's mind. Through performances, technique demonstrations, carefully prepared radio interviews and lectures to women's clubs, she strove
to present modern dance as a serious art whose vitality came from the
rich vocabulary of human expression. Attired to perfection, she was often
heard at Seattle society gatherings expounding her views with deep
conviction. She was equally skilled in the practical work of supervising
layouts, stencils and poster silkscreening, or adding to her 3000-name
mailing list to publicize her concerts. All these activities helped gather
enthusiastic followers who filled the seats at her concerts. Her high
standard of professional accomplishment, accompanied by a good business head, meant that her performances paid for themselves and even
netted a small surplus for the school.

But her efforts were not enough. The businessmen who made up the
board of directors insisted that the institution should be profitable; Aunt

Nellie maintained they were shortsighted and shirking their duty to raise money. After a final falling out, Miss Cornish resigned in the spring of 1939. She was replaced the following season by a woman whom Bonnie thought nice enough, but without vision.

In June Bonnie again taught in New York at the Graham Studio. She also acted as stage manager for a dance cabaret presented by the Theatre Arts Committee in the Teresa Kaufmann Auditorium of the 92nd Street Young Men's and Young Women's Hebrew Association. The dancers included Agnes de Mille, Dorothy Bird, Esther Junger, Bill Bales, the German dancer and mime artist Lotte Goslar, and the young Shawn and Humphrey-Weidman dancer Jack Cole, then at the beginning of his remarkable career in jazz dance. The program note, an oblique reference in that fateful summer of 1939 to the war looming over Europe, read: "The hopes of humanity are most sensitively reflected in the personalities and works of its artists."

At the end of the Studio course Martha asked Bonnie if she would drive Erick Hawkins west with her. Bonnie was heading for Berkeley, where Ralph was teaching for the summer. During the long journey west she found Erick extremely heavy going. Suffering the dust and discomfort of long hours in the driver's seat, she was annoyed that he always looked impeccable in his all-white tennis outfit, and entirely too beautiful when he took off his shirt in the intense heat. People could not keep their eyes off him.

Her other passengers were two Group members, Thelma Babbitz and Frieda Flier, both from Jewish working-class families and active in leftist organizations. To pass the time the girls, both non-drivers, took turns reading aloud from *The Grapes of Wrath,* John Steinbeck's latest novel about impoverished sharecroppers who had left their eroded farms in the Midwest in search of a better life in California. Bonnie was actually driving along Route 66 described in the story, seeing firsthand the displaced people of the Dustbowl. Their ancient Model Ts, the first Ford cars ever produced, were chugging along, held together by bailing wire and loaded with people and possessions. Many overheated vehicles were steaming and had come to a stop on the roadside in the shade of large billboards. *Grapes of Wrath* was happening in front of their eyes, but Hawkins was not moved. He insisted that people did not live in the way Steinbeck described and found the book's language insulting.

In their hotel room at night Thelma and Frieda brought Bonnie up to date on Studio life. Although Martha had admitted it to no one, it was obvious to everyone around her that she was deeply in love with Erick. Bonnie was shocked. She found it difficult to believe that Martha could fall for such a man, regardless of how intelligent he was said to be. Of his positive qualities during the dozen or so years he was with the Company she said: "He was not a bad mover, although rather wooden, which Martha handled by building special roles for him as a kind of prototype male. And he photographed well." She came to value Erick only after he left the Graham Company and pursued his own dance career.

The 1939 Bennington summer dance session took place at Mills College. Dance had been in the PE program headed by Rosalind Cassidy since 1925. She wanted to make Mills the West's center of dance and by 1934 a program for dance majors was underway, headed by Wigman-trained Tina Flade. When Cassidy visited Bennington in 1936 she was inspired by what she saw and soon afterward plans were made for a joint enterprise between Mills and Bennington.

Although Bonnie was not teaching in the Mills summer session she had arranged for Merce, Dorothy and Syvilla to participate in Holm, Humphrey-Weidman and Graham classes. By the time Martha arrived to teach the last two weeks Bonnie's three students were looking very good. A photo of Merce and Dorothy in a duet Bonnie had made for them at Cornish, which they performed in a noontime outdoor program at Mills, shows a lanky boy with the alert quality of a deer in flight, so characteristic of Merce's best dancing years. "Even though he was still raw, he had a magicial quality that wowed people," Bonnie said.

Because good male dancers were scarce, feelers were already out for Merce from Holm and Humphrey even before Graham's arrival. But having had a man in her Group for a year Martha wanted another, and when she saw Merce she immediately invited him to join her. Merce sought Bonnie's consent to leave his four-year course at Cornish and go to New York. She remembered his first class with her as a self-conscious, hollow-chested boy. Her whole effort for two years had been to get his legs working, his chest open and his carriage correct. She knew she could not refuse him, but she teasingly said, "You're just not finished. I haven't finished your arms!" "I tell him to this day," she said, "that I never did finish them. Nobody did, because he still uses them like flippers! Half his style comes out of those unfinished arms."

Merce was thrilled to be with Graham. By December, 1939, he was dancing the role of the Acrobat in *Every Soul is a Circus* (Paul Nordoff). His letters to Bonnie over the next few years, however, reflected his diminishing enchantment He remained a soloist with the Graham Company until 1945, but by 1944 he had already begun presenting his own solo recitals, with John Cage as his music director.

Entering her third year at Cornish in the autumn of 1939 with only one dance major and an unimaginative administration, Bonnie realized that the school held little further promise for her. She made a last effort to build up the dance department with a project to attract teenagers to dance while they were still in high school. This was her own early version of an Arts-in-Education program which the National Endowment for the Arts and Humanities developed three decades later. She auditioned more than a hundred young people from schools all over Seattle and chose 30 who were given a month of free classes. From this group she selected 16 to join her regular students in a further six weeks of intensive classes and rehearsals, culminating in the performance of a new twenty-minute choreography, *America was Promises*. It was to be presented in a concert planned to take place two weeks before Graham's Seattle appearance to help stimulate interest in her work.

America was Promises, set to Archibald MacLeish's poem, was spoken and sung by the Repertory Playhouse actor Gerald Van Steenbergen, with a piano score for four hands by John Cage. The themes of its eight sections were *Voyage, Discovery of the Land, Corruption, Westward Movement,*

America was Promises, Cornish School, 1940. Photo: Phyllis A. Dearborn (Bonnie Bird Collection).

Building, Restlessness, Realization, and *Declaration.* The poem and the dance were about being an American through difficult and trying times. Nazi Germany and the Soviet Union had signed a non-aggression pact that opened the way for their joint invasion of Poland in September, 1939, the beginning of the Second World War. America remained neutral. In choosing this theme, Bonnie was demonstrating her growing awareness of international affairs and her realization that even her American heritage might be at stake.

The concert began with *Spiritual* (Cage) danced by Syvilla Fort, followed by *Four Songs of the Moment* (Cage), danced by Dorothy Herrmann, and *Imaginary Landscape No. 2* (Cage), danced by Bonnie Bird, Syvilla Fort, Dorothy Herrmann and Cole Weston, and culminated with *America was Promises.* It was finely organized, well danced and enthusiastically received. Nothing less would have satisfied Bonnie. It paid its own expenses, and, as usual with her programs, made some money for the school. Despite her success Bonnie was no longer interested in continuing at Cornish; without Miss Aunt Nellie she felt the school had lost its way. In the spring of 1940 she handed in her resignation, effective at the end of the season. She had decided to open her own school and pursue, at her own risk, a rounded, creative program in dance education.

John Cage also left Cornish at the end of the school year. He was eager to have contact with the Bauhaus School artists who had fled to America after the school's closure in Nazi Germany in 1933. He and Xenia went to Chicago, where László Moholy-Nagy had founded the New Bauhaus.

After returning from the 1940 Graham June Course, Bonnie opened her new school, the American Dance Theatre, at 4140 University Way. Classes were linked with the Seattle Repertory Playhouse, a short walk away, where her dance performances also took place. The range of the curriculum reflected Bonnie's determination to give her students a rounded education in dance and theater. There was a two-year course for dance majors with classes in music, acting, theater background, makeup, speech, stagecraft, and painting (with Mark Tobey). There were also dance classes for children, teenagers and non-professionals. Four guest professors from the University of Washington made up the associate faculty. The photographer Phyllis Dearborn occupied a small front room in the building. She made some lovely photographs of Bonnie's dances. Performances consisted of new pieces as well as works Bonnie had created at Cornish. Several of her former Cornish students also participated in her concerts. Among Bonnie's new choreographies were: *Theme and Variations on Children's Folk Songs* (Johann Georg Reutter); *Of Ancient Significance* (Arthur Honegger), *From Statements About Ourselves* (Lopatnikoff), and *Every Man's Saga* (McKay), based on the drawings of James Thurber.

During the season the Seattle Artists' League, which Bonnie had helped establish the previous year, found its stride. She was very pleased with a recital by Syvilla Fort which included *Prelude to Flight*, *Haitian Rhythm*, *Bacchanale*, and *Spiritual*, all four works composed and accompanied by John Cage.

But Bonnie was feeling increasingly depressed. The administrative burden of the school exhausted her and modern dance itself seemed an uphill, often futile, struggle. She was upset by what was happening in Europe: Hitler's Germany had subjugated northern Europe, left deep wounds in Great Britain after an unsuccessful attempt to invade it, occupied Yugoslavia and Greece, and in June, 1941, invaded the Soviet Union. Her marriage to a social psychologist showed her there was more to life outside the narrow confines of dance. Because of Ralph's widespread activities their home was an oasis for intellectuals and artists. "The great Negro bass Paul Robeson frequently stayed with us when he visited Seattle, but only after registering at the best hotel so that others of his race might also do so," Bonnie said. Earl Robinson, the 'music for the people' composer and balladeer, was a guest, as was Eva Curie, daughter of the discoverers of radium. Detroit trade unionist Keith Sward, author of *The Legend of Henry Ford*, a firsthand account of his experience of Mafia infiltration into the Ford automobile factories, was incognito when he stayed with them because the Mafia had a contract out of kill him. Spaniards working with Ralph to find foster homes for orphans from the Spanish Civil War often filled the house.

Bonnie grew despondent over the failings of her own education. Her dreams of a life in dance inspired by Caird Leslie and Anna Pavlova, fostered by Nellie Cornish, and realized by Martha Graham for a few marvelous years, had come to very little. What was the future for a dancer? Had all those years been for nothing?

Drained of incentive and aspiration she closed her school and turned away from dance. Her childhood notion for a career, before dance took over her life, had been to become a doctor. She decided to study medicine, but not having had a college education she faced seven years of hard study. In the summer of 1941 she took a course in Ralph's classes under her maiden name and directly afterward became a fully-enrolled student at U.W. By then she was totally anti-dance and did not even want to be recognized as a dancer.

Studying, taking more time to raise a step-daughter with whom she was extremely close, and taking flying lessons – something she had always wanted to do – kept her happy and busy. The day she was to make her first solo flight, December 7, 1941, the Japanese bombed Pearl

Harbor. All civilian flights were grounded. Four days later Germany declared war on the U.S.A. Suddenly, America was at war on two fronts.

In the scramble to get onto a war footing there was a sudden shift among university faculty members all over America. Many went into government positions or joined the armed forces. When the noted social psychologist, Robert Tryon, joined the Office of War Information Ralph was invited by the University of California at Berkeley to teach in his place for the duration. Ralph was delighted to be able to teach social psychology, his area of greatest interest. He had tenure at U.W. and would return there after the war.

In January, 1942, the Gundlach family rented their home and headed south for California. An early morning silver thaw covered the roadside fences in glittering streams of ice and made the fields sparkle in the blinding sunshine. Bonnie's land was dancing for her. She knew it, was grateful to it, and would never forget this performance.

8

AMERICA AT WAR

The Second World War Years

Bonnie was happy at Berkeley. Her medical studies were going well, she loved her house on the north side of the campus and she felt secure in her choice of a new career. When a request instigated by some of her new friends came to teach evening dance classes at the local Y she had no qualms about returning to dance as a sideline and readily agreed.

In the late spring of 1942, however, there was strong pressure on undergraduates to take war jobs. Only those who were within sight of graduating were encouraged to continue their studies. Bonnie postponed her studies to join in the war effort and applied for a job as a pilot with the Civilian Aeronautical Division, which was employing women to fly practice targets. Although she met the stiff qualifications, she was rejected on the grounds that she had a daughter under fifteen. She decided that if she could not fly planes she would work on them. Certain of finding a job at the nearby Treasure Island aircraft repair center, she went to night school to learn how to dismantle and reassemble airplane engines; however, on learning that women were first assigned the midnight to eight o'clock 'gaveyard shift' she began looking for some other kind of work. Those hours, she felt, would be too hard on Ralph and Joan. A friend recommended her as an interviewer for the newly created Office of Price Administration and Rent Control and while she was waiting for confirmation she took a short-term job as a dispatcher for a pile drivers' union. She quickly learned about shoring up buildings and dispatching pile drivers with the tools they needed for their particular skills. "I stayed a month and even enjoyed the work," she said. "I had left the dance profession in a big way."

In the Western Division of the Office of Price Administration and Rent Control, she was one of a team of women chosen because they were adept at meeting the public and getting along with people. She found the job interesting and made life-long friends among her colleagues, bright and lively college graduates, as well as the division's head lawyer who later became godfather to her son.

The well-established trade unions in the San Francisco area put a great deal of effort into raising money for the War Chest and organizing a sound and flexible civil defence system for the city. It was during this time that federal workers began organizing their own union. Bonnie, increasingly restless because she was no longer pursuing her pre-med studies, was interested in any new role she could play. She became a union member and shortly afterward a representative to the Congress of Industrial Organizations, the CIO.

In September, 1943, she went to Mexico for the Western Hemisphere Conference on the Care of European Refugees, representing both her own union and the San Francisco Chapter of the Spanish Refugee Appeal. Delegates included trade union representatives and polititians as well as volunteers from all walks of life who had worked in refugee organizations. The conference chairman was Lombardo Toledono, Director of the Mexican Federation of Labor. Dr. Edward Barsky, former head of the International Brigade's team of doctors, and the Chilean poet Pablo Neruda were also present.

At that time the Spanish Refugee Appeal was helping Spaniards who had reached southern France escape the clutches of the Vichy government. Since the bombing of Bilboa in 1937, Mexico had been taking in refugees, among them hundreds of children for whom they provided hospitals and orphanages. Bonnie visited many of the hospitalized children and wrote a report on the situation that dramatically increased support for refugee care. Her interest in this work was also personal. In 1939 she and Ralph had 'adopted' Victor Neijo, a small, wizened, Spanish child living in a refugee colony on the French coast near Bayonne. He and other orphaned children had disappeared into the concentrations camps of the Vichy government, and he was never heard of again.[1]

A chance encounter brought Bonnie back to dance. While in Mexico she met a group of politically oriented young sculptors, lithographers and illustrators who had recently formed themselves into a collective, *Taller de Gráfica Popular*, Popular Graphics Workshop. The group of about two dozen included Leopoldo Mendez, Pablo Higgins, Malcho Igirie and Juan O'Gorman. Workshop members were so poor they could often afford neither a stone for making a lithograph nor a printing press. The leading revolutionary graphic artists of Mexico, David Alfaro Siqueiros, José Clemente Orozco and Diego Rivera, championed their work. All of these artists were communists and anti-church. The government, led by President Cardenas, a powerful force for reform in a country that had been dominated by powerful landowners and the Catholic Church, had begun a huge program of public education. One of the ways the young Graphics Workshop artists could use their skills was by accepting poster assignments sponsored by the trade unions. These poster campaigns were designed to improve the lives of the peasants by educating them about the agrarian reforms that were being put into effect, from land utilization to flood control.

"When Workshop members discovered that I was a dancer they were wonderful to me. They wouldn't listen to anything about my not being a dancer. They knew about modern dance: Anna Sokolow had already made a big impact in Mexico; she had a company there and everyone knew who Anna was. 'If you are a dancer these are the things you can do', they said to me." They persuaded Bonnie to prolong her stay and visit some of the villages with them to observe how they worked on mural assignments. When an artist was asked to paint a mural on a public building he first spent time finding out about the peasants' lives and history, and their present attitude to the landowners. The artist's inter-action with the local community enabled him to understand the problems of the people and convey their feelings with clarity.

Bonnie was deeply moved. An artist's concern for the people around him and his dedication to improving their lives through his work was a totally different concept from that of the artist whose personal vision was the supreme motivating force. The members of the Taller de Gráfica Popular gave her pause to think. She had held high hopes and worked hard for a dance career of her own, but everything had petered away. The war had frustrated her plans for a future in medicine. She was very unhappy. "I began to feel more and more that I wanted to go back to dance;" she said, "that there was another way of working in which one didn't have to work in isolation, but collectively and cooperatively. My whole patterning had been 'do it yourself'. Not that I can say that I had any notions about how to work collectively in the way that we think of it today." She wondered if she had the potential to succeed within, as well as beyond, the perceived boundaries of dance. It would take time. Above all, she needed to keep her mind fresh and rediscover her spirit of adventure. About one thing she was certain: working for the govern-ment held no future for her.

Bonnie was twenty-nine. "Along with my work, my marriage had begun to feel like a kind of an entrapment," she said. "I felt I needed to be able to move freely, if only for a while. Luckily, I had a tolerant husband, although the arrival of a telegram saying I was going to New York may have caused him to wonder whether he was losing me." A friend sent her the air fare and she stayed with the Kulka family, taking classes at the Graham Studio and teaching occasionally for Martha. She also took several part-time jobs, one of which included being a leg-woman for an interior decorator. After two months she flew back to San Francisco, having decided to open her own studio again and use it as a base for new career initiatives. She remembered a building in San Francisco where May O'Donnell and José Limón rehearsed and opened her school there.

Because trade unions in San Francisco were supporting adult education for the increasingly large number of wartime waterfront workers and their dependants, the California Labor School, with which Ralph was affiliated, started developing recreational programs of all kinds and asked Bonnie to organize and teach its dance classes. Having large groups of adults and children of all ages gave her the opportunity to try out her own ideas and methods for teaching recreational dance, a new area for her.

Within the school's program Bonnie also taught four- to five-year olds for the first time, and in several of her teenage classes she found she had to deal with seriously disturbed young people. She tackled these new challenges by reading, asking questions, listening, thinking, and putting ideas into action. Ralph was never far from immediate and supportive involvement in her work. Family life also played its part in her creative classes for children: there was many a time during a story telling exchange over the dinner dishes when Joan's fresh imagination brought imagery into play that gave Bonnie new input.

Bonnie also became a committed fund-raiser for the Russian War Relief. She conceived an uniquely successful program of events in large private homes which were loaned for the occasions by their owners. Her charm and know-how persuaded visiting artists, such as the violinist Isaac Stern, to join members of the Berkeley faculty, often leading physicists, in friendly, well-catered evenings of quartet music in magnificent surroundings. In June, 1944, shortly after D-Day, a huge gala she coordinated was given in San Francisco's Civic Auditorium. Participants included the San Francisco Symphonie Orchestra; Hollywood actress Olivia de Havilland; Bonnie's own studio group of 20 dancing to a movement from Tchaikowsky's *Symphony Pathetique*; one hundred folk dancers; and the Jewish Chorus from nearby Petaluma, made up of 80 Jewish chicken farmers who sang Russian, Ukranian and Yugoslavian folk songs.

Bonnie's first experience in the embroyonic field of dance therapy came early in 1945 when she worked at Pinehaven Institution, a home for emotionally disturbed youngsters, with the renowned German-born psychoanalyst and one-time disciple of Sigmund Freud, Erik Erikson. Erikson was working with Ralph in the Psychology Department at Berkeley. His American wife, a former dancer, and their little daughter were taking classes with Bonnie at her studio. The lessons were full of games drawn from daily life: one game was designed to develop kinesthetic reactions, such as walking to the store while playing left foot, right foot, left hand, right hand; another had mother and child acting out stories and then reversing their roles. Through this game a real cameraderie developed because the mother was not always in the position of authority. Erikson often observed Bonnie teaching while waiting to take his family home and decided that what she was doing might also help some of his patients reveal the frustrations at the root of their anti-social behavior.

The Pinehaven psychiatric social workers and analysts worked with children from the ages of three to eighteen, whose problems ranged from emotional dependence to schizophrenia. Bonnie went there twice a week for six months, working mostly with children from nine or ten upwards. She knew she was not going to be able to teach anything she had ever taught before, but she had already learned that putting on a production was vital to the success of her work with children. At Pinehaven it would be a first-time-ever event, as these children had never before succeeded in concentrating on one particular goal long enough to produce a result.

The first thing she did was make costumes. Bare midriffs and feet were in vogue, so she made the girls full skirts which could be worn with shirts tied at the midriff. She asked them to crayon a motif around the bottom of their skirts so that she could find out how well they were able to follow a project through. Because they were unable to sustain their concentration most of the skirts finished up with only one portion of a design.

When she taught the first dance class, she did not allow the boys into the classroom. They were sent away to do something else. This made them jealous of the girls, which was exactly what she wanted. By the second class she had them all. Meanwhile she had arranged with the Pinehaven stenotypist to take down everything that was said in her classes. She told the children, who could be very testy, that she had a very short memory and needed the notes as reminders.

Having read up on their personal histories, Bonnie began with structured improvisations related to the particular problems of each child. Through improvisation, each child's genuine personal movement, expressive quality and individual rhythm became instantly visible. The movement was rudimentary, but talking through each improvisation with the child revealed more information about his or her problems. After classes Bonnie wrote descriptions of the physical actions in the margins of the typist's notes which were useful both to class development and to the psychiatric social workers who looked for anything that might be meaningful. For the performance she built movement sequences using the improvisations. Erikson was enthusiastic about her work and said that the information coming out of the improvisations, especially the fantasy, afforded him new ways of reaching the inner lives of the children which had hitherto been inaccessible.

Using movement to further an individual's emotional and physical integration was another facet of dance for her to explore. Dance therapy in America was still in its early years, although primitive cultures have used and treasured this aspect of dance since time immemorial. "There were a few forward thinkers in this field," Bonnie said, "mostly led by Marian Chace who was working in the Washington D.C. area. It sometimes attracted the interest of medical doctors, but another twenty-five years passed before dance therapy even began to be recognized by other disciplines."

During 1944 and 1945 Bonnie ventured into dance criticism, writing under the name of Tess Egert for the San Francisco *People's World.*[2] She was also active in developing the San Francisco Dance League which gave concerts and workshops. Its original members included Ruth Hatfield, Marian Van Tuyl, Eleanor Lauer, Mimi Kagen and the Danish dancer Bodil Genkel.

In the summer of 1945 the Gundlachs left San Francisco for their Seattle home. Ralph went back to work at the University of Washington, but Bonnie found it difficult getting started again. The war and living in San Francisco had given her many opportunities for a broader career, but there was very little activity on the Seattle dancescape. She accepted a position as head of dance and movement at the Seattle Repertory Playhouse mainly because she liked Florence Bean James who, with her husband, Burton, directed its activities. She taught dance to actors, choreographed an original musical play about early Seattle settlers, *Calico Cargo* (George F. Mackay and Helen Litty), and made dance and dance-drama productions for the Playhouse touring unit. In the spring of 1947, however, she resigned after a series of disagreements with Burton James over working methods. "I was not going to continue with someone I considered a dictator," she said.

Bonnie decided to take a year off, read more about psychology and child education, and make clothes for Joan, who was about to start her freshman year at Reed College in Portland, Oregon. She also spent a great deal of time planning the summer course she was going to give at Reed in 1948, and taking care of a young Repertory Playhouse actress living in her home whose Christian Scientist family would not believe she was dying of Hodgkin's disease.

During the autumn she heard talk of a 'witch hunt' about to be set up by the Washington State Legislature to seek out communists. It would involve, among others, the U.W. faculty. The hearings were to change Bonnie and Ralph Gundlach's lives, but first they had to endure an ugly sequence of events they thought could never happen in America.

The Un-American Activities War Years

The Un-American Activities Committee was set up by the Washington State Legislature, with Albert Canwell as its chairman.[3] It held its first hearing early in 1948, when it attacked the Washington Pension Union which represented the interests of old age pensioners, alleging that it was dominated by communists. When the Canwell Committee failed in this attempt, it turned its attention to the University of Washington, the first university in the United States to be attacked as part of a red-baiting exercise. In June, 1948, Ralph and more than 40 others were subpoenaed to appear before the Committee. One of several charges against him was that of being a communist, based on his membership of organizations included in a list of alleged communist fronts published by the Federal Attorney General's office.

The subpoenas were issued just after Bonnie left to teach the summer session at Reed College and the hearings started on July 19th. "It was supposedly a hearing," she said, "but it was really like a Salem witch trial. And so began a pretty horrendous year." Ralph taught summer school in Seattle and spent weekends with Bonnie in Portland trying to sort out how he would fight the charges. From the way in which the hearings were focused on particular professors, they realized that, whatever the outcome, there would be no point in their staying on in Seattle after it was all over. In the meantime Bonnie had been asked if she would accept a position teaching dance for the 1948–1949 academic year at Smith College in Northampton, Massachusetts, in the place of a friend who was taking a sabbatical. After considerable thought and discussion with Ralph she accepted. There was little she could do to help him in Seattle, but perhaps she could mobilize support for the Seattle professors in New England.

"The Fifth Amendment guaranteeing due process of law and protecting the rights of the accused was not understood in those days," she said. "It had not really been tested, nor did people know what their rights were under the First Amendment [freedom of speech, religion, the press, petition and assembly], or whether they could refuse to appear and testify before a legally established committee. Even the lawyers were not clear on these points at that time. So Ralph was testing the waters. He said the Canwell Committee was illegal and had refused to accept the subpoena until his lawyer said he could not do that. He was battling every step of the way." The lawyers themselves were trying to sort out how to defend their clients because Canwell made it clear that their position was strictly an advisory one. They might counsel their clients whether or not to answer a question, but they could not argue before the hearing, nor could they cross-examine witnesses. No debate was allowed regarding the constitutionality of the committee nor its method of procedure.

At first the University of Washington stood behind its professors and said it would provide legal assistance. But as the State Legislature was about to review U.W.'s budget, it was thought that questions about activist faculty members might damage the university's reputation and endanger the state grant on which it depended. Raymond B. Allen, U.W.'s President, soon came under pressure from some of the trustees who were themselves pressurized by the right-wing American Legion. So Bonnie had to find lawyers not only for Ralph, but also for others ordered to appear before the committee, and raise the money to pay their fees. The Gundlach phone rang constantly with all kinds of abuse from self-appointed vigilantes out to discredit Ralph. Some threatened to harm Joan in order to hurt him. "We had to circumscribe her life. It was a living nightmare," she said.

Six professors and several public servants had been singled out for the fiercest attack by the Canwell Committee. Also under attack were Burton and Florence James and others from the Seattle Repertory Playhouse, which stood on university land but was funded from its own box office receipts. "Although they were blackening people's names and creating a hell of an atmosphere in the city they weren't getting anywhere with the hearings," Bonnie said. "It was pretty awful to hear people get up and say that so and so was at a communist cell meeting in a house on such and such a night, and you couldn't answer. Many of the people were paid to testify. Informers paid by the Federal Government were brought in from New York. There was a lot of lying. It was a very fascist sort of thing."

The deliberate misrepresentation of the proceedings by journalists feeding the fears of their readers was a sure-fire way of increasing circulation. Because most newspapermen were still unable to distinguish between communists, liberals and advanced social thinkers, the Seattle newspapers provided the public with sensational stories based on slur and innuendo. "The hearings made headlines every day and you couldn't do anything about it," Bonnie said. "It wasn't long before news of the hearings broke in the national press.

"Ralph felt that the hearings were primarily designed to stop liberals from participating in civic affairs. He was aware that he was particularly vulnerable because of his range of activities and his non-repentant attitude. He maintained that no committee of the State Legislature had the right to ask about anyone's personal beliefs or associations. By the Canwell definition, anyone who supported such progressive causes as old age pensions, better living standards, human welfare and civil liberties was a communist. If a non-communist was a supporter of these causes, but denied being a communist, he would be leaving himself open to the charge of perjury." Because of his uncooperative stance the Canwell Committee considered Ralph devious and a crypto-communist and judged him in contempt of the hearings.

The University of Washington would not support anyone who refused to answer the committee's question as to whether they were or had ever been a communist. It appointed its own committee, the Faculty Committee on Tenure and Academic Freedom, which held follow-on hearings to determine whether the six professors named by the Canwell Committee should be allowed to continue at U.W. or be fired.

"The university brought in some of the same stooges that the Canwell Committee had used. It was very disheartening," Bonnie said. "Ralph had strong backing, probably not to his benefit, from organizations of which he was a member but that were suspected of being communist fronts, like the Teachers' Union Local 401, which he had headed." Other organizations and groups in which he was active were also suspected of being subversive, such as the Consumers Union, the Medical Bureau (neither of them on the Attorney General's list), the Northwest (Seattle) Labor School (from which he had resigned before it appeared on the list), the Spanish Refugee Appeal, the National Federation for Constitutional Liberties and the Joint Anti-Fascist Refugee Committee. Ralph had huge support from students and professors from his own and many other universities throughout America, but not from the university hierarchy, which took the same position as the Canwell Committee.

He endured the Faculty Committee hearings and the Board of Regents hearings that followed, and in February, 1949, he was fired from the University of Washington, regardless of the fact that he had taught there for 22 years and held tenure. "It was a complicated situation," Bonnie said "but in any event they found that he was not a communist. It cost us $6000 in lawyers' fees. Three professors were fired and three were put on probation for two years, which was even worse because they were expected to grovel. The hearings broke several of those men."

After Ralph was fired, Bonnie spent every weekend rushing from Massachusetts into New York City where she was bringing a suit for a million dollars against *The New York Times* for having printed libelous statements about her husband made by U.W.'s President Allen while on a visit to New York. "A retraction was ultimately printed, but in the back pages where it didn't make much difference anyway," she said. "I brought the action on principle. That was very expensive, too, and I had to pay all the costs."

Ralph stayed with Bonnie in Northampton while he and the rest of the 'Seattle Six' were awaiting a third trial, this one for contempt of a legislative committee. His air fare was paid from money raised at a big party given by Bonnie's circle of dance friends. The trial began in March, 1949, before a jury at the King County Court House. It dragged on and on because it involved six people and a battery of lawyers. Ultimately, having exhausted all attempts to reject the charges, Ralph was convicted, fined $250 and imprisoned in June for one month, at exactly the time President Truman was trying to calm the wave of anti-communist hysteria sweeping the nation.

Ralph was put in a big cell in the county jail. When he told Bonnie that the benches were too hard to bare, she sewed padding into his underpants during college coffee mornings at which money was raised for his expenses. There were forty men in his cell. Some of them were waiting to be tried while others had been picked up for vagrancy or drunkenness. A friend got the library services, an atrophied prison right, back into operation and Ralph ordered so many books that the other prisoners thought he had a special privilege. "By showing the men how to order their own books he helped them recognize their rights as prisoners," Bonnie said. "None of them could understand why he was in jail; he hadn't stolen anything or murdered anybody. He had just lost his trial and been given a thirty day sentence for something called 'contempt'."

* * *

Before she had started work at Smith College, Bonnie thought she should let the college faculty know that she was Mrs. Ralph Gundlach. She wrote to both Edith Burnett, head of dance in Smith's theater department in which she would be working, and Hallie Flanagan Davis, head of drama at Vassar, Smith's sister college, and former head of the Theatre Section of the Works Progress Administration. "I received wonderful letters saying that they did know he was my husband and that they were following events in the Northwest with great interest because they felt that independent liberal arts colleges had a long history of academic freedom which had to be upheld."

At this time dance featured in two departments at Smith; the other was in PE, which had hired Martha Myers, a brand-new young instructor who later became a dean of Connecticut College. "We weren't expected to like each other, but we did," Bonnie said with a smile.

Bonnie was again in the familiar New England countryside she had not seen since her summers at Snake Hill Barn and Bennington. She stayed in an old house in Northampton and bicycled to the campus every day. She taught dance technique, dance composition, dance history, and directed the dance group. She was a professional and worked as a professional, consulting when appropriate; however, she encountered difficulties with her immediate boss who wanted to be involved in all decision-making, artistic included.

Bonnie danced a solo in a faculty concert for which she asked Columbia University's Jack Ashelomoff, whose work she had admired at Reed College the previous summer, to write a piece for a small chamber orchestra. For a concert by her nine dance majors she choreographed *Almanac of the Seasons* (Thomas Arne, Johann Mattheson, John Bull and Henry Purcell), based on Nicolas Breton's medieval verses and a 16th century series of woodcuts. During the dance an on-stage narrator, hidden by moveable screens on which slides of the woodcuts were projected, read about each season's activities. She also presented a pre-classic dance suite linked with the work in her choreography class. The performance took place in the black and white tiled Alumnae House concert room, accompanied by a harpsichord and the music department's madrigal group.

Over the year she gave several well-received student concerts in which, along with her daily classes, she encountered artificially-created problems, sometimes even sabotage, which she suspected arose from internal departmental jealousies. It did not take her long to be convinced that college teaching was not for her.

By carefully organizing her teaching and rehearsal schedule Bonnie was able to find time to mobilize support for Ralph's cause. At leading universities from New Jersey through Massachusetts she spoke to teachers' unions, university faculties and groups concerned with the issue of academic freedom. Ralph's friend Colston Warne, head of the Department of Economics at Amhurst, suggested approaching all the university professors acquainted with his work who could verify his competence. Bonnie met with as many of them as time and money would allow and gathered their signatures on a letter that went directly to the U.W. Board of Regents. Among the signatories was the Harvard astronomer, Harlo Shaklie, who, she said, "...enjoyed tilting at the windmills of academic conservatism."

Interest in Ralph's case grew among the Smith College students and they began pressing for his appointment to the faculty. "Smith's President Davis felt it was terribly important that the liberal colleges which were not land-grant colleges, not politically subject that is, should be bastions of support for university faculties who were beginning to be hounded in this way. He was ready to do all he could to get Ralph a temporary appointment, but due to the reactionary attitude of the head of the psychology department it never came off."

When J. Robert Oppenheimer, head of the Los Alamos Project, visited Smith to accept an honor, President Davis arranged a private meeting with Bonnie at which he offered to help Ralph. Oppenheimer had been a good friend of theirs from their Berkeley years. "Robert had been speaking out strongly for civilian control of atomic energy, which had incensed both politicians and the army. He was also being investigated by a Congressional Un-American Activities Committee, which ultimately, but not until 1964, cleared him. I felt he had enough problems of his own and did not want him to be compromised, even by being seen talking with Ralph. Robert was going to have a tough enough time as it was. It turned out to be a dreadful time. So we didn't stay in touch. I never did see him again."

* * *

Reed College

Bonnie returned to Reed College in Oregon in 1949 for a second summer course. Named for the radical modern thinker and writer, John Reed, it was a small liberal arts college with a reputation for scholarship that belied its size. Many Rhodes Scholarships to Oxford were won by Reed students.

Before the war Ralph had been an external examiner at Reed and had good friends on the faculty. Shortly after their marriage Bonnie became acquainted with the college and its faculty. She thought Reed would be an ideal place for a six-week summer school of music, theater and dance, so she developed and presented a detailed proposal which, because of the war, came to nothing. Her ideas, however, had attracted much interest and when she again suggested a session for the summer of 1948, one of the college deans took hold of the idea, sponsored it and took the crucial responsibility of administrating it.

Over her three summers at Reed teaching technique and dance composition and conducting production workshops, Bonnie also continued developing approaches to teaching the very young based on her experiences in San Francisco and her continuous studies in psychology and child education. Her aim was to evolve creative ways of teaching dance to four- to six-year olds based on play so that the children not only took easily to dance, but also became more socially integrated and better balanced individuals. Her classes in 'dance-play' gave children the chance to express their feelings through movement and loosened the rein on their imagination. At the same time they helped the children learn how to function in a group. Five-year olds, for instance, might spend a whole lesson being sailboats. "Your spines," Bonnie told them, "are the masts of ships, stretching high into the sky and rocking gently from side to side until a sudden storm bends your heads almost to the floor." As she described the gulls that alighted on the rigging, the childrens' fluttering hands became birds; with darting movements they became fish around the ship. Paint-play and clay modeling also provided scope for creative expression and along with dance-play revealed the child's inner life, dreams, frustrations and abilities.

More importantly, dance could be made fun by a teacher sensitive to children's feelings who did not treat dance classes simply in terms of recitals or a parent's investment, but rather as a part of general learning and creative activity.

The student teachers on Bonnie's courses interacted with the children's classes. They were required to observe at least two children in each of two groups, assess their physical capacity for skills and sustained work, their mental ability to form concepts, their intelligence level and their emotional and character development. From their own evaluation of the children the student teachers created appropriate dance-play activities and used them in teaching 15-minute class segments. They also observed other student teachers as they taught, and made written assessments of their work. At the end of the course they handed in a detailed report of their impressions of the children they had been observing. A list of child education and psychology books was required reading. The teachers' course was very demanding not only on the students but also on Bonnie, who meticulously planned each session, taught, observed, made critical observations and kept copious notes. This thorough method of working became her hallmark.

Beginning with the summer of 1949 Bonnie's suggestion to Reed that it offer a number of scholarships to talented New York student dancers was put into effect. The recipients, who came from several different educational institutions, included Marion Sarach (who became a professional dancer), Abraham (Remy) Charlip (dancer, stage designer, illustrator, choreographer), Hope Lange (Hollywood actress), and Shirley Spackman (professor of history).

Lou Harrison, whose work Bonnie had first admired in the 1938 Mills College summer session, had built a solid reputation as a composer and he became her accompanist and musical director for the 1949 and 1950 sessions. During his first summer at Reed he composed the score for her choreography of Yeats' haunting poem, *The Only Jealousy of Emer*. Since her Playhouse days Bonnie had loved this poem about a Gaelic heroine's bargain to save her chieftain husband from the 'restless dwellers between life and death'. In this production an actor behind a screen projected the poetry for each of the dancers. She also restaged *Marriage at the Eiffel Tower*, with a new score by Harrison. Abraham Charlip designed the set and costumes and Ralph, having recently finished his sentence, again joined Bonnie as one of the phonograph voices. She also co-directed an open-air production of Purcell's *Dido and Aeneas*.

Meanwhile, although Ralph had received strong support from his colleagues in the Society for the Psychological Study of Social Issues and the American Psychological Association, it had become clear that he could not hope to get another teaching job in any university or college in the United States. For both Bonnie and Ralph, survival meant salvaging their careers and creating a new life together in the East. At the end of the summer of 1949 they packed up, rented their home, and headed for New York.

In the summer of 1950 Bonnie returned to Reed for the third and last time. For her workshop productions she created two new works: *Yesterday's Child*, based on Pavel Tchelitcheff's series of drawings, and *Hide and Seek*, with Robert Crowley conducting his own score. She also restaged *Almanac of the Seasons*, for which Harrison wrote a new score incorporating period music, and repeated *Marriage at the Eiffel Tower*. She again co-directed an opera, Gluck's *Orpheus and Eurydice*.

9

A PHOENIX IN NEW YORK

THE 1950s, '60s AND INTO THE '70s

"We decided to live in New York City because I could get jobs teaching," Bonnie said. "Martha Graham and other people in my field were very supportive. I got a well-paid job for three days a week at Cherry Lawn School in Darien, Connecticut, a private boarding school with a good reputation. I also taught at the Graham Studio, in city-run child welfare training centers, and I plunged right back into choreographing and producing a new work which was performed at Hunter College."

Bonnie and Ralph stayed with Dr. Kulka until they found a small apartment on East 74th Street. "By applying my skills in carpentry, it could also accommodate one of my students from Reed, Flo Peters, who had decided to study dance in New York."

It was financially a very difficult time. Ralph did a number of freelance 'underground' projects – psychological studies and research work farmed out to him by colleagues, but his name did not appear on any of his work. He was accepted for a three-year professional training program in psychotherapy at the Postgraduate Center for Mental Health, which was funded by the government for the treatment of seriously disturbed war veterans. At the end of this period he began practicing as a psychotherapist and maintained a private practice, as well as doing research several days a week at Down State Medical College and later at Metropolitan Hospital. "Ralph was lucky and knew it because there were areas of applied psychology outside the institutions of higher education that he could hope to move into. What he never lost was his curiosity and his sense of humor: his shirt could be rewoven."[1]

During that first season back in New York, 1949–1950, Bonnie staged *Marriage* and a new version of *The Only Jealousy of Emer* to Harrison's score for celesta, piano, flute, cello and bass. Presented on a benefit program by Trudy Garth's Choreographers' Workshop at Hunter College, Bonnie danced Emer, with Merce Cunningham as Emer's husband, Cuchulain. This was the last time Merce appeared in another choreographer's work. Supporting dancers were Ronne Aul, Dorothy Bird and Raymonda Orselli. Bonnie also used actors, including Colleen Dewhurst, a young Shakespearean actress on the brink of a brilliant career. "From the beginning of rehearsals the actors worked with the dancers," she said. "The dancers had their own speakers who were in the orchestra pit and moved from side to side exactly in line with the dancers. The dancers wore masks that covered only the upper face; they did not mouth the words, but because the voices moved with them the audience thought they were speaking." Dance critic Winthrop Palmer, in his summary of modern dance performances over the year at the Kaufmann Auditorium, Hunter College Playhouse, the Weidman Studio Theatre, the Juilliard Concert Hall and the High School for Needle Trades, cited *The Only Jealousy of Emer* as the best group work of that season.[2]

Cherry Lawn was a small school that put great emphasis on outdoor living, music, art and dance. Many of the children came from broken homes and were extremely difficult to handle. "It was quite a job," Bonnie remembered. "I had to get up at dawn, travel an hour on the train and be picked up at the station. In the winter it was rough. I taught every age in the school, from eight to eighteen. I was determined that my classes were going to be co-ed all the way through, although I was warned that I would probably have trouble with the older boys, partly because there was a very good football and soccer coach. But boys have just as great a need for expression through movement as girls, and by treating a part of the dance class as 'stage movement' and emphasizing falling, juggling and the more acrobatic aspects of dance, I won them over.

"The big ace up my sleeve was to begin with a production before starting dance classes. I chose a popular melodrama of the gay '90s I had once used in Seattle, *No Mother to Guide Her*, which we presented in the style of a silent film with musical accompaniment. It had everything in it, including a bank foreclosing on the family farm. The costumes, in imitation of early films, were black, white and grey. I found a music book compiled for silent film accompaniment that had excellent examples of chase music, love duets, villains' entrances and exits, storms and so on. Quite by chance I discovered a wonderfully gifted 11-year old boy I heard improvising on the piano. He had rebelled against his musically brilliant parents by hating music. He could not even read notes. But this production excited him, so I arranged for the accompanist of my New York classes to come out and work with him. He learned to play all the music I needed and became our pit piano player. He loved his costume – a sprung celluloid collar, a bowler hat, a black suit, and a cigar for chewing. I think that as a result of this experience he began studying music seriously. Today he is one of America's most prominent composers."[3]

The rehearsals, which took place directly after dance classes, were tough competition for the football program and very soon the coach lost all his players. He begged Bonnie to change the production, but it was in full swing and nothing was allowed to get in the way of the two performances at the end of the year.

The experience at Cherry Lawn was positive in other aspects, too. An analyst of note who was treating one of Bonnie's students was impressed with the results of her approach to the dance experience and came to watch classes. "The feed-back was good and gave me an opportunity to get some sort of interaction with someone who was extremely well-regarded."

A part-time job that included a big production became more than full time, and the travel was exhausting. Bonnie thought very carefully about opening her own studio again before deciding she could make it work.

In September, 1950, Bonnie opened her Dance Drama School at 115 West 52nd Street, above a steak house whose cooking odors permeated the building. "It was not the best area for children to come to, but amazingly enough I got all the classes going." She took a three-year lease and put in a new 1500 square foot maple wood floor costing $5000. This huge debt caused her continued anxiety. The school offered a large range of classes appealing to professionals, amateurs, children and teachers: Ronne Aul taught modern dance; Margot Mayo, ballet; Joseph Antony and Morris Carnovsky, acting; Lou Harrison, music; Remy Charlip and Flo Peters, dance- and paint-play; Bonnie, music and movement in teaching the child.[4] There were also classes in recreational dance and American dances, games, songs and stories. Among the guest lecturers were drama teacher Herbert Berghof, playwright John O'Shaughnessy and dance critic Doris Hering.

Bonnie started a small dance group to provide the school with a professional company into which its advanced students could progress. It immediately attracted students from the Graham Studio and dance graduates from the High School of Performing Arts. The group appeared at Hunter College later that winter in a cooperation with the arts department in which the sets were designed and built by Hunter students – among them the young painter and precursor of pop art, Larry Rivers.

Bonnie also made time for other choreographic assignments. She took ten days away in November to stage a musical, *Acres of Sky*, at the University of Arkansas, and in May she presented a dance based on a poem by William Blake, *Nonage* (Hall Overton), at the Juilliard School of Music, on a program using music by young Juilliard composers. Choreographies by the young dancers Katherine Litz, Helen McGehee and Daniel Nagrin also featured on the program that heralded the establishment of the Dance Division of the Juilliard School a few months later.

During that year Bonnie spent two or three evenings a week at Merce Cunningham's studio, where she, Merce and John Cage were studying Labanotation[5] together. Her interest in this method for writing dance movement had first started in the mid-1930s when Marva Spellman, a member of Hanya Holm's Company, gathered members of the Graham Group together for practice in Rudolph von Laban's developing system. When professional activities prevented Bonnie and Merce from continuing their studies, John worked by himself and notated *Totem Ancestor*, which was later copyrighted.

Although the Dance Drama School quickly earned a good reputation, Bonnie had overstretched herself to create the model school she wanted and it was running at a deficit. A gift of $1000 from the Katharine Cornell Foundation helped, but she owed a lot more. To her surprise she found she was no fund-raiser. "If it had been for somebody else, I would have been fighting mad, but I couldn't fight for myself and was often close to tears. It took me a long time to learn to get tougher and more objective and to detach myself from the 'me' part of it." The theft of a suitcase containing original scores by John Cage and Lou Harrison was the final straw. The strain of the situation was intolerable. She needed a regular income to pay off her debts and decided to accept an offer from Dr. William Kolodny, director of the 92nd Street Young Men's and Young Women's Hebrew Association, to chair the dance training program there.

Dr. Kolodny had been an educator in Pittsburg before his appointment to the YM-YWHA in 1936. He understood little about dance, but he knew that good teaching was essential for children. He consulted with John Martin who told him that Martha Graham had the most important training program in dance. Martin also suggested that Kolodny establish the Y as a center for modern dance performances. Over the years the Y's reputation grew as many established and aspiring dancer-choreographers made critically important appearances in its small but excellently equipped Teresa Kaufman Auditorium.

Bonnie had met Dr. Kolodny in 1937 shortly after his appointment, when evening classes were first offered to business girls. Graham was beguiled into teaching them because of John Martin's recommendation. Although she loathed anything to do with 'amateur' teaching, she liked Kolodny's ideas and felt they were important. Bonnie demonstrated and taught for Martha when Graham had to miss classes, which was often, until she left the Graham Group six months later and returned to Seattle.

Almost all the children from her Dance Drama School transferred to the Y with Bonnie for the 1951–1952 season. Her first task was to tackle the well-subscribed but chaotic dance training program. Doris Humphrey was ostensibly its director, but was so involved in the newly established Dance Division of the Juilliard School and the José Limón Company that she did little more than act as artistic adviser. The faculty was an unsupervised collection of people teaching whatever they wished. Some of the better teachers, like José Limón, had good reputations, but there was no teaching continuity. Classes were regularly taken by substitutes when the teachers toured. The faculty had never had a full meeting or even talked about principles or goals; there was no coherent program and no progress from class to class. Bonnie was disturbed by the laisser-faire attitude. "The whole program was anarchical, disorganized, boring to the children and non-productive." she said. Dancers, however, liked teaching at the Y because it was in New York City. Although the pay was generally poor, teaching three or four classes a couple times a week helped pay their rents. Bonnie did not want to be regarded as chairman of such a dance program until, with a committed faculty behind her, she could make something of it.

She immediately set up regular meetings and asked the faculty's cooperation "in improving the quality of the school by working together in a democratic way to establish a systematic progression of attainment for the students while maintaining a flexible approach to teaching."[6] The word 'democratic' had seldom been used by dance teachers in relation to their work together, but for Bonnie's immediate purposes it meant sharing leadership in proportion to what each teacher had to offer toward group goals. Hence, a leader shared power and was not the sole decision-maker, allowing unselfish attitudes to flourish and a stronger group cohesion to develop.

The teachers who regularly attended the faculty meetings found that the discussions and exchange of experiences made them feel much less isolated. Gradually Bonnie also interested parents in becoming involved with the progress of their children and they, too, became an integral part of the work. With the enthusiasm of both the students and the parents, and the support of most of the faculty, she was soon able to begin directing a coherent program, and by the end of the first year was clearly recognized as chairman of the department. She then dropped those professional dancers who were simply using the school as a convenient place to earn extra money.

Lucy Venable,˙a teacher at the Y working with the Dance Notation Bureau, often talked with Bonnie about what the goals of the Y as a responsible training center should be. In discussions about the latest methods of teaching children Labanotation she renewed Bonnie's interest in dance notation and it quickly became an integral part of dance study for both faculty and children.

Because the mainly middle-class Jewish families living in the area wanted their young children to take dance classes, the Y had quite a large number of four-to-six-year olds. For the older children the work was phased in an open system of progression entirely in modern dance. Bonnie took over a class of nine-year olds who formed an honor workshop in their third year with her and, in their fourth year, ages 13 to 14, excelled in her special teacher-training course for young dancers.[7] They also created and notated their own dance works. Bonnie said the success of these children helped break down older teachers' hang-ups. Most of this group remained with her until they were 16 and a high proportion entered the dance profession: Sally Hess became soloist with Dan Wagoner; Ann Vachon and Rosalind Pierson became heads of university dance programs; several others became professional dancers, choreographers and teachers. All remained Bonnie's life-long friends.

From her first year at the Y Bonnie made her teacher-training course[8] obligatory for the faculty, but she also offered it to outside teachers with a college education or a good dance background. "Most dancers tended to take their own training and impose it on children in a 'cut-down' version, but children are not 'cut-down' adults," she said. Her course was built on the growth of the child psychologically, creatively, socially, physically and emotionally, and covered goals and objectives, problems and projects for teaching each different age group. Because it was the only course in Manhattan for the training of children's dance teachers it filled a growing need and prospered. Bonnie tried to give away her course to universities and specialized schools offering degrees in dance, hoping students might get academic credit for it. But because institutions at that time were mainly concerned with training professional dancers, nothing developed from this initiative.

Doris Humphrey might have been a little apprehensive about working with a former member of the Graham Group, but, because Bonnie had enormous respect for her they were able to work easily together. With Bonnie steering the program, a reinvigorated Humphrey began to involve herself more actively as artistic director and even took Bonnie by surprise when she suggested an end-of-year performance for all 200 children. The faculty supported Doris' proposal for a work with an open theme, *Coming and Going*, to which each teacher contributed a section. The performance gave a focus to the year's work and, to Bonnie's relief, was not labeled a recital or a sales pitch for the next year's crop of students.

From the beginning of her second year at the Y the terms of teachers' contracts were revised to ensure that their time, energy and concentration were fixed on their jobs. A number departed, but those who remained had their teaching hours increased. More and better accompanists were hired. The faculty was happier and more cohesive, although some members were restless because they had no opportunity to produce their own work. To try to solve this problem they met with Doris and discussed what kind of program might be initiated at the Y within the limits of space, time and budget. Often mentioned was the fact that there were few dance performances in the city to which children could relate. Not even New York City Ballet's *Nutcracker* was as yet on offer. Parents, desperate to find dance diversions for their children, naïvely asked if they should take them to see Jerome Robbins' new, powerful, shocking, definitely adult ballet, *The Cage*.

Bonnie and the faculty began looking into small companies. Eddie Strawbridge ran a touring company for children, but his work did not attract quality dancers and they felt that poor dancing made it difficult for young audiences to understand his ballets. But Alwin 'Nik' Nikolias made wonderful productions of story ballets for children on Saturday programs at the Henry Street Playhouse. His dancers were good, and kids who came from all over the Lower East Side had a marvelous time for just ten cents. Several other companies had fallen by the wayside because they served mainly as ego trips for their directors. The Y investigating group concluded that a company was successful only when its choreographies were outstanding, its dancers of a high calibre, it had its own training school as a support system, and each company member was able to make an artistic contribution.

The idea of forming a Y-based professional repertory company with young dancers of advanced technical achievement began to take shape. A very small honorarium for performances would be offered and all the members would be responsible for their own technical training. Faculty members might also dance in it, but only as regular members, while other faculty might act as unpaid staff and get their creative satisfaction from running the company – "in as democratic a way as possible," Bonnie said. Rehearsals could take place from 10 a.m. to 1 p.m. in the Y studios before the beginning of scheduled classes an hour later. The company would have a two-fold purpose: to provide children from five to twelve with unusual and stimulating dance entertainment expertly performed, and to give young dancers the opportunity for frequent performance experience.

As the working details of the company took shape so did the idea of having a merry-go-round as the fanciful theme of each program. Populated by colorfully painted and plumed horses bobbing up and down to the strains of a street organ, the merry-go-round offered exciting adventures for children of all ages. What better name for the company than the Merry-Go-Rounders!

Finding the money for this project was the next task. Dr. Kolodny said that it was impossible to ask his board for help. There was only one thing to do; he would let Bonnie use the Y charge account! One of the first things she did was to find a young costume designer, Eleanor de Vito, who had a fine eye for dance. As Artistic Director of the Merry-Go-Rounders (MGR), Doris Humphrey was quick to propose a work for the first program based on Gilette Burgess' *The Goops*, a book on manners that she had enjoyed as a youngster. The pie-shaped little Goops in Burgess' drawings never did anything correctly, and many a child in her day was admonished with "You don't want to be a Goop, do you?" Bonnie took one look at the book and thought it punitive and unsuitable, but if it was what Doris wanted she was not going to veto it. Doris suggested Eva Deska as choreographer. "If anybody could make something entertaining of it, Eva could," Bonnie said.

Doris also suggested inviting Alwin Nikolais to produce a work. Since his own group was very successful he was not interested in having a rival, but he did allow the Merry-Go-Rounders to have *The Fable of the Donkey* for one year. It was a short time to have such an expensive production, but it was right for the company. The story involved silly clowns, gossips and brats who advised a farmer and his son how – or how not – to ride their donkey.

The third dance was made by Fred Berk, who headed the teaching of Jewish Folk Dance at the Y. His *Holiday In Israel*, about the recently created State of Israel, the different countries from which its inhabitants came and the dances they brought with them, was the first of several popular works he created for MGR.

Auditions for the new company were held in November, 1952. The first performance took place in the Kaufmann Auditorium on February 1, 1953. It had 96 costumes and cost nearly two thousand dollars to mount. From the very first performance audience participation was an integral part of MGR performances, with the children responding in song and movement while sitting in their seats. Doris Humphrey was at first very doubtful about this idea, but Bonnie was convinced that the children should have the experience of moving even while sitting down and she kept pushing this aspect of the program. All kinds of movements relating to the story dances using the head, arms, and upper torso were explored, and the children even learned mudras for La Meri's *The Celestial Element*.

Within the motif of the merry-go-round two central characters were developed: the Ringmaster and the Magic Mechanic. The Ringmaster (James Paul was the first) started every show in front of the curtain by leading the children in a charming theme song composed by the school accompanist, Beatrice Rainer. Then the curtains opened to reveal marvelously gaudy clowns riding up and down on hobbyhorses with brightly colored ribbons running from their heads to the top of a pole in the center of the stage. As they revolved around the pole, the dancers' movements made the scene look like a lively fair-ground carrousel. Suddenly the merry-go-round broke down and all the clowns and their hobby horses came to a standstill. The Ringmaster was unable to get it started again. Luckily he remembered his friend, the Magic Mechanic (originally Bernice 'Bunny' Mendelsohn), and fetched her on stage. The Magic Mechanic took a look, got out her little tool kit and tried various things, but nothing worked. Finally, she discovered the real problem: the children in the audience were not participating in what was happening on stage. She told them that they were the only ones who could get the merry-go-round going again and to enable them to start up the motor she taught them magical arm movements. With their help the stage came alive with movement once more and the merry-go-round was restored to its former glory. As the curtain slowly closed behind them, the Ringmaster and the Magic Mechanic began telling the children the story of the first dance and leading them in the movements its theme inspired. The whole house was in motion with children prepared and eager to experience the dance itself. Before each of the next two works the story telling and movement adventures were again led by the Ringmaster or the Magic Mechanic, or both, until they brought all the Merry-Go-Rounders back on stage to lead the audience in a high-spirited finale of movement and song. The program had whirled by in one hour and twenty minutes.

The Merry-Go-Rounders was an immediate and smash success. Educators hailed it as something fresh and special on the dance scene. Over the years MGR presented an increasing number of Tuesday morning shows that became traditional school outings to which thousands of children were bussed or came with their teachers on public transport. From early November through May the company toured two or three times a week to schools in the New York City area, and on weekends it played the suburbs. With its own staff handling the work, MGR was regularly booked by cultural and community groups and PTA's. The company gave Christmas seasons sponsored by the Board of Education of four or more shows at Public School 44, as well as performances of a single ballet for organizations and children's television.

MGR never claimed their programs were appropriate for adults, but parents and friends enjoyed coming to see the shows; they were done with panache and skill and were great fun. With success came awards from the Dance Business Group of America whose president, Ben Sommers, was 'Mr. Capezio': in 1955 "for distinctive furtherance of dance in America" and in 1956 "to encourage the Merry-Go-Rounders in its work".

The Merry-Go-Rounders in *The Goops*. Clockwise from left: Jeff Duncan, Roberta Singer, Rima Sokoloff, Manon Sauriau, Gloria Spivak, Pat Cooper, Barbara Shivitz and Flo Peters. Photo: Lionel Freedman.

During its first summer, MGR created innovative programs for young-sters on the Lower East Side using Joseph Papp's first outdoor theater; however, the dancers often injured themselves on the cement stage and the administration was exhausted from the work of bringing in audiences through social workers and community centers, as well as seeking financial support. This was MGR's only attempt to keep going through the summer.

As Co-Director, Bonnie was responsible for administrative coordina-tion and rehearsing the dances. She took over as Artistic Director on Doris' death in 1958. For the thirteen years until 1966, "I was the one who kept things together and turning over," she said. Along with Bonnie, MGR's original founder-members were Lucy Venable, Labanotator for MGR's dances; Fred Berk, Assistant to the Director; and Bernice Mendelsohn, Production Coordinator. Eva Desca was Company Director and the Music Director was Beatrice Rainer. On tours the company traveled with its ten dancers, two narrators, two understudies, accom-panist, stage manager and company director.

The young dancers, many coming out of Y classes over the years, received five dollars a performance, and travel, food and accommodation while on tour. They had to learn discipline, projection, how to sustain performances in awkward situations and how to use their energy to win the audiences' concentration. They had total responsibility for the care and packing of their own costumes. They also learned the political implications of leaving a messy dressing room. Bonnie was a self-confessed 'crab' when it came to this, continually reminding the company members as she checked the clean-up that "If they wanted to be asked back they should not offend the janitor." She also insisted that the company should establish a clear, responsible mechanism for dealing with the inevitable complaints that arise from within a group.

The Merry-Go-Rounders believed it would only survive if its dancers' skills increased. Company members were periodically evaluated on their attitude, imagination and performance. They learned that their response to each choreographer affected the creation of a work; there was never any marking in rehearsals. Learning to use their own initiative they enhanced their ability to work with ideas of all kinds. During the first year they were expected to improve their technical level by attending technique classes at their own expense; by the following year MGR provided early morning classes four times a week with guest teachers including James Truitt, from the Lester Horton Dancers, and the former ballerina, Ruthana Boris. Robert Joffrey was company regisseur for a year (1955–1956) before he started his own company. Bonnie brought in the drama director Howard da Silva to improve the dancers' acting and voice skills and occasionally he chose some of the dancers to

The Merry-Go-Rounders: The Ringmaster and The Magic Mechanic. Photo: Lionel Freedman.

appear in his own productions. Stanislavsky and Boleslawski were suggested reading.

The list of well-known choreographers who made works for the company grew steadily. Soon it had a repertory of 14 works, of which five or six were shown each season. They included Donald McKayle's 1, 2, 3, ... Follow Me!, Sophie Maslow's *The Snow Queen*, Lucas Hoving's *A Love for Three Oranges*, Geoffrey Holder's *Cakewalk*, Eva Desca and Lucy Venable's *Ballet Charades*, Bernice Mendelsohn's *Forest Adventure*, and Bonnie's *The Enchanted Balloons*. "We never had a shoddy bit of choreography," she said with pride. Choreographers received a fee of $25 for each work and a two dollar royalty per performance. MGR did more than 50 works and had more than 150 dancers during Bonnie's years with it. There was hardly a dance artist in New York City who did not have contact in one way or another with what was happening at the Y. Because of this MGR proved itself an excellent training ground for a career in dance. Many stayed in the company for two or three years and several became members of the Y staff. Because MGR offered its dancers repertory experience it was also a showcase for their talents. Many of its dancers were invited to join leading concert groups or made it into Broadway shows.

The devotion and support of the Y faculty while continuing to teach was unwavering, and because of their interaction with the company their own teaching skills steadily improved. They became role models for the students, a part of the plan Bonnie had envisioned for MGR's continual growth and renewal. Soon a Junior MGR was formed as a support group for the company. Its members were the eleven-to-fourteen-year old students. They were allowed to watch company class and rehearsals when their own schooling permitted and help with the costumes. The Junior MGR focused the work and ambitions of all the children in the school.

MGR also pioneered public relations know-how in dance education. This enabled the company to make increasingly longer tours that took them to New England, and once even to the Midwest. The scale of charges for performances ranged over the years from $250 to $350 for larger theaters charging admission, to schools where, with the agreement of MGR members who considered they were performing a community service, only expenses of about $50 were charged.

With all the publicity accompanying MGR's initial success, Dr. Kolodny and the Y faculty were warmly congratulated on their imaginative undertaking that was so admirably filling a gap in the education of young people. But when the board of directors discovered the bills he had tried to hide he was called to account. "Well, what do you want me to do? Cancel it?" he asked.

At the end of the first season the Y absorbed MGR's outstanding debts. Thereafter, the company led a precarious but self-sufficient existence. As problems with office space and costume and set storage grew, Dr. Kolodny started gently pushing MGR out of the Y premises. By 1955 the group had moved around the corner into a dreary little shop that was a kind of solution for its immediate problems. Generously, the Y let MGR continue using its rehearsal studios without cost from September through May. With eyes twinkling, Bonnie said, "We were not supposed to rehearse on Saturday mornings, the Sabbath, but sometimes we did sneak in."

MGR always battled to break even. Along with several fund-raising activities run by the staff and occasional private gifts, the company also received money almost every year from a mysterious 'anonymous donor'. Founder-member Lucy Venable had a family trust fund and Bonnie was sure it was she who helped to cover the deficit.

Because MGR was expensive to tour, a compact off-shoot was formed in 1962 – the Merrymobile, 'a new kind of program for elementary school children'. It had three dancers, a narrator, a pianist and a stage manager who presented 45-minute programs of dance theater that were carefully related to the school curriculum and performed in elementary schools during school time. Its first presentation, *Weather Or Not*, conceived by Billie Kirpich, with music by Norman Curtis, used song, dance, narration and audience participation to dramatize the phenomena of weather.

In the summer of 1962, and each year through 1966, Bonnie taught the Dance Educators Workshop at Connecticut College during its modern dance festival. Assisted by Jennifer Tipton, Ann Vachon and other Y alumnae, she worked with up to 50 kindergarden and community dance teachers who studied her methods as she taught local children aged four to sixteen. In 1963, she was accompanied by the members of the newly-formed Merrymobile, who gave classes, workshops and performances.

The following is an excerpt from Bonnie's opening address to the students of the 1964 Dance Educators Workshop: "To me what is so important in teaching dance is that the teacher be aware of her responsibilities. She should be fully acquainted with the capacities, the limitations and the creative needs of each age level, from the youngest to the oldest students, and utilize this knowledge as a guide and a stimulus to design the best and most effective classes for each age group.

"The teacher should have a clear knowledge of what the attainable goals are for each class and understand the manners and methods that can best be employed to reach them because, really, the very best material poorly presented adds up to nothing in a class.

"Your responsibility is to acquaint yourself before you go into teaching with how children grow. This means some understanding of their development physically, mentally and socially. What often happens in teaching is that you have set yourself goals for a 'perfect product', a vision we all have for children, and the tendancy, unless we know what a child can do, is to want the end results immediately. Why don't they keep their legs straight? It's as if the child is trying to thwart you in achieving your goals for the child. It soon ceases to be the child's goal; you are trying to fit the child into some mold of your own making."[9]

The development of Bonnie's career during the 1950s was also a time of great personal happiness. Six years after the Gundlachs had left Seattle for New York, Ralph's new career took shape when he became an associate research director of the Post Graduate Center for Mental Health, one of the world's largest mental health centers, based on a training school and an out-patient clinic. "He became a real wage earner," Bonnie said. In December, 1955, at the age of 41, under the care of her long-time friend, Dr. Kukla, she gave birth to her first child, Heidi. Bonnie's group of Y students took a special interest in her pregnancy and a loving hand in Heidi's care, making clothes and blankets for her. The baby became a regular part of class life. A year later the Gundlachs moved to Hastings-on-Hudson where John Scott was born in October, 1957. Six months later four-and-a-half year old Michael, Joan's son, came to live with them

The Gundlach family: Michael, Heidi, Bonnie, Scott and Ralph, California, 1961. Photo: Bonnie Bird Collection.

permanently after the breakup of his parents' relationship. The sudden arrival of an unplanned third child sent Bonnie into a panic. She sought the help of a psychotherapist, but spent the sessions discoursing about her plans for MGR. "All I needed was to talk my work problems out. It really did make me feel better," she said. Acquiring a full-time housekeeper, for the next 17 years a beloved member of the family, helped tremendously. Michael quickly became 'big brother' to Heidi and Scott and in 1962 Ralph and Bonnie officially adopted him.

The upbringing of the young children became an integral part of life at the Y while Bonnie continued teaching, choreographing and administrating without interruption. During these years Lucy Venable became company director, followed by Lucas Hoving, and later by his assistant, Jennifer Tipton. "The quality and contributions of the people attracted to working at the Y were outstanding," Bonnie said with pride.

When Heidi was six years old Bonnie began Saturday morning classes for young children in Hastings, mainly so that Heidi could have dancing lessons. By the following spring there were eleven classes in progress. Because she was not interested in a commercial school, she established a non- profit organization so that she and her teachers could be properly paid. Out of this framework grew the Hasting's Creative Arts Council, which broadened its activities by building up band and orchestral programs in the area. Bonnie's Honor Workshop performances, accompanied by a 40 piece band, were the highpoint of each year's work.

Another layer of Bonnie's work had begun in the early 1950s when Lucille Nathanson invited her to join the parent-sponsored South Shore Community Workshops on Long Island which she directed. A close working relationship between them began when Bonnie set up a dance component throughout the various South Shore communities. She taught Saturday morning classes, and Nathanson also became a member of the Y faculty.

Because Nathanson was interested in Bonnie's training program for children's dance teachers, the two women decided to run a one-day workshop on the creative teaching of dance for children, the first of its kind, which the Y agreed to sponsor. Bonnie invited Lucas Hoving, the Dutch-American dancer, choreographer and former principal dancer with José Limón who was teaching in Westchester, and both he and Bonnie gave demonstration classes. By the end of the day the gathering had proved so successful that it was decided to continue exchanging ideas and information. A committee was formed with Bonnie and Lucille as co-chairs, and soon an organization was established dedicated to the creative teaching of dance as an art form. After several name changes, it is known today as the American Dance Guild.

The Guild grew rapidly because teachers of dance unconnected with academic institutions or major professional schools needed a meeting ground to communicate their ideas to other dance teachers and educators. At first the Guild's concentration was on workshops for teaching children, but it soon broadened its scope to include teenage and adult dance education. Professional dancers were also encouraged to become members.

When it was known as the National Dance Guild, Bonnie became Chairman-Elect (1964–1965), National Chairman (1965–1967) and Past Chairman (1967–1969). "We were genuinely concerned with the problems of educators in the art of dance. I began to realise when I was chairman that there were other dance organizations – huge, monied and top-heavy with executives – that were actually trade associations. They treated dance as a commodity, not as an art. Their members put stickers in their windows like good-housekeeping awards and used conventions run by these organizations to gather teaching material. I was invited to teach at some of them. They always wanted my classes written out in advance in order to duplicate them and hand them out to their members. I would not do this, but instead made a statement about what the approach and content of my class would be. Nothing else. Fifty students would arrive with notebooks, ready to write down everything I said and did, only to find that they had to put their notebooks away and start working. They didn't much like that. These organizations usually went for 'stars' in modern dance or ballet. They wanted them for their names and not really for the material they gave in classes."

The Guild's purpose was to act as a clearing house for new ideas leading to better teaching standards. High on its agenda were unified grades of payment in different areas of dance teaching, such as community centers. It eventually ran a large range of workshops, some of which involved three-day sessions featuring guest teachers such as Helen Tamiris, who became very involved in its work, and Margaret H'Doubler.

From its inception the Guild sought to cooperate or affiliate with other organizations to benefit dance, among them the National Conference on Children and Youth and the Theatre Research Institute. It produced a popular *Newsletter* and soon launched a magazine, *Dance Scope*, whose first editor was the young dance writer, Marcia B. Siegel, whom Bonnie had met at Connecticut College. The editorship of such a magazine was a plum. Siegel's career was given a flying start.

By the mid-1960s, after 20 years of lobbying by arts organizations, national government funding was becoming a reality. America's large corporate businesses had long been reducing federal taxes on their profits by forming charitable foundations which gave generous donations to scientific research programs. These programs often happened to benefit the donor company. In time the corporations were pressured to endow educational institutions and the performing arts. In 1963 the Ford Foundation gave seven million dollars to George Balanchine to promote dance in America. Other foundations and institutions followed. Donations were given to ballet, theater, opera, symphonic orchestra projects, and for the production of arts programs on television. Because the costs of sponsored projects often exceeded the initial donations, pressure grew for the government to provide additional support.

In September, 1965, America formally acknowledged its commitment to the arts world when President Lyndon Johnson signed the Arts and Humanities Act, which established the National Endowment to provide financial assistance through the Arts Councils of America. At about the same time the Elementary and Secondary School Act came into effect, providing support for the arts in education through the Office of Education (OE). The OE had the most money immediately at its disposal.

"I didn't think the dance field itself realized the importance of the Endowment. Thinking back on its emergence, it is important to bear in mind that for at least two decades there had been government organizations in the various art fields that were moving in the direction of taking equal financial responsibility, as well as trying to establish organizational means through which the voice of the arts could be heard at the highest levels of government. Just after the war I participated in a research project that my husband Ralph coordinated for the Seattle Repertory Theatre. We made a survey of arts funding and arts support in different countries of the world where we knew something existed. We found that the Arts Councils of Great Britain and Canada were well ahead of us. Even though there were many arts organizations in America in which state governments were taking some kind of financial responsibility, nothing was done on a national level with any sense of vision because Congress wasn't interested. At times pockets of arts activity appeared through the Office of Education, only to disappear again. I think the only time dance was mentioned in the Congressional Record before 1965 was when the strip-tease artiste, Sally Rand, whose act combined Lois Fuller and the Folies Bergère, performed a fan dance that caused a ruckus in the Midwest and became one of the national jokes."

With Bonnie as National Chairman, and with Manon Souriau, former Y student, MGR member and now colleague as editor-in-chief, the Guild's *Newsletter* started featuring front-page editorials and detailed articles intended to wake up dancers to the significance of this new era. Because the situation was so important they were urged to stop acting like second-class citizens and begin to take responsibility for their art.

Articles alerted the profession especially to what the OE's Elementary and Secondary School Act was offering, such as support for the education of low-income families, authorization of one hundred million dollars for a five-year program to meet supplementary educational needs in the schools, and 45 million dollars for educational research and training. Great emphasis was put on the fact that the government was to draw on the resources of professional associations in implementing the projects.

In order to participate in these highly-funded programs dancers had to organize themselves and show what benefits dance projects could bring to education and the community. Guild members were appointed to liaise with each agency of government at local, county, state and federal levels whose programs would benefit from including dance. *Newsletter* space was set aside for disseminating information about these agencies.

In recognition of dance's potential contribution to total education, the OE had already awarded three grants to dance projects initiated by dancers themselves. One was for $195,000 to Guild member Nadia Chilkovsky and the University of Pennsylvania for the "Development of a Comprehensive Graded Curriculum in Dance Training for Secondary School Students." Another was for a pilot study in elementary schools presenting the way of life of people in West and Central African societies through their dance, music and sculpture, under the direction of Pearl Primus and supervised by the NYU School of Education. The third was for a program initiated by Guild member Betty Rowen through Teachers College, Columbia University, "An exploration of the Uses of Rhythmic Movement to Develop Aesthetic Concepts in the Primary Grades."

By March, 1966, the National Endowment, through the National Council on the Arts, had awarded seven out of eight matching grants to modern dance companies: Martha Graham, $181,000; José Limón, $23,000; Anna Sokolow, $10,000; and $5000 each to Alvin Ailey, Merce Cunningham, Alwin Nikolais and Paul Taylor. The Guild itself received a small grant in recognition of the important role it played in developing written communication on dance: the New York State Arts Council awarded it a grant for $1500 to facilitate the organization of a conference on writing for the dance.

The new-found abilities of dancers to unify and advance their own cause greatly contrasted with their history of not having been able, through lack of means or know-how, to work together. Bonnie remembered a meeting held at the New Dance Group in the early 1950s at which an attempt was made to organize dancers into a trade union. "A trade union is essentially a defensive organization, not one that is far-seeing. But Martha, Doris and Charles were all for unions. They had a common wish to organize in some way like everyone else and have representation. I found that funny because, when it came to the crunch, who was the enemy? There just wasn't one. But the socially aware New Dance Group people asked Marty Popper, a bright young lawyer sympathetic to their ideas, to talk to the dancers about how they could organize a union. A well-attended meeting was held and, typically, nothing happened afterward. Twenty years later I met Marty and reminded him of that meeting. After sharing a laugh over it, he said, 'That was a very salutary experience for me in working with dancers'. I asked him what he meant and he answered, 'I learned something about dancers. I made a serious mistake. The studio had mirrors in it, and I stood facing the dancers with my back to a mirror while they sat and looked at themselves. They were all doing their thing in front of the mirrors. They didn't even hear me!'"

'Organization' and 'cooperation' became dancers' bywords. The Endowment approached dance company leaders, both modern and ballet, and asked if a service organization might help in building larger audiences, finding financial support from the community, providing technical aid for productions, creating more performance opportunities, stimulating the exchange of information among companies, and in presenting the 'image of dance' to the public. With a membership made up of dance companies this new organization would serve the entire field of dance. The idea found favor with everyone attending a conference to discuss the proposal. Bonnie, serving on the by-laws committee, wrote, "It was a rewarding experience in mature democratic process to participate in the committee's deliberations."[10] The Endowment soon established the Association of American Dance Companies (AADC) and the Guild followed this up by establishing its own Performing Division to act as spokesman for the dancers themselves.

In 1964, before the Endowment was established, money had been made available through the Office of Education to establish a program in dance research. The OE's Katherine Bloom and Dr. Esther Jackson attended a meeting of the National Council for the Arts in Education, hoping to talk with dance organization or college and university dance department representatives. The only dance person they found at the gathering was the Guild's Lucille Nathanson, and soon afterward Bloom telephoned Bonnie, who had recently been chosen as the Guild's Chairman-Elect. She knew Bonnie from her MGR activities and, recognizing her ability to rouse people to action, asked her to convene a meeting of key dance educators so that she and Dr. Jackson could tell them about money that was to be made available for dance research and how they could apply for it. About twenty directors of major university dance programs in the New York vicinity came. "I can remember that meeting so vividly! It was like a tower of Babel. I couldn't believe how backward these heads of departments were. Bloom and Jackson were stressing the need for research and that this money had to be spent on research, but the dance department directors didn't think anything could be done. It was incredible. I was mad. Afterward I said we couldn't allow this to happen. Such an amazing opportunity! The first time we were being invited to present material! We were being invited to learn how to function professionally! Ralph just laughed. He was in a field that was doing research all the time.

"I insisted we call another meeting and got a number of prominent people in dance behind me. The second gathering was almost as bad, but gradually it was decided we should have a national committee. We arbitrarily chose one hundred names from around the county – heads of large and small dance departments and a few other key people – and invited them to become members of a new committee on research in dance. Seventy accepted. We identified who was doing research in different areas and invited them to give papers at a three-day conference we organized called Dance Research: Problems and Possibilities. It was a very rewarding and exciting experience at which we began to shape what later became the Congress on Research in Dance (CORD). The first thing we did was to publish a report of the conference. We identified areas of research that were beginning to emerge – history, anthropology, ethnology and dance therapy and then ran a conference on each of these topics."

Bonnie was CORD's first chairman for two years, then past chairman, also for two years. She remained an active member of its board of directors until 1974. "CORD's work has given a new dimension to dance," she said. In an article entitled "The Dancer's New Responsibility," Bonnie explained her vision: "I believe Dance encompasses everything to do with the art – its history, its practices, its applications and its development, not just its physical techniques. This implies that the profession of dance includes the training of its performers, its choreographers, its teachers and its special craftsmen, and should also imply a serious commitment to the development of its articulators and explorers. Articulators would include notators, historians, critics, aestheticians and administrators. Explorers would devote their efforts to dance research in its application in many areas outside that of performing, such as recreation, education, physiotherapy and psychotherapy."[11] Her breadth of view has become a reality in today's ballet, contemporary and ethnic dance worlds, and CORD still provides opportunities for the continuous exchange of ideas among scholars in a wide range of related fields.

In the years Bonnie was organizing and directing the Guild and CORD she was also involved with the Y, the Merry-Go-Rounders, running her Hastings dance school and raising three children. "It was pretty mad. But I slowly withdrew from my activities with the Y and the Merry-Go-Rounders, and more and more people became involved with the work of the Guild. It took on a life of its own. People grumbled about the Guild all the time, but I said that the only way you can make yourself heard is by becoming a member, getting inside and doing something about it. Dancers are great at taking pot-shots from the outside! At CORD there were many long-time colleagues whose contribution to dance has been remarkable – Marian Van Tuyl, whom I had first met on Louis' course at Bennington, Eleanor Lauer, one of my first summer course students at the University of Washington and Jeanette Roosevelt, head of the dance department at Barnard and a good friend, to name but a few. People stay a lifetime in dance."

As soon as one of Bonnie's activities tapered off there was always another in the offing. Her continued interest in dance therapy led her to accept an invitation to visit Blythdale Hospital in Valhalla, New York. Sponsored by the Federation of Jewish Philanthropies, the hospital's original purpose had been to treat orthopedically and neurologically handicapped children. When Bonnie joined it the programs had been enlarged and included children with post-operative problems. She was impressed by the positiveness of the hospital's programs and was very pleased when the medical section, which had priority over the educational program, invited her to join the hospital staff.

For three years from 1969 she spent three days a week working at Blythdale with small groups of children. She met with them first in classrooms, but for her productions she brought them together in a larger space two groups at a time. In her third year the new head proposed an open-plan layout using free-standing partitions to separate teaching areas. Bonnie was totally against this plan and voiced her concern, not only about the problem of concentration for her own students which, at best, was a minute at a time, but also about having dance classes in an open room while other students nearby were trying to study. "I thought the new man had obviously not previously worked with handicapped children," she said. "At he same time I was highly complimented when the teachers in the education division, some of whom had hardly allowed me into their classrooms when I first arrived, made it clear to the head that of all the recently developed programs mine should definitely be continued. During the summer the situation deteriorated when the head did not contact me, and I resigned. Within a year he was fired. It was

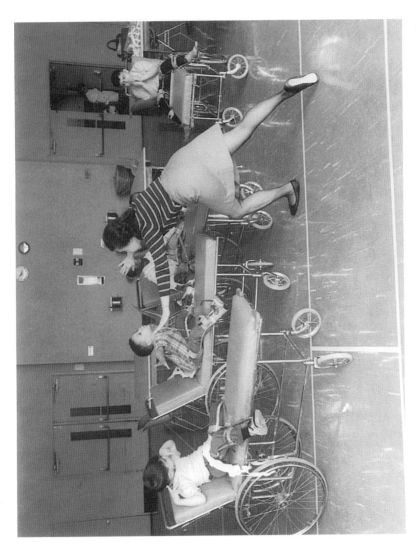

Bonnie teaching at Blythdale Hospital in Valhalla, New York. Photo: Marion H. Levy (Bonnie Bird Collection).

the remaining teachers who saved the situation as far as the youngsters were concerned. Sadly enough, some projects fail."

While working at Blythdale, Bonnie, still representing CORD, gave a report on her work with handicapped children before the National Council for the Arts in Education. It interested Herb Kummel, executive director of the Dance Notation Bureau (DNB).[12] He wanted to change the focus of a large summer camp he had inherited from his parents and asked Bonnie if she would run a training program for dance teachers there. After looking at the camp, she agreed to work two days a week at the DNB offices with Kummel to develop the project. It was already too late to get a program ready for the coming summer, so Bonnie began sitting in on meetings with Irmgard Bartenieff[13] whom she had first heard about at Blythdale, where Bartenieff had earlier achieved excellent results working with children with infantile paralysis. "Irmgard had applied Laban principles to her care of the handicapped," she said, "and through exercise patterning and repatterning had succeeded in giving them the correct exercises to get them walking. She developed dance therapy for aesthetic reasons – to help children who were cut off and disabled emotionally."

At the DNB Bartenieff was developing an Effort/Shape program. Effort/Shape is a system describing movement quantitatively and qualitatively, based on the work of Rudolph von Laban.[14] For years Bonnie had been curious about this system and its use as a complement to Labanotation. "Kummel did not understand Effort/Shape because Irmgard talked in a vague and circuitous way," she said. "He was a product-oriented person, something I had not expected in a former ballet dancer. He could understand Labanotation because it was something solid and marketable, but he did not understand anything about changing people through an educative process." He recognized, however, that Bonnie might fill a new role at the expanding Bureau in its Effort/Shape program. The summer camp training project was dropped. "I acquired several different titles over the years," Bonnie said, "but in general I acted as director of educational services."

Laban's two systems, Labanotation and Effort/Shape, were developing simultaneously at the Bureau. Kummel did much to package DNB functions in a saleable way by publicizing Labanotation, instigating crash training programs and placing qualified notators with dance companies to record or reconstruct dances. New dance scores were continually being added to the Bureau's 'Masterwork Library'. Kummel also became very interested in setting up a program typing Labanotation that IBM was developing. That program faded, however, with the coming of computers and the introduction of software which meant that notation could be fed into a computer and seen on a display unit. "New possibilities were coming up fast," Bonnie said, "but the hardest person to drag along was the dancer, because dance is about doing and not about recording!"

Meanwhile Bonnie struggled to define an Effort/Shape study program and articulate it in ways that Kummel, the DNB board and the public could understand. To justify its existence, short three-month courses for dance therapists were offered three times a year. Bartenieff and her team developed a certificate course in movement analysis in a full-time year-long certificate program at graduate level. Bonnie felt the courses fulfilled their purpose by contributing to a person's growth and learning and providing tools that students could use in their teaching. "The Effort/Shape program broke even most of the time," Bonnie said, "but it did not produce a saleable product in the same way as the notation courses."

Bonnie approached New York State University at New Paltz, York University in Canada, Brooklyn College and Antioch College to explore the possibility of Effort/Shape being accepted as a complementary program in dance anthropology, dance therapy, or in the array of other courses that were developing. She also saw it as a potential post-graduate research project. "The biggest difficulty was to work out how to bring the program under a university's umbrella while it still functioned from the DNB," she said. "Kummel would not cooperate and Bartenieff became frustrated because of insufficient financial backing. She felt that in order to grow the division would have to leave the Bureau altogether, which it finally did in 1978, becoming the Laban Institute of Movement Studies."

A part of Bonnie's work was to strengthen links between English and American dance institutions. She read a great deal about what was going on in the teacher-training programs influenced by the work of Rudolph von Laban, who had settled in England shortly before the Second World War.[15] That is how she came to know about Marion North, Laban's brilliant teaching and research assistant during the last ten years of his life, first at the Art of Movement Studio (AMS) in Manchester, and then at the Laban Art of Movement Studio (LAMS) in its home in Addlestone, Surrey.

Marion North was highly regarded for her work in movement analysis, industry, the community, dance education, teacher training, therapy and child development. She had been head of teacher training at Sydney Webb College in central London in the 1960s, where she developed a movement and dance department training teachers for colleges and work in the community. In 1972 she was appointed to replace the retiring head of the Movement and Dance Department at Goldsmiths' College, University of London. Created in 1944, it was the first college in the United Kingdom to provide a diploma course in dance teaching not under PE but in the Division of Humanities and Creative Arts. In 1973 North was appointed Director of the Laban Art of Movement Studio on the retirement of it founder-director, Lisa Ullman. Because of the long and beneficial association between the two institutions, a year after North's LAMS appointment the University of London, acting on behalf of Goldsmiths', became the Studio's sole trustee.

North had often been invited to the United States and had taught all over the country. Early in 1973 she was scheduled to speak at a conference on notation systems and dance research at the University of Illinois. Bonnie wrote to North before she left England, asking if she would stop off in New York on her return journey and teach a short course for the Bureau's students and key teachers.

"To keep the costs down and because I was having to do everything on a non-budget, I asked Marion to be my house guest. It was cold and the snow was only slowly turning to slush, so there was plenty of time to talk about dance in front of a roaring fire and during our trips to and from the city. Laban's ideas about teaching dance to children, teenagers and adults were very different from what was happening in the States. They were also very useful. They gave dance a language, a coherent approach. In the course of our conversations Marion also began to understand my background. She spoke of the kinds of programs she thought ought to develop and I think I made contributions to the discussions that led her to invite me to do some guest teaching. I soon arranged an unpaid leave and went to England to teach the 1973 autumn semester at Goldsmiths' in the inner-London borough of Lewisham, and at the Laban Art of Movement Studio 25 miles to the south-west in the green Surrey countryside."

During that visit the two women found so much common ground and formulated so many ideas that North asked Bonnie if she would consider moving to England and working with her. An official letter from Goldsmiths' College arrived on Bonnie's return to the States inviting her to become a Principal Lecturer and develop a new Dance Theatre Department at the Laban Art of Movement Studio.

At the age of sixty, when most dancers would already have left the field or developed their careers as far as was possible inside the expanded concept of dance, Bonnie was about to return to active technique teaching and all its related activities, but now with British students and 40 years of pioneering work behind her.

Her family gave their whole-hearted support. Five years after moving to Hastings the Gundlachs had moved to a larger house where Ralph was able to see his patients. Having suffered two heart attacks and a broken neck in a taxi accident, he felt the move to England would provide an

Bonnie Bird and Marion North at the start of their unique collaboration, England, 1973. Photo: Marion North.

excellent opportunity to retire and concentrate on his writing. "His positive attitude and good humor in adapting to a sharp restructuring of his activities buoyed the whole family, making it possible for each of us to view the necessity for change as natural in the evolution of our lives," Bonnie wrote in 1974 in her annual Christmas Letter from England to all her friends world-wide. The two older children, Michael and Heidi, were already at college: Michael was a civil engineering major at the University of Washington, and Heidi, after transferring from Earlham in Indiana, was about to start her second year at Sarah Lawrence College in a dual program of dance and liberal arts studies. Bonnie's younger brother in California also had a teenage son and agreed to become John Scott's surrogate father, which worked out very well since English schools would not have suited him.

Bonnie left the Dance Notation Bureau in mid-April, 1974, and for the next five months crisscrossed the Atlantic between teaching assignments in England in preparation for the big move. The house in Hastings was rented and she found "a comfortable if humorous" purple-trimmed bungalow in Addleston handy for the Studio and for journeys to London. Ralph arrived in September, just after she had taught a two-week summer course at the Studio. Her sense of adventure was as keen as ever, and they explored the countryside in her Morris 1300, "driving on the wrong side of the road from the wrong side of the car."

10

BUILDING SONG

A visionary who brings her own Western lands
with her wherever she goes

Off a busy thoroughfare in a depressed inner London borough, up a
narrow street of old terraced houses used by Goldsmiths' College as
classrooms and offices, straight ahead there suddenly appears a modern
two-storey brick building. It is the Laban Centre of Movement and Dance.
Next to it is a complex containing recently built studios regularly
transformed into The Bonnie Bird Theatre where, one day in April, 1994,
Bonnie was filmed watching and commenting on a student demonstration of past and present exercises from the Graham technique. "The
struggle to get the Graham work across is the same now as when I worked
with Martha," she said later. "Understanding the contraction and release
not only as concepts but as physical realities is still difficult. How Martha
expressed human emotion! The 'laugh', 'pleading', 'cry', 'call' – all
involve the body totally and must be exaggerated to project their deeper
meaning. The use of images, analogies and motivation to link the inner
and outer reasons for the movements and make them believable has
succeeded very well with these students."

During 1994 Dr. Marion North[1] celebrated her 21st anniversary as
director of the Laban Centre. It was also Bonnie's 20th year of close
work with North during which, as head of the Centre's Dance Theatre
Course, she returned to the States again and again to renew contacts
from among her huge network of students, colleagues and friends, hire
teachers, arrange for visiting lecturers, view new works by young
American choreographers, and invite artists and groups to the Centre
to teach, perform or choreograph. In her role as Artistic Adviser to
Transitions Dance Company, she expanded the school's educational
activities into Europe, North America and the Far East, all the while
working closely with the company during its heavy performance and
teaching schedule.

What was the history of the Centre and Bonnie's role in making it a
leading institution of higher education in the dance world?

Transitions dancers in *An Etude*. Choreography: Amanda Miller, 1995. Photo: Chris Nash.

In 1941 Rudolph von Laban and his close colleague, Lisa Ullmann, began teaching modern dance on short courses during holiday periods in various institutions around Great Britain. In 1943 the Art of Movement Studio (AMS), under Ullmann's direction, was set up in Manchester. By 1946 its teacher-training program, which offered a three-year Laban Diploma similar to that first developed in pre-war Germany, was recognized by the Ministry of Education. Laban himself was involved in many different projects at once during this period. As well as being on the Studio staff, he continued his influential work with actors and his time and motion studies for industry. His concept that movement and dance enhanced child development coincided with the views of John Dewey and others on the British post-war education scene, and Lisa Ullmann attracted a great deal of support from all over the country for this aspect of his work. In 1948 the Ministry of Education approved a one-year course at AMS for PE teacher-training.

In 1953, with its official name now the Laban Art of Movement Studio (LAMS), it moved from Manchester to Woburn Place, an old Victorian mansion situated in 17 acres of countryside in Addlestone, Surrey, which Leonard Elmhirst's son, William, had bought for it. In this setting Laban was better able to relate his concepts of fitness and health, work and play directly to nature. In 1955 the Laban Art of Movement Centre, with Laban as director, was established as a parallel institution for research purposes. The Studio's diploma program continued, along with one-year teacher-training courses for students from other colleges. Over the next 20 years, despite Laban's death in 1958, its teacher- and post-graduate training courses in dance and movement studies prepared generations of teachers for British schools and colleges. The government was especially satisfied with this type of dance education as it did not compete for the big subsidies that British ballet companies, who brought world-wide artistic acclaim to British choreographers, dancers, musicians, and designers, were getting.

Meanwhile American modern dance had been given a kick-start in Britain in 1966 when Robin Howard founded the London Contemporary Dance School and invited American teachers from the Graham Studio to London. Howard based his school on the technique and theater of Martha Graham, whom he greatly admired. By 1973 its London Contemporary Dance Theatre had graduated from performances in its own small theater at The Place and other similar venues to London's Sadler's Wells Theatre, where it met with national recognition. The rumblings that would produce Britain's contemporary dance explosion in the 1980s had begun.

The fortunes of the Laban Art of Movement Studio were, however, at a low ebb when Marion North, who had left it after Laban's death, took over as its director in 1973. Forward looking and with a vision of a new kind of dance education, she posed the question of the Studio's future. She saw her mission as securing the survival of Laban's work in the contemporary world, but did not believe it should be limited to any one part of his work, such as teacher training. She was strongly supported by Dr. Glen Wilson, Warden of Goldsmiths' College, University of London, who shared her belief in the importance of dance as a serious study in higher education.

LAMS focus was going to change, and for this she needed outstanding people. "As I got to know Bonnie," she said in an interview in 1992, "I appreciated that she was doing a good but limited job in New York, where I felt she did not have the opportunity to put all her unique experiences in the field of dance to best advantage. If you can give me credit for anything, it was recognizing that she was the person we needed to develop a dance department that would prepare well-educated students for careers in dance. It has been a very good partnership of sharing ideas, of imaginative and creative thinking and, as it were, chewing over possibilities, with one or the other of us developing our random thoughts into some kind of shape and then working them out together. I think it must have been this kind of imaginative and creative thinking that stimulated Bonnie throughout her life as a performer, choreographer, director of dance companies and teacher of dancers.

"If I look at what we do now at the Centre, it is exactly what the range of Laban's work and attitude to dance were, developed and done differently. It is not what he did in the '30s or '40s; it is what he would have done today. But nevertheless it covers theater, education, therapy, community work, special education for children with special needs, and many more aspects of dance and movement, academic study and research – the whole range of his life's work. About the only area we don't touch because it has been taken into the commercial field is the application of his work to industry and commerce."

And for Bonnie, all her hopes for sensitively educated dancers in a wide range of dance-related studies came together under one roof. "Here, at Laban, I have found my one university for all these special courses. That has been very exciting because we offer so much and we have been able to develop a coherent and flexible program with a faculty of specialist teachers for dancers, all within the one institution."[2]

What were Bonnie's impressions on her first visit to England in the fall of 1973? "Laban's training was based on his movement concepts. He was a real taskmaster and the execution of his movement patterns amounted to a kind of technical training, but as the Studio's emphasis was on training for educationalists, it was really a bonus if a student developed into a dancer. Dance technique itself was looked down upon. I had American friends who had studied at the Studio and were frowned on for doing warm-ups and barres! I think the problem was that there was no concentration on skill coordination outside the range of the particular Laban studies. No importance was given to leg and foot development, but there was a heavy emphasis on the students' 'act of creation', so to speak. The Studio seemed not to have recognized that the art of dance itself was changing and developing, and it had become increasingly insular and defensive."

In the autumn term of 1974, a three-year full-time Dance Theatre Diploma Course worked out by Bonnie and Marion North was initiated. Its core studies were technique, choreography and Laban Studies (movement analysis through Labanotation). Graham technique formed the basis of the first two years of contemporary dance study, followed by a choice of other American techniques such as Limón, Nikolais/Louis or Horton. Bonnie wanted the choreography course, up until then the domain of the specially gifted student, to be at the heart of dance study. Her premise was firmly rooted in the belief that creative dancers were better equipped to take responsibility for their future as artists. "It was stimulating and tough going. The first year I taught just about everything the faculty couldn't itself provide. I taught all the technique classes, as well as the classes in choreography and costume making, and did all the production work except some of the lighting. Within three months there was such a marked difference that I was soon driving students around to local schools in a rented station wagon to present lecture-demonstrations on the practice of dance. I did the works!

"Attitudes quickly began to change. Quite early on students in teacher training began asking why they didn't have the courses offered on the Dance Theatre program. Over the next few years teacher training was phased out and finally dropped altogether except in a one-year post-graduate course. Soon we began adding to the staff of the Dance Theatre Course. Patricia Mackenzie, a fine ballet teacher, was one of the first, and my former American colleagues began joining us for short courses and residencies." Among them were Bessy Schönberg, head of dance at Sarah Lawrence College and former member of the Graham Group, and Lucas Hoving, director [1971–1978] of the Dans Academy of Rotterdam.

In September, 1976, The Laban Art of Movement Studio, now called the Laban Centre of Movement and Dance, moved to Goldsmiths' College,[3] situated in New Cross, a racially-mixed area of inner London. Here it could participate in the London dance scene as well as incorporate into its activities Laban's ideas on dance as a community expression. An old Victorian building to the rear of Goldsmiths', St. James' Primary School, had been given to the Centre to reconstruct, but its new studios were not ready in time for the autumn term arrival of 190 students from Great Britain and abroad. The faculty and students had to shuttle between an assortment of borrowed classrooms, gymnasia, halls and ballrooms.

By June, 1977, the first crop of Dance Theatre students graduated. The list of American guest teachers already included Alwin Nikolais, Anna Sokolow, teacher-choreographer-educator Eleanor King, Richard Kuch from the Graham Company and Don Redlich, Holm-trained dancer and choreographer.

With the move from Addlestone, Bonnie and Ralph decided to sell their Hastings home and bought an apartment in Bloomsbury in central London. It had four good-sized rooms off a long central corridor, a large kitchen and two bathrooms. Marion and her husband, 'Mac' (Francis MacNamara), lived across the hall which made it easy for the two women to carry on their discussions exploring new ideas for the development of the Centre away from the bustle of the school. The new Gundlach home was large enough to accommodate visiting family, friends and guest artists, and was within walking distance of the British Museum and Oxford Street and easily accessible to all parts of the city. In her yearly Christmas Letter of 1976 Bonnie wrote, "What a joy it gives us when you who are so special to us come our way! We feel refreshed and reconnected to our roots. What sprawling ones they are, embracing both coasts of that big, crazy, beautiful American continent!" Ralph was always busy writing in his large study with a fine view over the rooftops of London, or attending international conferences as well as son Scott's high school graduation in California, or traveling through Great Britain and Europe with Bonnie, Marion and Mac.

The next phase in the growth of higher dance education in Britain came at the beginning of the 1977–1978 season with the introduction of the Centre's Dance Theatre BA (Hons.) It was the first degree course of its kind in the U.K. and was to be awarded by the Council for National Academic Awards (CNAA), the validation body for degree courses in non-university institutions.

Bonnie played a major role in the development of this course and was especially pleased with the positive reactions of the student body. At the same time the degree course was established the Centre added five new faculty members, bringing the total to 25. As the Centre grew, Bonnie instituted democratic procedures in all stages of decision making with committees for management, planning, choreography, teaching, and technique. "Greeted the first class of B.A. Honours students in October: 26 delightful young people from seven different countries. They have a real sense of pioneering, as indeed they should, since it is the first such degree in dance in the United Kingdom." (Christmas Letter 1977)

More Americans arrived at the Centre, including John Cage and Ruth Currier, formerly of the Limón Company. Talented graduates of London Contemporary Dance School were given opportunities to teach and choreograph. Centre Dance, a small performance unit of graduate students and faculty members (echoes of the Merry-Go-Rounders, and the forerunner of Transitions Dance Company) gave several performances.

Visitors and exotic journeys also filled Bonnie's life. From her dancing past came Muriel Stuart, Lucy Venable, Shirley Wynne, Anna Sokolow and Dr. Ernst Kulka. In March Ralph went with friends on a month-long tour of France, the Low Countries and Germany and Bonnie caught up with them on a trip up the Rhine from Amsterdam to Lake Constance and Munich. They all returned to London where they left Bonnie to get on with her work at the Centre before setting sail on a Baltic Cruise to Stockholm, Helsinki, Leningrad and Bremerhaven. Heidi, fresh from her Sarah Lawrence graduation ceremony (attended by brother Mike and former housekeeper Velma Reese, both of whom had flown in from Seattle), said a warm hello and then went off to pick strawberries in Norway for a month. After the Centre's summer course Marion, Mac, Bonnie and Ralph arrived at a friend's home in Palma, Mallorca for two weeks of sun and good wine. With dates for the following Easter to teach at York University in Toronto, Canada, visit friends in San Francisco and teach in New York before returning to London, Bonnie was enjoying a wonderful time of new ventures and warm camaraderie.

From Bonnie's Christmas Letter, 1978

"It is nearly Christmas and until this very day, December 15th, I have not had one minute to devote to writing the Gundlachs' annual letter of greeting. It is harder to manage without Ralph, but it shall be done because the children and I want you to know that we shall be saluting each of you with a special toast on Christmas day. I am flying to New York on December 20th, where Heidi, Michael and, I hope, Scott will meet me for a week of being family.

"As most of you know, Ralph died on August 15th in London. He was alert and responsive until minutes before he died. His heart gave out after coping with several minor but debilitating set-backs in the preceding month.

"Happily, he had enjoyed to the fullest a trip to San Francisco in late June, where he saw many dear friends and spent time with his sisters, Jean and Betty, and sons, Scott and Mike. Heidi arrived in London only a day after he flew back from San Francisco following 10 days in Kaiser Hospital due to the collapse of a leg artery. Though the English weather was behaving like a mild winter on Puget Sound, the days were filled with laughter and talk.

"The first of three celebrations honoring Ralph's life was held in London on August 20th. It was a bright, flower-scented day as friends gathered in Golders Green. Frank MacNamara, Marion North's husband, spoke of Ralph's gift for friendship, as did Jerry Tyler, retired ILWU official from Seattle. Jerry's recollections stemmed from Ralph's support of the early trade union struggles in the Northwest where he earned recognition as a 'stand-up guy' from the men and women on the picket lines.

"The celebration in San Francisco took place on August 27th. Ralph's sister Jean had arranged that it be held in the Unitarian Church. Members of our families and a wonderful number of dear friends came from far and wide to hear Hugh de Lacy, Harry Bridges, Ralph Granneberg, Earl Robinson, Bill Roark, John McTernan, Keith Sward and Nikki Bridges (reading a tribute written by Jean) speak. How surprising it was to learn that four of them had been students of Ralph's at the University of Washington. I was thrilled that our three children were there to hear the personal recollections about Ralph by these men and women because it gave them so many new insights into the dimensions of their Dad's life in the years before they were born.

"The next day I drove Jean and the children to the top of Mt. Tamalpais and there, on a promontory overlooking San Francisco glinting radiantly in the sun, we let the winds scatter Ralph's ashes over a part of the landscape he so loved. Mike carried some ashes back to Washington to scatter in the high meadows of Mt. Rainier which Ralph was proud to have twice scaled.

"On the evening of September 5th more than a hundred of our close friends and colleagues gathered at the Postgraduate Center for Mental Health in New York City where, following his precipitous break with the University of Washington in 1948, he had trained as a psychotherapist and become a member of the Research Department. Ted Riess, Ralph's long-time friend and associate, chaired. The sense of loss felt by everyone over Ralph's absence was tempered by the warmth and wit of those who did speak: Albert Ottenheimer, Oscar Smith, Robert Schrank, Chester Feurstein, Irving Bieber, Howard Da Silva, and Sheldon and Barbara Waxenburg. Each illuminated the unique way in which he perceived and lived his life. His pursuit of life, whether in work or play, was never disconnected from the realities of the world nor concern for the people in it. His was a truly generous and productive life. The children and I, each in our own place in the world, are the richer and, perhaps, some day will be the wiser for having had him as father and husband."

By September, 1978, three more studios had been completed at the Laban Centre, one with a moveable wall so that two studios could be combined as a performance area. A real theater that ultimately would seat 120 was coming into being; even in its unfinished state it attracted many visiting artists. Remy Charlip, then appearing in London's first version of the American contemporary dance festival, Dance Umbrella, opened the concert series in November, 1978. Americans Elizabeth Walton, Jennifer Scanlon and Laura Glenn soon followed.

The following July the Centre commemmorated the centenary of Laban's birth with two major events: an international summer school and a four-day international symposium. It was a grand coming together of American and European dancers and educators to celebrate their heritage. The American guest teachers included dancer-choreographer Murray Lewis and his company and the dance writer Marcia B. Siegel. The symposium was attended by 150 people from all over the world led by Sigurd Leeder, Lisa Ullmann, Irmgard Bartenieff, Anna Jooss Markard, leading American dance therapist Clair Schmais, long-time Laban colleague Sylvia Bodmer, the Dance Notation Bureau's Executive Director Muriel Topaz, and Valerie Preston-Dunlop, expert in Laban dance analysis and dance documentation methodologies who had recently joined the Centre.

At the beginning of the 1979–1980 season the Centre had two third year groups, Dance Theatre BA degree and Dance Theatre certificate students, working side by side to complete their studies and prepare for graduation. Meanwhile, educators and foreward-thinking organizations such as the Calouste Gulbenkian Foundation, led by dance advocate Peter Brinson, were laying the groundwork for higher education for the growing number of young people being trained for a professional dance career. With the Laban Centre's degree program already in place, the London Contemporary Dance School and the Royal Ballet School also soon started to provide the means for its students to gain higher academic qualifications.

In addition to her teaching and administrative tasks, Bonnie was involved with the difficult preparation of the Centre's submission to the CNAA for approval to offer a Master of Arts Degree (MA) in Dance. Although MA programs that contained dance were already on offer at a few universities, the Centre's was to be quite different. "What an education this exercise is for all of us! Our wits will be the sharper for having to contend with the ponderously academic and rigid pre-conceptions about what constitutes acceptable modes of learning (i.e. since dance is done with the body and not the tongue, it must follow that it is mindless, etc. etc. etc.)." (Christmas letter 1979) Dr. Dorothy Madden, well-known American dance educator, joined the Centre in 1979 as a permanent faculty member to teach dance composition and also advise on the future MA program.

In July, 1980, the annual summer school welcomed Merce Cunningham who taught technique, composition and repertory classes, and John Cage. One of the course's high points was a showing of *Imaginary Landscape No ???*, a complicated compilation of the joint work of 12 visual artists and 30 dancers, performed to 21 sound scores all played at once by Cage's students. It was a veritable musical circus, a far more complex version than that first created by Bonnie and John at Cornish more than a half century before! For the concluding performance, Cunningham and Cage presented *Dialogue* to an audience of 500 in the Great Hall at Goldsmiths' College.

In September, 1981, the graduate-level MA program came into effect. It offered a choice of three subjects from among the following: dance history, choreography, documentation and reconstruction, sociology and Laban Studies. Aesthetics of dance and education in dance were later added. More space for all the new programs was soon created through the conversion of the deconsecrated Church of St. James, Hatcham, directly behind the Centre. It provided six additional studios, tutorial and seminar rooms, an enlarged library and a student Common Room.

This period also saw the long process of the Centre's separation from Goldsmiths' College. "The idea had originally been to bring the two departments, Goldsmiths' and the Centre, together as one," Bonnie said, "but we quickly saw that to become a part of Goldsmiths' would not work for us. Once you are in a university setup, everything is done by committees that move very slowly. We had an independent and different series of programs. We were not in conflict with each other, but we were doing different things. With the teacher training cutbacks, Goldsmiths' went on to develop a lively and large dance department based on combined arts courses, which we do not offer. At the Centre everyone must take the core subjects, which are technique, choreography, and Laban studies. They can then select from the optional dance/movement courses we offer. As for teacher training, I believe that the dancers are

Transitions Dance Company members in *Standby*. Choreography: Rui Horta, 1993. Photo: Chris Nash.

better off completing a BA degree and then a year's teacher training to get a teaching credential, which is what we offer now."

Bonnie was a driving force behind the founding of the quarterly *Labanews* in January, 1981. From her work assisting Louis Horst on *The Dance Observer* early in her professional life she had learned the importance of spreading news and information about dance. *Labanews* soon grew into the *Dance Theatre Journal*, an internationally recogized magazine publishing a wide range of articles on dance. Many Laban graduates have developed their careers through their association with this magazine.

By the early 1980s the growing interest in choreography was reflected at the Laban Centre in the huge demand on its studio space from early morning until late at night and on weekends. Bonnie now concentrated on originating programs to facilitate the making and production of new works by young choreographers. In the 1982–1983 season, the one-year Advanced Performance Course was initiated with fourth-year Laban Centre students as well as graduates from full-time dance training programs in other schools. The heart of this on-going yearly program, Transitions Dance Company, consists of eight dancers drawn from the course, under the day-to-day direction of an American guest teacher-choreographer-educator. Through their work in a student company with professional standards, dancing new works by guest choreographers from Britain, America and Europe, its members hope to make the leap into professional dance. Transitions has developed into a fine touring repertory company offering workshops, lecture-demonstrations and residencies in educational outreach programs. Bonnie joined the tours abroad, spending much of the time teaching and networking. Choreographers who have developed in recent years through their work with Transitions include Lea Anderson, David Massingham, Matthew Bourne, Jacob Marley and Mark Murphy. Their companies are filled with Laban graduates.

In 1984 a fund was established on Bonnie's 70th birthday with gifts from her many friends and colleagues to honor her important contribution to contemporary dance in the United States and the United Kingdom. Because the needs of young choreographers were foremost in her heart, she requested that the fund should initiate a program of awards to support the development of choreography in the UK and elsewhere. With the money carefully invested, the Bonnie Bird Choreography Fund makes three sets of awards: the British Awards, given annually to three British-based choreographers to enable them to pursue research or projects that will contribute to their development as choreographers; the annual North American Award, which commissions a North American choreographer to make a new work for Transitions Dance Company; and the European Award, given to the most outstanding choreographer at the biennial Rencontres Choréographiques Internationales de Bagnolet, who is also invited to stage a work for Transitions. Since its inception the Fund has given awards to more than 30 choreographers.

Other courses were added to the Laban Centre curriculum in areas of dance which Bonnie had pioneered in America. When the Centre introduced its M. Phil. and Ph.D. Research Degrees in the early 1980s, she recalled her efforts to establish CORD and her years spent promoting dance research. Remembering the variety of teacher-training courses she had instigated she was delighted when the Community Dance Course, started in 1982 by Dr. Peter Brinson, began training community-based dancers for work with toddlers, teenagers, senior citizens and the disabled. Thinking back on her work with Erik Erikson and at Cherry Lawn School and Blythdale Hospital, she was very proud when, in 1986, the Centre initiated Britain's first MA in Dance/Movement Therapy to train therapists within the health, social and education services for work with the mentally, emotionally and physically disturbed. Because of her long-term effort to secure U.S. government recognition and support of the art of dance, she was especially pleased when the Politics of Dance Course was later initiated.

A new phase of Bonnie's work began in February, 1987, when she became head of International Development. Her journeys to establish contacts with universities and governments became so numerous that she was traveling more widely throughout the United States, Europe and the Far East than she had ever imagined possible.

"We are always amused and excited by the incredible range of people Bonnie knows," said Dr. North in 1993. "Practically any American mentioned in the field of dance was either her student, her assistant, her collaborator, her teacher, or participated with her on one project or another. When I travel with her I am fascinated by how people flock around her and ask, 'Do you remember when you taught me?' or 'when you worked with me', or 'when I danced with you' or 'for you?'.

During the 1980s and into the '90s Bonnie's life was a joyous mixture of work and fun. First and foremost was her base, the Laban Centre, with all the dance activities and academic life she loved; then teaching from Vancouver to Hong Kong by way of Europe; house exchanges on America's East and West Coasts during summer working visits and vacations; frequent reunions with Heidi, Scott and Michael on extended

Bonnie Bird, the dance educator, teaching in Taipei on one of the many Transitions Dance Company tours to the Far East. Photo: Tony Nanadi.

family occasions in Seattle and Berkeley; attending or chairing meetings of CORD, the American Dance Guild and various dance conferences; interviewing prospective North America students for the Centre; and returning to England before term time for the annual Bournemouth Laban Centre Staff Conference ("Trying to keep an independent institution like the Centre economically viable and maintaining its leadership in dance education is no small challenge").

In June, 1989, Bonnie decided that 75 was the appropriate age at which to retire. Each time she relinquished a role or level of teaching it was a matter of great pleasure for her to see how well her place was taken by a younger member of the staff. Earlier that year she had been greatly honored when the Centre's Studio Theatre was rededicated and became the Bonnie Bird Theatre. (She had only recently discovered that half way across the world her Aunt Grace had also been similarly honored in a ceremony of dedication that created the Grace van Dijk Bird Memorial Library on the University of California campus at Berkeley.)

But retirement did not greatly alter her life. She was immediately invited to become a Trustee of the Laban Centre and remained occupied as Adviser to the Advanced Performance Course and Transitions Dance Company, choosing the students and the company dancers, searching out new choreographers and still traveling back and forth across the world. In 1990 she was awarded an Honorary Doctorate of Arts by the Council for National Academic Awards for her work in the field of dance education.

It was not until comparatively late in her life that Bonnie came to know Rudolph Laban's ideas on the multitude of career possibilites open to a dancer, but he would have delighted in how she, herself, had pioneered unexplored territory and extended the frontiers of dance. Early on she had learned that dance's mental and physical training, its personal and shared experiences, open up the mind and imagination, enabling young people to expand their capabilities and redefine themselves in an ever changing world – and succeed in realizing their own, increasingly demanding, expectations. Bonnie never thought she was extraordinary for what she had accomplished, or even different. It was all part of the whole. The whole was dance and dance was life. Her great happiness in England was that all her life experiences had come together and were a source of continuous renewal.

"My work at the Centre has been very challenging. One dreams throughout one's life and wishes that one could make something work or bring an idea to life. I must say that I have had to call on practically every experience I have ever had in my entire life in the dance field, from turning a tomato can into a stage light to solving some kind of production problem, or working in some depressing situation in a community and learning how to cope with the janitors and the director and the crazy parents (all the coping you have to do!). All these experiences have been called on in one way or another in developing the programs here at the Centre.

"I think my contacts and knowledge over a lifelong career have been extremely important. People who knew me well in the States and have worked with me have had good experiences. I don't think many of them were sour. Sometimes we fell flat on our noses, but it wasn't because of anything nasty. It was just the collapse of a particular situation or the natural play-out of an idea.

"Trust has been an important factor. Artists and teachers have wanted to come to the Centre, even though we couldn't pay them very much, because they knew they might make a contribution to an exciting realization of an idea. And they feel that they have been really genuinely appreciated. Dancers are taken for granted so much of the time. Even though they know they have a place in history they don't often get a chance to feel it. It's wonderful to be able to provide the circumstances to enable them to function, even for a short period of time, so that they feel they are being genuinely recognized. That has been especially nice."

In Taipei, on the last leg of Transitions 1994 tour of the Far East, Bonnie fell seriously ill. Marion North accompanied her on the journey back to California to her recently acquired apartment in Tiburon overlooking Angel Island and San Francisco Bay. Medical tests revealed cancer of the liver, a terminal illness. Accepting this as one more challenge among so many, Bonnie underwent chemotherapy treatment. With her doctor's agreement she contacted a herbalist in South America whose special diet she carefully followed. She held mortality in abeyance. In October, Heidi gave birth to a daughter, Bonnie's first grandchild. The round dance of life was continuing. With her accustomed grace and good humor she let her friends know that she would be back in London in January, and she kept her word. Sparkling eyes and smiles greeted everyone. Her wig was most becoming; she was administering the injections herself. She soon returned to the States for a medical follow-up, with plans to join the Company at the end of March on their North American tour. In a letter dated March 19, 1995, she wrote, "The big news is that City Centre is presenting us in the Company's first professional showcase. Audrey Ross, head of publicity, has invited a wide range of presenters, critics, and dance professionals to come on April 3rd at 5 p.m., with a reception following. I am a little stunned that this break through has come after years of timorous door knocking. The Harkness Foundation is covering all costs! We will do our 'foreign' works which, I am told, are of most interest to New Yorkers. I am thrilled to have the works of these young choreographers seen in 'Mecca' by a group of experienced dance aficionados."

Bonnie was not able to fulfill these plans. In full flight almost to the last week, she passed away on April 9, 1995. A few days later, on a promontory atop Mt. Tamalpais, amid the wonders of nature and a man-made world that only her western lands could conjure up, the wind scattered her ashes over the landscape she so loved. Afterward Marion North carried a portion to the Laban Centre, on the other side of the world. Her round dance was completed. To the universe belongs the dancer.

NOTES AND SOURCES

Chapter 4. *The Cornish School*

1. *Miss Aunt Nellie: The Autobiography of Nellie C. Cornish*, edited by Ellen van Volkenburg Browne and Edward Nordhoff Beck. Seattle: University of Washington Press, 1964, p. 206.
2. *Ibid.*

Chapter 5. *Preparation*

1. *Miss Aunt Nellie: The Autobiography of Nellie C. Cornish*, edited by Ellen van Volkenburg Browne and Edward Nordhoff Beck. Seattle: University of Washington Press, 1964, p. 207.
2. Hedwig Müller, *Mary Wigman: Leben und Werk der grossen Tänzerin.* Weinheim and Berlin: Quadriga Verlag, 1986, p. 173.
3. Dorothy Bird Villard: quote from a letter to the author, July, 1989.

Chapter 6. *The Martha Years: From the Letters Home*

1931–1932: Launch
1. The history of the Neighborhood Playhouse began with Irene and Alice Lewisohn, wealthy sisters who wanted to bring the arts to the people of the Lower East Side, a community made up largely of European immigrants. In 1905 the sisters began their activities at the Henry Street Settlement School where they worked in conjunction with Lillian Wald, who had founded the school in the 1890s for the training of nurses and home carers.

   Early experimental productions incorporated elements of the colorful neighborhood pageants of Grand Street that centered on the immigrants' own customs, traditional singing and dancing. Performances of already existing theater texts only slowly become a major part of the activity. The first public performances were given in 1915 in the newly completed and excellently equipped Neighborhood Playhouse, which

seated 450 and included the first permanent plaster cyclorama instal-
led in an American theater.

The Neighborhood Playhouse achieved Irene Lewisohn's twin goals
of aiding social welfare and satisfying her own artistic aspirations. She
was an actress and had been trained by Genevieve Stebbins, a disciple
of François Delsarte, the 19th century French music teacher whose
analyses of the gestures and expressions of human movement also
greatly influenced the American modern dance pioneers. Working
with the neighborhood's young people in diverse forms of dance and
drama, she also acted and danced in plays and sometimes directed
them. She hired the best directors, dramatic coaches, actors and
actresses for the Playhouse productions, which catered primarily to
the residents of the Lower East Side, but also attracted audiences from
all sectors of the city.

The Neighborhood Playhouse closed in 1927 and 'Miss Irene'
undertook the direction of a series of orchestral dramas in which the
dancers she selected shaped their own roles. The first program was
presented in 1928 at the Manhattan Opera House and included Martha
Graham, Charles Weidman and Doris Humphrey in Ernest Bloch's
Israel, and Graham and Michio Ito in Debussy's *Nuages*. In the 1929
presentation, Graham and Weidman danced the lead roles in
Lewisohn's heroic conception of Richard Strauss' tone poem, *Ein
Heldenleben*, and in the 1930 production at the Mecca Auditorium (later
renamed the New York City Centre), Graham and Weidman were
featured in performances of Martin Loeffler's *A Pagan Poem*.

Alice Lewisohn Crowley, in her book, *The Neighborhood Playhouse:
Leaves from a Theatre Scrapbook* (New York: Theatre Arts Books, 1959)
wrote that Louis Horst gave credit to these orchestral dramas "for
having given dancers the necessary push to express dramatic and
emotional values which up to that time had been conceived more or
less abstractly." Graham's first extended dramatic work, *Primitive
Mysteries*, shortly followed her participation in this series.

At the same time as Lewisohn undertook these dance-drama
productions, she opened the Neighborhood Playhouse School of the
Theatre, whose curriculum incorporated all the theater arts. It began
with nine students, all of whom participated in the first orchestral-
drama production, and with Martha Graham and Louis Horst as heads
of the dance department.

2. Mollie Parkes, "A Tribute to Irene Lewisohn," *The Dance Observer*,
   Volume XI, May, 1944, pp. 155–156.
3. Louis Horst, *Pre-Classic Dance Forms*. New York: Kamin Dance Publishers, 1953; repr., Dance Horizons, 1968.

4. Henry Gilfond, "Louis Horst," *The Dance Observer*, Volume III, February, 1936, pp. 3 ff.

1933–1934: "Great times are coming!"
1. Hedwig Müller, *Mary Wigman: Leben und Werk der grossen Tänzerin.* Weinheim and Berlin: Quadriga Verlag, 1986, p. 181.
2. Frances Hawkins, *The Dance Observer*, Volume I, December, 1934, p. 87.
3. Ralph Taylor, *The Dance Observer*, Volume I, December, 1934, p. 89.
4. Mary P. O'Donnell, *The Dance Observer*, Volume III, February, 1936, p. 16.
5. Ralph Taylor, *The Dance Observer*, Volume I, December, 1934, p. 88.
6. Henry Gilfond, *The Dance Observer*, Volume I, December, 1934, p. 89.
7. Winthrop Sargeant, *The Dance Observer*, Volume I, May, 1934, p. 43.
8. John Martin, "The Dance: A Vermont Experiment." *The New York Times*, August 26, 1934.
9. George W. Beiswanger, "Physical Education and The Emergence of the Modern Dance." *Journal of Health and PE* 7, No. 7. September, 1936, pp. 413–416.

1934–1935: "Opening a door on a new and shining world"
1. Ralph Taylor, *The Dance Observer*, Volume I, December, 1934, p. 88.
2. *Ibid.*
3. *Ibid.*, p 89.
4. John Martin, *The New York Times*, November 19, 1934.
5. Under President Roosevelt's Second New Deal, a new set of sweeping social and economic reforms were put into effect early in 1935. Among them was the Works Progress Administration (WPA), which functioned from 1935 to 1943 and ultimately employed 8.5 million Americans. Approximately 4000 artists were salaried in its Federal Art Project to produce, among other things, murals, paintings and sculptures with an American emphasis for public buildings; drawings and paintings for the Index of American Design; and photographs of America. The Art Project also included many politically radical artists who painted themes of social protest.

The Federal Theatre Project of the WPA (1935–1939) was organized to help solve unemployment in the theater. Under the general direction of Mrs. Hallie V. Flanagan, it included the Dance Project, which was administered by supervisors in various cities. New York and Chicago were the most active.

Among the New York Dance Project choreographers were Doris Humphrey, Charles Weidman, Helen Tamiris, Gluck-Sandor and Arthur Mahoney. Martha Graham, in keeping with her policy of artistic independence, did not take part in any WPA programs, but her Group dancers, by working around her rehearsal schedules, were able to give their own WPA-supported concerts.

After eight months of preparation, the New York Project's first production, Gluck-Sandor's *The Eternal Prodigal* (Herbert Kingsley), opened in November, 1936, with a cast of over one hundred dancers. The Project's Young Choreographers Laboratory gave its first perform-ance in January, 1937, presenting works by Lily Mehlman, Nadia Chilkovsky and others. In May the Project opened a season of forty-one performances of Helen Tamiris' *How Long Brethren?* and Charles Weidman's *Candide*.

Chiefly because of the improved financial state of theater by 1937, Congress cut fifteen percent of the Theatre Project's funds. The last major dance activities of the New York Project were a festival for children, *Folk Dances of All Nations*, choreographed by Lily Mehlman, and a dance-drama by Tamiris and Harold Bolton, *Trojan Incident*, both produced in April, 1938.

In Chicago, the Federal Dance Project's first director-choreographers were Grace Graff (née Cornell, Bonnie's fellow student at the Cornish School), her husband, Kurt Graff, and Berta Ochsner. They produced a dance review in December, 1936, *O Say, Can You See*, which included tap and chorus routines. In January, 1938, Katherine Dunham, director of the Negro Unit of the Chicago branch of the Federal Theatre Project, produced a program with the Graffs and Ochsner. In June, 1938, the Project presented the Graffs' *Behind This Mask* (David Scheinfeld), and Ruth Page and Bentley Stone's *Frankie and Johnny* and *An American Pattern* (both with scores by Jerome Moross). Page and Stone produced another long-running program of dances in March, 1939, in which the young, future choreographer and Graham dancer, Pearl Lang, appeared.

The Federal Theatre Project came to an official end on July 31, 1939.

6. Henry Gilfond, *The Dance Observer*, Volume II, March, 1935, p. 30.
7. *Ibid*.
8. A movement among American modern dancers to use dance as propaganda began in 1932 when several members of Hanya Holm's lecture-demonstration group formed the New Dance Group. Their intention was to focus on America's social and economic injustices and work for change, not through political alignments, but solely through the power of dance. The founding members were Miriam Blecher, Edna Ocko, Grace Wylie, Nadia Chilkovsky and the pianist-composer Estelle Parnas.

A second propagandist group, the Workers' Dance League, was organized soon after the founding of the New Dance Group. It banded together various solo dancers and dance groups with leftist leanings and also functioned as a booking agent. About a dozen leftist dance groups, many with strong labor union affiliations, appeared under its auspices.

Of a concert by the Workers' Dance League, Paul Love wrote in *The Dance Observer*, Volume I, May, 1934, p. 43, "One comes away from a recital with the feeling of having seen excited, obstreperous children putting across their adolescent ideas in a virile fashion. The fashion may be all right, but the ideas are not, because they are romantic in the worst sense."

According to Henry Gilfond in his review of the Workers' Dance League concert at the Civic Repertory Theatre on November 25, 1934 (*The Dance Observer*, Volume I, December, 1934, p. 89), Sophie Maslow's dances were "well constructed," Jane Dudley moved "with precision and control," but "the works that received the most applause were those based on humor, satire or burlesque." Of these Anna Sokolow's, "whose work can hardly be termed 'red', was the evening's favorite." In the same article he described a piece Bonnie Bird had originally made for a Graham Studio showing, *Death of a Tradition*, as "slapstick", implying that it, too, was well received. In an article for *The New York Times* in January, 1934, John Martin had written: "The original aim of the movement was to produce propaganda under the guise of art. It is likely it will find it has produced art under the guise of propaganda."

Early in 1935 the Workers' Dance League changed its name to the New Dance League. It broadened its platform and raised its artistic standards, hoping to draw a larger number of high quality artists into the movement. By December its new members included José Limón and Letitia Ide. Mary P. O'Donnell wrote in *The Dance Observer*, Volume III, January, 1936, "In forsaking the path of literal social comment, the New Dance League is producing inestimably finer art, but at the same time defeating its avowed purpose of infusing dance with propaganda."

The Works Progress Administration was also succeeding in reducing support for Marxist theories of art and propaganda by providing work for artists in many disciplines throughout the United States during the Depression. By 1937, the leftist dance groups that had been forming and splintering, such as the New Dance League, the Dance Guild and the Dance Association, merged to form the American Dance Association. The ADA continued its commitment to social justice as a part of its activities.

9. Julien Bryan, a documentary film maker whose wife, Marion, was founder of the dance department at Sarah Lawrence College, made a silent, black and white film of a few short sections of *Panorama* at the time of its premiere. For the Graham Company season in October, 1992, the company director and former leading Graham dancer, Yuriko, used it to help her reconstruct eleven minutes from the last section of the 45-minute work. Because no one from the original cast could remember much about the piece, she had to work out the movement sequences, entrances and exits and how to cut the music. The revival had 33 dancers and one mobile, and the costumes were red skirts and short, boxy tops. Bonnie saw a performance and said, "It didn't matter to me that the wrong kind of mobile was used in the last scene because it was so much fun to see the very simple movement that Graham had selected to use in dealing with so many dancers plowing across the stage. It had such enormous spirit and was so fresh, young and positive that the audience rose out of their seats. It was yet another dimension to Martha's work and reconnected people to her philosophy during that period."

1935–1936 "A delicate receiving instrument"

1. In the performance for International Labor Defence, Anna Sokolow's *Strange American Funeral* was danced by the youngest of the evening's participants, the Dance Unit [formerly the Theatre Union Dance Group) of the New Dance League. Helen Tamiris and her group presented *Harvest*, a suite of three dances, and *Work and Play*, from her cycle *Toward the Light*; Doris Humphrey presented *New Dance* and Charles Weidman offered *Stock Exchange*, from his suite, *Atavisms*. Martha Graham presented *Celebration, Course*, and her latest solo, *Imperial Gesture*. In *The Dance Observer*, Volume III, January, 1936, p. 6, Henry Gilfond's review of the solo strongly rebuked those who admired only her delicacy of line, color and dynamic movement, and continued, "This is a dance that could not have been created by an artist who is not thoroughly aware of her social and economic environment....*Imperial Gesture* is definitely and simply an indictment of imperialism....Its implication for the audience is positive, convincing, and signals a healthy protest in the face of the tightening pressure of world conflicts."

2. Kurt Jooss, dancer and choreographer of an emerging new movement in German modern dance, 'dance theater', had fled his native Germany in August, 1933, one step ahead of arrest by the Nazis. He and his company toured Europe (excepting Germany) and America until the following spring, when the company was disbanded for financial reasons. In April, 1934, Leonard and Dorothy Elmhirst invited him to

establish the Jooss–Leeder School of Dance at Dartington Hall and in September, 1935, Ballets Jooss was refounded there.
3. *The Dance Observer*, Volume III, February, 1936.

Chapter 7. *Rumbles in the West*

1. This film shows Bonnie Bird dancing on the cement stage of the Mills College Greek Theatre during the summers of 1938 and 1939. A video was produced by John Mueller of the University of Rochester Dance Film Archive and copyrighted in 1985 by Bonnie Bird. The credits read: "Color footage shot on 16 mm film by Betty Lynd Thompson. Black and White footage originally shot on 8 mm film." Thompson was a Master of Arts candidate at the University of Idaho. The first part of the video, in black and white, shows Bonnie performing exercises from the Graham Technique. The second part, in color, shows Dorothy Herrmann performing technical combinations alongside Bonnie.
2. Erick Hawkins (1909–1994), born in Trinidad, Colorado, studied classics at Harvard University. His sudden decision to become a dancer came when he saw Harald Kreutzberg dance in New York in 1931. After a summer course with Kreutzberg in Salzburg, Hawkins enrolled for ballet classes at the newly-founded School of American Ballet in 1933. His first teacher there was Muriel Stuart. He was intelligent and quick to learn. Encouraged by George Balanchine, he began teaching classes at the school. From 1935 to 1937 Hawkins danced with Lincoln Kirstein's American Ballet, for which Balanchine was choreographer, and then spent two years with Ballet Caravan, a splinter group created to produce new works by young American ballet choreographers, for which Hawkins choreographed a solo for himself, *Show Piece* (Robert McBride). Kirstein sent him to Martha Graham, whom he greatly admired, feeling that Hawkins, as a late beginner, had a better opportunity to build a career in modern dance.
3. The first "Modern American Percussion Concert" on December 9, 1938, featured works by John Cage, Ray Green, William Russell and Gerald Strang.
4. Jean Cocteau, spokesman for the group of French composers known as *Les Six* (Georges Auric, Louis Durey, Arthur Honegger, Darius Milhaud, Francis Poulenc and Germaine Taillefer) contended that the new generation of French composers should derive its inspiration from the witty art of the music hall and the circus. Conceived by Cocteau, *Les Mariés de la Tour Eiffel* (1921) was their only collaboration.
5. In his article, *Relating Music and Concert Dance*, for *The Dance Observer*, Volume IV, January, 1937, pp. 1 ff., Henry Cowell wrote, "Music has

grown too top-lofty through its independence from the dance. Only by reassociation with the dance will modern music be prevented from decay. So the need of these arts for each other is mutual." He referred to his music for dance as being "elastic.... but having form and easily adapted to the changes and freedoms essential to the dancer's creation." According to his system, the score could be written with built-in flexibilities such as phrase length, repetition and instrumental interchange. Fitting the proper musical phrase to the dance phrase or making overlaps when necessary was the last step. He composed Graham's *Immediate Tragedy* (1937) in his way.

Chapter 8. *America at War*

1. *Ralph Gundlach: Social Psychologist*, Virginia Frost, Master of Arts Thesis, The Evergreen State College, Olympia, Washington, May, 1989.
2. "An Analysis of Antony Tudor's Important Contribution to the Ballet," 'Tess Egert' (Bonnie Bird); an excerpt from a review for *Peoples World*, San Francisco, 1944–1945:

"It appears to this writer that a deeper investigation of Tudor's ballets finds him doing several important things in a very logical way.... He thinks intelligently and with a real craftman's familiarity with his tools. He carefully builds the dramatic sequence of the ballet itself so that a full-valued climax is achieved. The result is that the reasons for a character moving in a certain way at a given time are consistent with the basic concept of that character.

"Thus it is that Nora Kaye in the role of Hagar in *Pillar of Fire* creates a woman of such depth and dramatic proportion that she might have stepped out of an Ibsen play. She is no stereotyped, bloodless creature – but a living, feeling human being.

"Tudor uses the corps de ballet in a completely unique way. Under his direction they not only support but actually enlarge the meaning of the ballet. They are used to create a special atmosphere against which the whole dramatic action develops, or as the projection of the character's internal reflections. Thus the corps de ballet becomes an integral part of the whole, giving dimension and range to the main action.

"This is but a brief analysis of the contribution Antony Tudor is making to the whole history of dance. His works point the way to a new and exciting era in ballet. He has proven that the expressive range of ballet can be expanded, that the classic combination of ballet steps can be safely abandoned for more exciting and meaningful uses of dance movement. Last, but by no means least, he has demonstrated that movement subordinated to ideas does not necessarily limit the artistry of either the choreographer or the dancer.... American audiences have more than expressed their enthusiasm in hailing the Tudor ballets. It is sincerely hoped that the Ballet Theatre will find its way to this city soon again. They have given San Francisco many days of fun and fine art."

3. Franklin Delanor Roosevelt died in April, 1945, and was succeeded by his Vice-President, Harry S. Truman. World War II ended a few months later and Roosevelt's critics hit out freely and fiercely against his New Deal and the vulnerable state of the American economy. When Winston Churchill's 1946 Iron Curtain speech revived old fears about the dangers of Communism, the wartime alliance with the USSR was finished. A newly elected republican Congress, which included Richard Nixon and Joseph McCarthy, declared Communism in government a major political issue. In February, 1947, President Truman ordered an investigation into the loyalty of federal employees.

Washington State, with many employed in its basic industries of forestry, farming, shipping and fishing, was considered progressive in its labor and welfare legislation. "There are forty-seven states and the Soviet of Washington," was a popular remark attributed to James A. Farley, Roosevelt's Postmaster General (1933–1940). The Washington Commonwealth Federation led the fight for legislation to fund social programs, but shortly after its founding in 1935 it was labelled a communist front organization. The University of Washington also had a reputation for radicalism. From the 1920s its faculty members were often involved in what were then considered controversial movements; they warned against excesses in government, sought solutions to the Depression and joined organizations against Fascism. From the early 1930s Ralph Gundlach had been an active member of many such organizations.

In the 1946 Washington State elections, the republicans defeated the democrats, whom they declared were 'communist-controlled'. The conservative democratic leaders, in order to rid themselves of any so-called communists in their ranks, formed a coalition of democrats and republicans which discussed the possibility of a legislative investigation into communist infiltration of the Democratic Party and state institutions. Special focus was put on the Washington State Pension Union and the University of Washington, where it was suspected that communists had infiltrated the faculty.

The Washington State Legislature set up an Un-American Activities Committee (UAAC) and chose the recently elected Albert Canwell, a former Spokane County deputy sheriff in charge of the County Identification Bureau, as chairman. His wealthy wife, hoping that he would make a name for himself, sent him to Washington D.C. to study the procedures of the House of Representatives Un-American Activities Committee. Canwell money underwrote the first few months of Washington State's UAAC's expenses before state funds became available.

The 'Canwell Committee' was made up of seven men, most of whom had little legislative experience. They had difficulty defining Communism, but settled on the definition that it meant anyone who was an agent of a foreign power and advocated and worked for the violent overthrow of the United States government. The first hearings, January 27th to February 5th, 1948, concerned the Washington Pension Union, which was accused of being riddled with communists and operating as a communist front. The UAAC represented the State's most politically conservative elements and wanted to discredit the Pension Union in order to prevent old age pensioners (OAPs) from having their minimum benefit fixed by law. "We take benefits for granted now," said Bonnie, "but in those days every state, every group of people had to fight – even for the recognition that they had needs. There were no OAP rights. Social Security in the U.S. in 1948 was very limited. The OAPs wanted a decent pension so they would not have to go on welfare. The battle to get proper consideration for OAPs was very fierce.

"The Canwell Committee failed utterly because the OAPs had nothing to lose. They could not be scared. They had no jobs, but they could organize and express their opinions lucidly and they had a lot of time to work. Those who weren't infirm were perfectly willing to go out and get signatures on petitions. The State Legislature was trying to emasculate them by exposing their leaders as reds and identifying them with communist ideas. The concept of having benefits and help from the state was considered communist. We can't imagine it now." The Canwell Committee lost the battle, blackening many names in the process. Soon afterward it began its investigation of the University of Washington.

Chapter 9. *A Phoenix in New York*

1. Letter from Bonnie Bird, February, 21, 1989, to Virginia Frost, author of *Ralph Gundlach: Social Psychologist*. The Evergreen State College, Olympia, Washington, May 1989. (Bonnie Bird collection.)
2. Winthrop Palmer, "Season's Summary," *Dance News*, Volume 17, No. 1. July, 1950, p. 6.
3. Composer and teacher John Corigliano.
4. From Bonnie's Dance-Drama School notes on Music and Movement in Teaching the Child, 1950–1951:

The Teacher's Role in Dance-play:

A. Her objectives for the class –

    1. *Technical*: (a) Improve group's level of coordination; (b) Heighten awarness of rhythm; (c) Conscious awareness of movement as means of communication.
    2. *Psychological*: (a) Create atmosphere for creative work; (b) Provide a flexible 'focus' for the group.
    3. *Social*: (a) Function as a group; (b) Provide channels for creative group activity.

B. Objectives for the individual child –

    1. *Technical*: (a) Improve child's level of coordination, sense of rhythm, and delight in expressive use of body.
    2. *According to child's needs*: (a) Reinforce weak ego; (b) Channel socially-aggressive, hostile behavior.
    3. *Special child*: (a) Provide problems challenging to his ability.

How the Teacher Accomplishes a Successful Role:

    – Observation of other classes and observational records of her own.
    – Informational records on each child.
    – Reading in literature on dance and children or related educational approaches.
    – Acquainting herself with what is being done in the field and related work.
    – Relation with child outside class.

5. Rudolph von Laban devised two systems of notation to record human movement. The first, 'Kinetographie Laban' (Labanotation) was set out in 1928 in the journal, *Schrifttanz*. This system is based on the structural analysis of movement and defines level, direction, speed and body part. It is written from the dancer's viewpoint, using a vertical center line representing the body, with vertical columns on either side for the right and left sides of the body. Symbols representing movement through space progress from the bottom to the top of the page within the columns which represent body parts. Included are signs for turning, touching, clapping, sliding, etc. Labanotation can, for example, record all varieties of steps, what arm or leg is moving, its relationship to any other part of the body, and group floor patterns. It is not only the most logical of all dance notations, but can also be used to record the full spectrum of human movement.

6. From Bonnie's notes on a YMHA–YWHA faculty meeting, September 28, 1955:

Present:

Bonnie Bird, Bunny Mendelsohn, Florence Peters, Melissa Nicolaides, Lucile Nathanson, Jacqueline Cecil, Beatrice Rainer, John Wilson, Janet Gay, Mary Ann Young.

Orientation:

The Y is an educational, not professional, institution. Our primary concern is with the cultural development of the child in relationship to dance as a vital form of creative expression.

However, we maintain a professional attitude and standard for work, for it is vital that what each child learns be sound and thorough so that a good foundation is laid on which to build a professional, should the child wish to follow dance as career.

As our catalogue indicates, we teach fundamentals of ballet and of modern technique in all classes. For educational, psychological and physiological reasons we do not teach strict, specialized forms of any 'school' of dance until the child has already had a thorough grounding and experience in a wider background of dance and is 'old enough' in training, body confirmation and interest to benefit by such special-ization. (Ballet is being introduced this year to Adv. I and II.)

Classes:

Beginning classes in dance should not only include the learning of specific exercises toward the development of sound technical control and facility in moving the body, but must be balanced with simple problems which introduce the students to the formal aspects of dance: rhythm, direction, dynamics, use of space, etc. Still another aspect of the class should include creative work in which the students are introduced to the handling of ideas in dance. At first the teacher may present the whole problem until the children understand what is required; then the teacher may, with a few suggestions, let the students individually or in small groups solve the problem. The problems set can stem from a formal or dramatic base, eventually involving both the compositional and ideational aspects of dance.

It is important to explain to the students why we don't wear shoes, why we discourage tutus or fancy costumes and why we have limited visiting days. Also, without frightening them, to help them realize that dance is an important art which requires considerable hard work in order to become adept in it.

Each age group, 4 and 5, 6 and 7, 8 and 9, 10–12, and teenagers, present their own unique problems of what they can accomplish and what they need. In a sense, each represents a grade advancement because more can be demanded.

Intermediate I–II, Advanced I–II, mean specific advancements within age groups. Don't hesitate to challenge all groups. Work to find what does stimulate them, what they can handle. Talk neither down nor up.

Specifics:

First few weeks watch for placement of children. Before moving [to a different class] discuss with child, parent and me. Don't be rail-roaded by parents. Changes must be made through Janet or Mary-Ann. Watch out for picking favorites, check yourself occasionally to see how often you get around to each child. Pay attention to the 'droops' the most at first – they usually need attention.

Take the roll. Introduce or incorporate the pianist (who can take the roll eventually).

If you have concern about a child, discuss it with me or with a parent (other than placement).

All children required to have leotard (on sale) so check on it by end of two weeks or so.

Items to be learned:

Directions: (a) Body (b) Space (use stage directions).

Basic coordination: walk, run, leap, skip, prance, hop, jump (both feet), galop, slide, turns.

Body coordination (principally torso): rounding and straightening back (contraction and release), twisting torso, bending and stretching (front, side, back), tilting.

Weak areas: back lifts (chest lift seems to be the most left out), rhythm during exercises and as conscious, distinct problems.

7. Teacher training for the 13–14-year olds used a different approach: Student apprentices acted as teachers' assistants while other students observed. Later, the observers joined in and acted as assistants to the assistants (big sister approach).

8. From Bonnie's notes on a training course for teachers (undated paper):

Basic Problems in the teaching of dance:

Factors for effective learning include: habits and skills, motivation and creativity, tension reduction of frustrations, discipline, growth, morale and group membership.

A teaching situation involves at least these persons: teacher, assistant and the accompanist; students, parents and the public. Various relations are set up through the interaction of these groups, but the teacher is primarily responsible for setting up the group interrelations, and through these interactions achieving the desired results.

The underlying and determining factors, then, are the goals and objectives of the teacher for the particular members of the class. These goals probably differ from the child's motives, the parents' hopes and aspirations, and the public's expectations. These differences need to be recognized and dealt with initially and throughout the duration of the student-teacher relationship.

The objectives of the teacher determine in large part what her procedures shall be. Our discussion of techniques will take place with regard to our fundamental orientation and our objectives.

(From another undated paper on teacher training)

Basic orientation and philosophy, goals and objectives, problems and projects for the year:

> Observation by each class member of teachers around NY. Projects to be presented and written up.
> Conference & observation of each class member (schedule).
> Matriculated students – projects observations written up. Book reports (4 per semester) a review and criticism, not a resume.

Class organization: number of sessions, number to a class, age distribution, space, parent observation, costume, length of class, equipment (mirror, barre, floor, black-board, paints, clay, etc.).

Overall year plan: what should a 4 accomplish, a 5, a 6, think to 16; get to know names; how to start class; how to end class; amount of technique; amount of composition; use of percussion, etc.

Age levels: physical, social, psychological, emotional, intellectual; type of teaching material for various age levels.

Community relations: to dance organization; to parents; to principals, etc.

Performance: costuming, accompanists, sets, organization.

Technique evaluation – Compositional devices – How to use accompanists and what to do without one – Integration with other arts – Special problems: discipline, injuries, rest periods, personality problems – Good teacher: voice, manner, dress, images, figures of speech, criticism, praise.

9. From Bonnie's notes on class assignments, Groups 1 and 2, Connecticut College, summer of 1964.

1st Week, July 6th:
Observe all three classes for *methods and materials*. Turn in work book Monday, July 13th. It will be returned with grade and comments Friday, July 17th.

2nd Week, July 13th:

Observe all three classes for *methods and materials* keeping in mind criticisms of written work. Turn in work books Monday July 20th. They will be returned on Friday, July 24th.

3rd Week, July 20th:

1. Observe Thursday class for M&M for 3rd and 4th weeks. Work book will be turned in Monday, August 3rd. Be particularly careful to be detailed, accurate, etc., based on criticism given in work books.

2. Observe two children assigned in Tuesday or Wednesday class. On Monday, July 26th, turn in as insightful a physical description of each child as possible. Note what she looks like (coloring, build physique, body tone, mannerisms, etc.) Record what she does and says. Note how she observes, listens and responds to teaching, how she takes criticism, relates to others and is able to work on suggestions, assignments, etc.

3. Observe Class Dynamics for next two weeks (general inter-group relations, teacher-group relations, progression of class – note up and downs).

A. How does the teacher:

1. Set tone of class at beginning?
2. Help children feel they belong to a group?
3. Keep discipline?
4. Build group morale?
5. Handle class interruption? (injuries, complaints, distractions, bathroom going, etc.)
6. Control the competitive, over-stimulated or aggressive child?
7. Handle the shy or resistant child?
8. Integrate holidays or special events into the plan of the class, (birthdays, Labanotation, etc.)?
9. Deal with discrimination or anti-social behavior or concepts?
10. Organize taking turns, having partners, etc.?
11. Prepare students for taking criticism from the teacher and classmates?
12. Get small groups in each class to function as a cooperative?

B. How does the teacher:

1. Introduce formally or spontaneously positive social values?
2. Utilize or incorporate facts about the world we live in?
3. Provide for the playing out of feelings, emotional conflicts, or even behavior that might be unacceptable in any other situation?

4. Help the child differentiate between fantasy and reality?

C. How does the teacher:

1. Use the aid she receives from the assistant in her role as demonstrator to motivate the class?
2. Use her accompanist as a person and a musician to motivate the class?
3. Use her own personal resources to aid, give insight to, and motivate the class about dance? What tangible materials does the teacher use?

This is not to be lengthy, but not superficial. Observe closely, compare with others, etc.

On Friday, August 7th, turn in paper with answers to these questions. Knowing the questions, begin to observe in all classes. Jot a note of something observed, but dig out answers specifically in class assigned for Dynamics.

4th week:

You will observe your two children with an eye to designing a section of a class (technical, rhythm, improvisations, etc.) which will involve all the class, but specifically aid one or both of those children. Due Monday, August 3rd: One exercise, one improvisation, etc. Note: preface plan with child's need as you see it.

5th week:

Free watching of all classes, bearing in mind questions in Class Dynamics due that Friday – and the planning of an assigned class due August 10th.

6th week:

Free watching of all classes.
Due Monday August 10th: class plan for assigned group.
Fri. August 14th: evaluation of course using these questions as guides:

(a) what you learned from it?
(b) what you would like to have emphasized, included, deleted, from course as given?
(c) what you consider might be most valuable next course to follow this one?
(d) any other comments or suggestions.

Group two people that are advanced might have class plan related directly to teaching problems they feel they have.

(From miscellaneous notes)
Questions for the dancer-teacher:

Who Am I? – a candid objective look at oneself, an appraisal of one's *skill and scope in dance, strengths and weaknesses as a teacher, shortcomings and abilities in relating to other human beings, and to the responsibilities of a job.*

What Have I To Contribute? – has my training, my performing experience, my education and related life experiences prepared me well enough to be an artist-teacher? What more is needed? Can I add to my knowledge to add to theirs?

What Do I Really Know About How Children Grow And Learn? Can I write out in an *orderly* fashion all I *really* know about the physical, mental and psychological growth of human beings from babyhood to adulthood and find I have a solid footing of facts upon which to operate and build?

How can I learn more? Study? Observation? Experimentation?

Am I Able to Take the *Stuff of Dance*, its movement substance and its craft and so translate it that my students experience the magic that illuminates the art?

Have I the resources, the creativity, the courage to dig deep and range far to find the ways that open the magic of dance to all my students whether amateur or professional, young or old, unsure or bold?

Am I, as a dancer-teacher, an artist-teacher?

How am I like other teachers and how different? Do I have more or different responsibilities (a) to the student – to integrate dance with student life? (b) to the profession – to be a part of the profession and work with it? (c) to the community – to understand dance and dancers in our society and to work to extend the value and understanding of dance?

10. *Newsletter*, National Dance Teachers Guild, Volume 11, No. 5. June, 1966, p. 3.
11. *Dance and Education Now.* San Francisco: Impulse Publications, 1965 (an annual), pp. 11–12.
12. The Dance Notation Bureau was founded in New York City in 1940 by Janet Price (Goeb), Helen Priest (Rogers), Henrietta Greenhood (Eve Gentry) and Ann Hutchinson (Guest). Ann Hutchinson was its first president and Hanya Holm and John Martin were advisors. Hanya understood Labanotation and was not suspicious of it like many American dancers. In 1951 her dances for the musical *Kiss Me Kate* became the first notated dance score in American commercial theater, largely because of Hutchinson, who was in the production at the time and notated the dances herself. In 1952 *Kiss Me Kate* was

the first American musical dance score to be copyrighted. Hanya's *My Fair Lady* and Gower Champion's *Bye Bye Birdie* were later notated. Professional dance schools, such as New York's High School of Performing Arts, which had started teaching Labanotation in 1948, introduced it to generations of dancers.

13. Irmgard Bartenieff, born in 1900 in Germany, was 25 when she first encountered Rudolph von Laban, movement and dance theorist, practitioner and philosopher. His work encompasses the study, analysis and notating of movement and dance, training for the professional dancer and actor, dance in the community, dance in education, dance therapy, and effort control in industry. Bartenieff studied with Laban and his colleagues Albrecht Knust, Dussia Bereska and Ruth Loeser, and taught dance and Laban's system of notation, Labanotation, before leaving Germany with her Russian-Jewish husband in 1936.

    In New York, Bartenieff, an early member of the Dance Notation Bureau, became a physical therapist. By the 1950s she was adapting Laban's wartime work on effort and shape to the handling and rehabilitation of polio victims in her work at Blythdale Hospital. During this time she made several visits to England to strengthen contact between the DNB and its European associates, where she also met and studied with Marion North, Valerie Preston (Dunlop) and Warren Lamb. More people, including dancers, came to her and she continued to expand and clarify her understanding of how Laban's concepts could best be applied to anatomical functioning. In 1965 she started the Effort/Shape Program at the DNB.

14. Bartenieff was developing Laban's second notation system which looked at elements of movement quality in terms of effort and shape. Laban had begun working on this system while making time and motion studies in England for F. D. Lawrence during World War II. The notation uses eight symbols built out of one small configuration of intersecting lines to describe the ongoing effort flow (free or bound) of movement, and records the variations in basic movement energy out of which arise the six effort qualities: indirect and direct (space), light and strong (force) and sustained and sudden (time). Symbols for the ongoing shape flow of movement record the basic changes in energy (dynamic) and shape qualities. These can be added to Labanotation or used by themselves for wider application in disciplines which are concerned with the quality of movement – its expressivity rather than its structural exactness. The symbols can be written at great speed for, like handwriting, they are written across the page. (When combined with Labanotation, they are written in vertical sequence to match the structural movement of the notation.)

Laban was the instigator of these and many other movement-related studies; over two following generations his many colleagues further developed his work, keeping in touch with him as circumstances allowed. Among his early pupils were Mary Wigman, who had begun her studies with him in 1913, and Kurt Jooss, a close colleague from the 1920s, who reflected Laban's ideas in his own choreographies for the Ballets Jooss. Another close colleague, Albert Knust, became the leading exponent of Labanotation in Europe.

15. By 1938 the Nazis had effectively stopped Laban from working in Germany. Kurt Jooss found him in Paris in a poor state of health and with Dorothy Elmhirst arranged an invitation to Dartington Hall, where the Jooss–Leeder School was then based. Laban recovered and began to teach again.

Chapter 10. *Building Song*

1. Dr. Marion North is director and chief executive of the Laban Centre for Movement and Dance. She holds a Laban Diploma and an Advanced Diploma in Child Development from the University of London; she is a Master of Education in Dance and Education at the University of Leicester; Doctor of Philosophy in Psychology and Movement Study at the University of London; and Doctor of Arts *honoris causa* of the Council for National Academic Awards. She taught with Laban and Lisa Ullmann and was assistant to Laban in his industrial research, his Youth Advice Bureau and his work for dance education and dance in the community. Her own research included a study of movement characteristics of young people from babyhood to adolescence, as well as the application of Laban's principles and findings in industry, which involved establishing and operating an arts center for employees and their families in a north London plastics factory. Her publications, continuously in print over 20 years, include *Introduction to Movement Study*, 1971, *Personality Assessment through Movement*, 1972, and many articles for professional journals in the United Kingdom and the United States of America. Dr. North is adjunct professor at Hahnemann University, Philadelphia, and lectures and conducts workshops at many other colleges, universities and centers throughout America. (My thanks to Dr. Peter Brinson's booklet, *21 years of change*, published by the Laban Centre for Movement and Dance: London, 1993.)

2. Subjects offered by the Laban Centre of Movement and Dance for the 1993/1994 academic year: Aesthetics of Dance, Arts Administration, Ballet, Choreography, Choreological Studies (including Laban Studies

and Notation), Contemporary Techniques, Community Dance Studies, Pilates Based Technique/Anatomy, Costume for Dance, Dance Culture and Communication, Dance History, Dance Movement Therapy, Education/Special Education/Teaching Methods, Improvisation, Music for Dance, Production/Lighting/Stage Management, Repertory, Research, Sociology of Dance and Politics of the Arts.

3. Among the teachers who moved with the Centre to London were Marion Gough, known for her work in primary teaching, adult education and teacher training, who was the first Inner London Education Authority dance specialist in a London secondary school, Walli Meier, special education expert, known for her practical work with handicapped children; and Simone Michelle, authority on the technique of Sigurd Leeder and co-director of the Leeder School for seven years.

BIBLIOGRAPHY

Allen, D. *Indians of the Northwest Coast*. Blaines, Washington: Hancock House Publishers, 1977.

Armitage, Merle. *Martha Graham*. New York: Dance Horizons, reprinted 1968 from the 1937 first edition.

Ashwell, Reg. *Coast Salish: Their Art, Culture and Legends*. Blaines, Washington: Hancock House Publishers, 1978.

Bartenieff, Irmgard, with Lewis, Dori. *Body Movement*. London: Gordon and Breach, 1980.

Brinson, Peter. *Dance as Education*. London: The Falmer Press, 1991.

———. *21 years of the change*. London: The Laban Centre for Movement and Dance, 1993.

Calouste Gulbenkian Foundation. *Dance Education and Training in Britain*. London: Calouste Gulbenkian Foundation, 1980.

Cohen, Selma Jean. *An Artist First*. Middletown, Connecticut: Wesleyan University Press, 1972.

Cornish, Nellie C. *Miss Aunt Nellie – The Autobiography of Nellie C. Cornish*. Edited by Ellen van Volkenburg Browne and Edward Nordhoff Beck. Forward by Nancy Wilson Ross. Seattle: University of Washington Press, 1964.

Coton, A. V. *The New Ballet: Kurt Jooss and His Work*. London: Dennis Dobson, Ltd., 1946.

Crowley, Alice Lewisohn. *The Neighborhood Playhouse: Leaves from a Theatre Scrapbook*. New York: Theatre Arts Books, 1959.

Countryman, Vern. *Un-American Activities in The State of Washington – The Work of the Canwell Committee*. Ithaca, New York: Cornell University Press, 1951.

De Mille, Agnes. *Martha: The Life and Work of Martha Graham*. New York: Random House, 1991.

———. *America Dances*. New York: Macmillan, 1980.

Drew, Leslie. *Haida – Their Art and Culture*. Blaines, Washington: Hancock House Publishers, 1982.

Graham, Martha. *Blood Memory*. New York: Doubleday, 1991.

Horst, Louis. *Pre-Classic Dance Forms*. New York: Kamin Dance Publishers, 1953; repr., Dance Horizons Inc., 1968.

Hughes, Glenn. *A History of American Theatre, 1700–1950*. New York: Samuel French, 1951.

Humphrey, Doris. *The Art of Making Dances*. New York: The Grove Press, 1959.

Kriegsman, Sali Ann. *Modern Dance in America: The Bennington Years*. Boston, Mass.: G. K. Hall, 1981.

Leatherman, LeRoy. *Martha Graham: Portrait of the Lady as an Artist*. Photos by Martha Swope. New York: Alfred A. Knopf, 1966.

Madden, Dorothy. *You call me Louis, not Mister Horst*. Amsterdam: Harwood Academic Publishers, 1997.

Markard, Anna and Hermann. *Jooss – A Documentation*. Cologne: Ballett-Bühnen-Verlag Rolf Garske, 1985.

Maynard, Olga. *American Modern Dancers; The Pioneers*. Boston and Toronto: Little, Brown and Company, 1965.

McDonagh, Don. *Martha Graham – A Biography*. New York: Praeger Publishers Inc., 1973.

Miller, Leta E. and Lieberman, Fredric. *Lou Harrison: Composing a World*. London: Oxford University Press, 1997.

Morgan, Barbara. *Martha Graham – Sixteen Dances in Photographs*. Dobbs Ferry, New York: Morgan and Morgan, 1980.

Müller, Hedwig. *Mary Wigman: Leben und Werk der grossen Tänzerin*. Weinhein and Berlin: Quadriga Verlag, 1986.

Sanders, Jane. *Cold War on the Campus – Academic Freedom at the University of Washington, 1946–1964*. Seattle and London: University of Washington Press, 1979.

Shawn, Ted. *Every Little Movement*. New York: Dance Horizons, Inc., 1963.

Shelton, Suzanne. *Divine Dancer: A Biography of Ruth St. Denis*. New York: Doubleday & Co., 1981.

Sorrell, Walter. *The Dance Through the Ages*. London: Thames and Hudson, 1967.

Stanislavsky, Constantin. *An Actor Prepares*. Geoffrey Bles, London, 1936; repr. 1942.

——. *The Art of the Stage*. London: Faber and Faber, Ltd., 1960.

Stodelle, Ernestine. *Deep Song: The Dance Story of Martha Graham*. New York. A Dance Horizons Book, Shirmer Books, 1984.

Wald, Lillian (R. L. Duffus). *Neighbor and Crusader*. New York: Macmillan, 1938.

INDEX

California Labor School, 128
Canwell, Albert, 131
Canwell Committee, 131–33
Carnovsky, Morris, 141
Cassidy, Rosalind, 119
Cecchetti, Enrico, 68
Centre Dance, 172
Chace, Marian, 130
Chandler, Charlotte, 93, 95, 97
Charlip, Abraham "Remy", 137, 141, 174
Chávez, Carlos (Graham's *Prelude*, Nov. '32, p. 33) (Bird's *Contemporary Challenge*, March '39, p. 114)
Cherry Lawn School, 139, 140–41, 178
Chilkovsky, Nadia, 80, 157
Choreographers' Workshop, 139
Civic Repertory Theatre of Eve Le Gallienne, 42, 50
Concert Dancers League of New York City, 22, 45
Congress on Research in Dance (CORD), 159, 160, 162, 178–79
Copland, Aaron (Graham's *Dithyrambic*, December '31, p. 30), 44, 47
Cornish, Nellie Centennial, "Miss Aunt Nellie", chap. 4 passim; 22, 23, 25, 69, 70–71, 81, 92, 99–100, 106, 118, 121–22
Cornish School of Fine Arts, chap. 4 passim; 43, 69–70, 81, 88–89, 120
Cornell, Grace, 19
Cornell, Katharine "Kit", 34, 37–38, 40, 64–67, 71, 89, 142
Council for National Academic Awards (CNAA), 172, 180
Cowell, Henry (Graham's *Four Casual Developments*, Feb. '34, p. 49), 50 (Flade's *Dance in the Early Morning*, July 1935, p. 76), 108, 111 (Bird's *Marriage at the Eiffel Tower*, March '39, p. 116)
Creston, Louise, 49
Cunningham, Mercier (Merce), 99–100, 103, 106, 108, 110, 113–114, 116–117, 119, 139, 142, 157, 175
Curie, Eva, 122
Currier, Ruth, 172

Curtis, Norman (Kirpich's *Weather Or Not* for MGR, 1962, p. 152)

Dance Drama School, 141–42
Dance Educators Workshop, 152
Dance Notation Bureau (DNB), 143, 162–63
Dance Repertory Theatre, 13
Dartington Hall, 9, 12, 86
Da Silva, Howard, 149
Davis, Hallie Flanagan, 134
Dearborn, Phyllis, 121
Debussy, Claude (Graham's *Maid With The Flaxen Hair*, April '26, p. 17)
Deja, Lore, 22
Dello Joio, Norman (Graham's *Diversion of Angels*, August '48, p. 67)
Dewhurst, Colleen, 139
Denishawn Company/School, 11–13, 16–17, 93
Der Blaue Reiter, 102
Deska, Eva, 146, 149, 151
Dessoff, Margareth, 38
De Havilland, Olivia, 128
De Mille, Agnes, 37, 118
De Remer, Dini, 31, 55, 109
De Vries, Mary Aid, 102
Diamond, David (Graham's *Praeludium No. 2*, Nov. '35, p. 82)
Dudley, Jane, 74, 80, 92
Duffy, Mrs. Homer N., 40–41, 57–58, 97, 107
Dunham, Katherine, 100

Effort/Shape, 162–63
Elementary and Secondary School Act, 156
Elliott, Laura, 37–38, 70
Elmhirst, Dorothy and Leonard, 9, 12
Engel, Lehman (Graham's *Ekstasis*, May '33, p. 43) (*Transitions*, Feb. '34, p. 48) (*Imperial Gesture*, Nov. '35, p. 82)
Enters, Angna, 45
Erikson, Erik, 128–29, 178
Evans, Edith, 64–66

Fanchon-Marko Review, 11

Other titles in the Choreography and Dance Studies series